To An...
with m...
Eva M...

Butterflies & Demons

December 2020

Eva Maria Chapman

Other Books by

Eva Maria Chapman

Sasha & Olga

Russian Roulette 20:20

From Russia to Love

Sexy at 70: A Spiritual Journey

Butterflies & Demons

Eva Maria Chapman

DoctorZed
Publishing
www.doctorzed.com

Published 2020 by DoctorZed Publishing Pty Ltd

DoctorZed Publishing books may be ordered through booksellers or by contacting:

DoctorZed Publishing
10 Vista Ave
Skye, South Australia 5072
www.doctorzed.com

ISBN: 978-0-6487107-6-9 (hc)
ISBN: 978-0-6487107-5-2 (sc)
ISBN: 978-0-6487107-4-5 (ebk)

A CiP entry can be found at the National Library of Australia

Cover image © DoctorZed Publishing Pty Ltd

Printed in Australia, UK & USA

DoctorZed Publishing rev. date: 14/04/2020

Testimony for Butterflies & Demons

"As well as reading *Butterflies & Demons*, I have also read Eva's book, *Sasha & Olga*, and was struck by how hard her own life was. I appreciate how she has weaved her life story in with the story of my people and recognises us as the healers and educators we are.

I enjoyed showing Eva many of the Kaurna historical features of Adelaide, especially the painting of Murlawirrapurka's last stand, which she describes so well in *Butterflies & Demons*. We also visited our commemorative bricks in the South Australian Migration Museum, not that my people were ever 'migrants', but she was happy that her family's brick was near that of Murlawirrapurka."

Eva o'Brien

Uncle Yelopurka Lewis,
Kaurna Elder
16th March 2020

Chapters

Acknowledgements

I *loved* researching and writing this book. It came out of a vison I had in Peru. My parents and I came to Adelaide in 1950, escaping war torn Europe. It was such a healing process to intertwine my Adelaide story with that of the Kaurna who had lived there for 40 thousand years. They are a beautiful people and I am so happy to have made their acquaintance; especially Kaurna elder, Uncle Lewis Yelopurka and his son Michael O'Brien. I loved all our chats. What generous and beautiful people they are.

People in the 19th century were great diary keepers and prolific writers of letters, which shed so much light on early Adelaide. I am especially indebted to Teichelmann and Schurmann, the Lutheran missionaries who did so much to document their time in Adelaide between 1838 and 1842 (Lutheran Archives, North Adelaide.) Not only did they write a comprehensive Kaurna grammar book (1840), but recorded many observations and priceless conversations with the main Kaurna people of the time especially their elder, Murlawirrapurka (also spelt Mullawirraburka in the history books). I want to acknowledge Rob Amery, a gifted linguist who has done so much to bring forth the Kaurna language, as well as a history of the early days, in *Warraparna- Kaurna Reclaiming an Australia Language,* Adelaide Press 2016. I drew heavily on many letters written at the time, for example between Governor Hindmarsh and the first Aboriginal Protector, Bromley, as well as the newspapers *The Colonial Register* and *The South Australian Register*. A wealth of excellent information was found in *History in Portraits. Biographies of South Australian Aboriginal people*, editors Jane Simpson & Luise Hercus, 1998.

William Cawthorne who befriended Murlawirrapurka, wrote diaries between 1842-1846 *Cawthorne Papers* ed. RKG Foster 1991. Cawthorne also sketched the scene in 1844, capturing the last Kaurna battle 'Shields & spears of the Natives on the Battlefield', which hangs in the Lounge Gallery of the Kaurna Building in the University of South Australia.

I really wanted to have an Adelaide publisher for this book and was delighted to find Dr. Scott Zarcinas of DoctorZed Publishing, who has done such a good job in helping to bring out this fascinating local Adelaide history and whose team produced an arresting cover.

Thanks to my husband, Professor Jake Chapman, who supported all my trips to Adelaide to research this book and was a great critical reader, as was my daughter Sophi Bruce, sister-in-law, Wendy Bruce and ex-husband, Peter Bruce. Thanks to Sonya Rankine and Nungga Wangga Radio in Adelaide for supporting me.

My greatest acknowledgement is to Murlawirrapurka, a great and wonderful Kaurna elder in the early days of Adelaide. I am trusting that this book will give credit to his magnificence.

Cast of Characters

Captain Collet Barker: Military Officer and explorer charged with finding the mouth of the River Murray as a possible harbour for the potential colony of Adelaide.

Captain Walter Bromley: First Protector of Aborigines in Adelaide.

John Brown: Emigration agent for South Australian Colonisation Commission.

James Cronk: Labourer from Tottenham who befriended Adelaide Aborigines.

Robert Cock: A Scotsman, early settler and explorer who was the only South Australian to offer the Aborigines recompense for loss of their way of life.

James Hurtle Fisher: Resident Commissioner.

Governor George Gawler: Second Governor of South Australia following John Hindmarsh, 1838.

Osmond Gilles: First colonial treasurer.

Robert Gouger.: Edward Wakefied's secretary.

Governor George Grey: Third Governor of South Australia following George Gawler.

John Barton Hack: A wealthy Quaker who kept an eye on the welfare of the Adelaide Aborigines.

Captain John Hindmarsh. The first Governor of South Australia.

Sir John Jeffcott: The first Judge of the Adelaide colony.

ix

Judge Henry Jickling: The second judge of the Adelaide colony following Sir John Jeffcott.

Colonel William Light: Surveyor General of the City of Adelaide.

John McLaren: Manager of the South Australian Company.

George Milner Stephen: Acting governor when George Gawler was called away.

Charles Moon: A sailor from the *Buffalo*.

George Stevenson: Private secretary to Governor John Hindmarsh and editor of the *SA Register*.

Robert Thomas: First Government printer.

Edward Gibbon Wakefield: Advocate of Systematic Colonisation.

Edward Wright MD: One of first doctors in the new colony.

Other Characters in the 20th Century Adelaide Story

Dr Hugh Birch: Medical superintendent at Parkside Mental Hospital 1954-1961.

Dr Bill Cramond: Medical superintendent at Parkside Mental Hospital following Dr Hugh Birch, 1961.

Charles Duguid: Started the South Australian Aborigines Advancement League in the 1930s and was a leading light well into the 1980s.

Sir Robert Menzies: Prime Minister of Australia from 1949 -1966.

Sir Thomas Playford: Premier of South Australia from 1938 -1965 and founder of the City of Elizabeth.

Other Characters in the Kaurna Story

William Cawthorne: Teacher and artist who sketched the scene in 1844 capturing this defining moment in Kaurna history, Murlawirrapurka's last stand. *Shields & spears of the natives on the battlefield* is hanging in the Lounge Gallery of the Kaurna Building in the University of South Australia

Lillian Holt: Head of Taoundi College in Port Adelaide in the 1990s.

Samuel Klose: Lutheran missionary from Dresden who took over from Teichelmann and Schurmann.

Vincent Lingiari: A Gurindji from the Northern Territory who stood up to the Vestey brothers in Northern territory in the late 60s.

Uncle Lewis Yerlopurka O'Brien: Chief elder of the Kaurna people and direct descendant of Kudnarto. He wrote *And the Clock Struck Thirteen*, Wakefield Press, 2007.

Lowitja O'Donohue: He fought to become a nurse in the hallowed white halls of the Royal Adelaide Hospital.

Charlie Kumantjayi Perkins: An Arrente man from near Alice Springs and a trailblazer for Aboriginal rights.

Mongarawata: A Milmenrura man who was hung for the massacre of the survivors of the shipwreck in the Coorong, South Australia, in 1842.

Christian Teichelmann and *Clamour Schurmann:* the Lutheran missionaries who came to Adelaide in 1838 to teach the Aboriginal children at Piltawardli. Teichelmann was dubbed Kertamerru, like Kertamerru, Murlawirrapurka, firstborn son.

Yerricha and Wang Nucha: Yerricha should have been more correctly written as Yerraitya, which meant secondborn, and Wang Nucha as Wangutya, the seventhborn male.

Kaurna Glossary

Banbabanbalya: where neighbouring clans gathered in Adelaide for discussions.

'*Birkibirki*': literally means 'lots of little bits' peas.

Jultiwirra: the stringy bark trees at the top of the gully which marked Permangk.

Kartanya: means firstborn girl, and *Kudnarto* thirdborn girl.

Kadlitpina: an important Wirra man.

Karraundongga: the red gum spear place.

Kakirra: the moon

Karta: Kangaroo Island.

Kua Mullawirra: Kua Kertamerru Mullawirra now pronounced Murlawirra. Murlawirrapurka's name when he finished his scarification rites.

Kalta: sleepy lizard.

Kamilya: my daughter's daughter.

Kammammi: maternal grandmother.

Karndo Wirra: forest men, a northern Kaurna group.

Karra Wirraparri: red gum forest river

Kirilla: 'the shine of the full moon'.

Kudlilla: cold season.

Kungurla: yabbies.

Kaurna Glossary

Kuri: a dance of Kadlitpinna's people, the Kaurna Wirra.

Mari Yertabulti: the Eastern Cascades

Midlaitya: fifthborn son.

Midlato: fifthborn girl.

Milmenrura: one of the Ngarrindjeri clans.

Moorundie: the river people, hated enemy of the Kaurna.

Mudlunnga: a nose shaped protuberance where Kaurna hunters trapped emus, entered an inlet near Port Adelaide.

Murlawirrapurka: esteemed wise purka of the Tandanya group. Mullawirraburka was the original pronunciation and is on his commemoration brick at the migrant museum.

Narungga: peoples in the north and west of Adelaide.

'Ngaityerli': means 'papa'.

Ngai wangandi marni' Welcome, you are at home.

Ngaltingga: Aldinga, Murlawirrapurka's home country.

Ngadjuri Ngarrindjeri clan in the south

Ngakallomurro: 'parakeet ashes', known to whites as the Magellanic Clouds

Ngano: Kaurna ancestor embodied in the Adelaide Hills.

Ngunyawaietti: literally means 'a moving-with-joy event'

Paltis: dances.

Pangkarra: local land.

Parna: As this star became more visible it signified the end of the hot season.

'Pepa meya': paper man, or judge. Was an insight into how the Kaurna saw British justice – just a pile of paper.

Peramangk: Adelaide Hills people, enemies of the Kaurna.

'*Pilyabilya*': a stunning butterfly with black, white, red, and yellow markings.

Piltawardli: possum place.

Pindi-meyunna: pit men – white man who has come back from the grave.

Pindi-nantos: pit men's horses.

Pitjantjatjara: peoples in the north of South Australia.

Pitluri: tobacco found in northern Australia.

Puri: pebble

Skilgolee Creek Block 346: owned by John Adams and Mary Ann Adams. Tim and Tom and part of what is owed to current Kaurna elder Uncle Lewis Yerlopurka O'Brien

Tambawordli: where the Kaurna traditionally held inter-clan gatherings and contests.

Tandanya: or Red Kangaroo people

Tarnda: the totemic kangaroo Tarnda Kaurna dreaming story of a young boy, Tarnda, who brought joy to the life of his aged parents and went on to become a great hunter. In old age, he was transformed into an old man kangaroo and was a great and respected teacher of all the Kaurna men, and was named Monana.

Tarndanyagga: Victoria Square.

'*Turnkiwardli*': tent, an amalgamation of two concepts, cloth and hut; 'parasol' was 'kurotura', a combination of 'kuro', crown of head, and 'tura', shade or shadow. '

Tindo: the sun

Tjilbruke: the great Tandanya ancestor.

Yammaiamma: the word for teacher and doctor was an extension of the word *yamma*, which meant foolish.

Wardli (wodli): hut fashioned by Aborigines.

Wauwe woman: kangaroo woman.

Willanga: 'the place of green trees'

Wilyaru: scars, the honoured special markings of.

Wiltutti: spring.

Winbirra: flute.

Winda: heavy fighting spears.

Wirra woman: woman from the Wirra, north of Adelaide.

Wodliparri: the Milky Way.

Wongayerlo: now Spenser's Gulf.

Yartta: the land.

Yartapuulti: Port Adelaide

Yoko worta bokarra: the tempestuous north-westerly winds.

Yudna wilyaru: the final ceremony for a Kaurna warrior.

Yurrebilla: the ears of the giant ancestor Ngano, who lay sleeping above the wide Tandanya plain.

Wakkinna: bad

Wangutya: a kinsman of Kadlitpinna who was hung unfairly by the British

Wardliworngatti: spring

Worltatti: summer

Windas (fighting spears) and shields, *kylahs* (hunting spears) *midlars* (woomeras), *wirris* (clubs), *cuttas* (fighting sticks).

Court of the Red Kangaroo

A circle of black, wizened women confronts the author.

Grandmothers: Who do you think you are? Are you attempting to write about the Kaurna, the Red Kangaroo people?

Author: Hey who do you think *you* are? I am trying to write Chapter One.

Grandmothers: We are the Kaurna Grandmothers. And we want to know why you are writing about us? We exist in an oral tradition. We are here to protect our sacred Kaurna heritage. We don't want white, nosy know-it-alls, poking their pointy snouts into our business. We've had it with you whites – a long line of interfering busy bodies – Methodists, Anglicans, eugenicists, doctors, missionaries, entomologists, Darwinians, anthropologists, sociologists, you name it. Why are you writing about us?

Author: Well it's not just about you – I'm juxtaposing what happened to your people in the Adelaide area in the 1830s, with what happened to my people, Eastern European refugees, in the 1950s.

Grandmothers: Uh oh, you sound like an academic.

Author: Well I'm not.

Grandmothers: Thank our ancestors for that! Save us from the academics. They are the worst of the lot. Academics have prodded, dissected, and analysed us to smithereens. But you *are* a PhD!

Author: Yes, I learnt to be a researcher, but as you will discover, that skill can come in handy.

Grandmothers: Well at least you're not descended from the British Imperialists who did us in. But we don't take kindly to being 'researched'. We are fed up with the number of trees it takes to pile up the feasibility studies, flow charts, and bureaucratic nonsense you whites seem so enamoured with. And then you ignore crucial research, as witnessed in the Northern Territory today! So why *are* you writing this book?

Author: Well if you must know, I had a vision to write it.

Grandmothers: Ah, a vision. Now that's more interesting. We can relate to visions. Tell us about it.

Author: In the vision I was accosted by a bunch of 1950s Adelaide Australians, looking like the gauche country bumpkins they were.

Grandmothers: Doesn't sound much of a vision. More like a second-rate nightmare.

Author: Just hold your horses – er kangaroos! As a result of what I saw in the vision, I knew I had to confront where destiny had placed me. These misfits were the people into whose lives I, as a small child, had been thrown. I was terrified of them. Can you imagine? I had just finished writing a book about what my family had escaped from, and now I felt compelled to write a book about what we had escaped to. And that's how you guys come in.

Grandmothers: Us guys? We weren't even around in 1950s Adelaide. We were virtually extinct. Dispensed with. Put away.

Author: Yes, I know. I didn't even see an Aboriginal person until I was twelve, and I only recently discovered the existence of the Kaurna race.

Grandmothers: So how do we come into it then?

Author: Ah well, that's what this book is about. In the vision, your story and my story intertwine inextricably. But if you must have a clue – I saw terrifying images. I clearly saw something disturbing about these 1950s Adelaide people who influenced me and tried their hardest to assimilate me into their way of life; they carried a dreadful legacy. And it took a vision over fifty years later for me to finally understand something that had always lurked around the edges of my consciousness; a truth I am now richer for knowing.

Grandmothers: And that obviously involves us.

Author: Absolutely. Where Adelaide stands was originally your country... for at least forty thousand years, before white man ousted you.

Grandmothers: So you shouldn't be surprised that we have made our appearance.

Author: I guess not. In fact, I am delighted and I welcome you. I invite your comments and input as the story unfolds. I would like you, as keepers of deeper knowledge and dreaming, to act as a kind of chorus, a conduit between the action and the audience.'

Grandmothers: Yes, we like the sound of that. Like our own plays, our *Ngunyawaietti*, which always endeavoured to make sense of what was happening around us.

We Kaurna loved educating through plays. We sang, we acted, we danced.

Author: Also, I hope you can influence and have a part in the action, as well as challenging me. Anyway, please introduce yourselves.

The grandmothers confer amongst themselves and put forward two spokeswomen.

Wauwe Woman: I am Wauwe Woman. *Wauwe* is Kaurna for 'female kangaroo'. I am a *ngangiburka,* a wise woman elder from the central Adelaide area.

Wirra Woman: I am Wirra Woman – *ngangiburka* from the Kaurna *Wirra* clan, just north of Adelaide.

Wauwe Woman: So, you're saying we can challenge you?

Author: Absolutely.

Wawe Woman: About your racism?

Author: My racism? What do you mean?

Wirra Woman: Were you brought up in Australia?

Author: Yes.

Wauwe Woman: Are you white?

Author: Yes.

Wauwe Woman: Then you are a racist. It is imbued in every cell of your body. Takes a lot more than some fancy reconciliation ideas to wash that clean.

Anyway, whack us with the first chapter.

CHAPTER 1

Impact

Adelaide Environs, 1820s

Kirrila scooped up crabs in the gentle surf of Ngaltingga. A movement along the shore caught her eye. She straightened her back and scanned the edge of the bay, shaded at this time of day by tall cliffs.

Just a pelican diving into the sea, she decided. Her daughter poked her *katta* into the wet sand, fascinated at the flurries of 'surf vermin', as her language described crabs, scuttling away from Kirrila's net. An unusual sound distracted her mother, but before Kirrila could look around, an arm grabbed her.

'Moorundie,' she hissed, surmising wrongly that these enemy river men had chanced on her, a lone woman, while they raided the sea cliffs for red ochre. Her child let out a squeal. She twisted around and saw the girl slip from the grasp of a pale man with strange garb all over his body. Terror gripped her – ghost-skins from Karta: just as the Ngarrindjeri had warned. She screamed at her daughter to run. Both assailants bundled her roughly towards a boat that appeared around the edge of the rocks. Gagging at their odour she clawed at the sand with her toes, willing it to suck her back. A thumping resounded behind them. Could she be saved? A ghost-skin picked up what looked like a shiny *katta*, and pointed.

Crack!

Thunder ripped apart the blue of the sky. She glimpsed her uncle, a beloved wise *burka*, as he fell. Her head banged on the edge of the boat as it heaved into the sea. She retched.

Adelaide, 1950

Billy put on his cowboy suit and placed both guns in their holsters. He had an execution to perform. Reffos had dared move into his street. He swaggered out into the blazing sun that flooded Commercial Road. The other kids were waiting. He saw the refugee standing outside number 48. Gee she was tiny! Couldn't be more than three years old. She smiled shyly. He hesitated.

'We don't like you,' he heard his sister say. 'We don't want you here. Go back to where you came from. You smell. We're gonna shoot you dead.' Billy saw the uncertainty flicker over the small girl's face. She obviously didn't understand English. Spoke some awful gobbledygook language, no doubt.

'We're gonna shoot you dead!' repeated his sister, pointing to Billy in his cowboy regalia. The reffo looked at him – looked at the guns in their holsters. Terror strafed her face. Billy's hands rested lightly on his weapons. He knew what he had to do. The other kids stepped back. The asphalt of the road shimmered in the heat. Billy strode towards his prey.

Kua rushed on to the beach. His isolation in the Murlawirra gully, customary after his recent circumcision, had been interrupted by cries and explosions that shattered the peace of the summer day. He saw the boat disappear into the Wongayerlo, the water where the sun always sank. He saw the fallen body of his uncle, his blood staining the white sand. He rushed forward, but stopped at the old man's signal, 'There's nothing you can do.'

Kua gaped at the hole in his uncle's stomach. He watched the slow ooze of blood, remembering its warmth on his own body as it bathed him during his first initiation. How proud he had felt to be anointed by the grace of this precious fluid which was now draining away. The old man's eyes steadily met his. Kua trembled at their power, his body still resonating with the chant his uncle sang during his second initiation. It charged his every sinew with potent energy, and overrode the searing pain at the core of his budding manhood. How honoured he had been, to be intimately branded by the male dignity and wisdom of his ancestors. The young man drank in what his uncle was communicating with his eyes.

'It's now up to you, Kua Kertamerru Murlawirra. A heavy burden is placed on your young shoulders. The white man is here in our sacred land. It falls upon you to take on this new and unknown challenge. Just look to the stars, look to the land, look into the wellsprings. All will be revealed.' The lustre faded from the dark eyes. Kua was left implacably alone.

―⁓―

Svitochka was very excited about being in Adelaide. She had spent the first week in a Displaced Persons' Hostel on the banks of the River Torrens. She was enraptured by the black swans that glided by. At last her endless travelling was over. Sharp imprints of a tumultuous past were beginning to fade. Glimmers on the water triggered flashbacks of the searchlights of border guards, when she escaped from Czechoslovakia; grunts of swans reminded her of two men who seemed to be hurting her mother, on a dark night in Austria; the azure of the sky echoed the blue monotony of the sea voyage to Australia.

She felt peaceful sitting by this river. The land was welcoming her, caressing her. She half shut her eyes and imagined kangaroos drinking at the water's edge. She hadn't seen any of these exotic creatures yet, even though fellow migrants on the boat claimed they would be hopping all over Australia. Svitochka was oblivious to the fact that she was sitting on an Aboriginal site, where Tandanya Rock once stood. For thousands of years this had been the sacred centre of the Tandanya, or Red Kangaroo people. In 1950, nothing commemorated the fact: no plaque, no sign. Unbeknownst to Svitochka, the ancient energy was seeping into her bones, giving her a strength she would need for the arduous years ahead.

—⁓—

Kangaroo Island, as it was dubbed by white-skins, was known by Kirrila's people as Karta – the land of the dead. It was uninhabited for generations before white sealers and sailors landed there. Kirrila was thrown into a loathsome existence; used at night for the carnal gratification of her captors, and by day as a slave. She was forced to hunt, cook, fetch and carry. Other black women on the island suffered the same predicament; harlots and slaves to a motley bunch of pirates and sealers, who, here at the end of the world, traded with passing ships. Some slaves had been captured from Van Diemen's Land and others from Ngarrindjeri country. Many tried to escape, but were shot while running or savagely beaten when caught. Some drowned as they swam out to sea, their bodies washing up a few days later.

A child of one of the unfortunate women attempted to run away. He was caught and his ear sliced off as punishment. Kirrila tried to ease his pain as he writhed in agony from the wound. Hungering for her own children, she cradled him tenderly until death released him. At night while her captors snored, she walked down to the sea and sluiced out her insides, to rid her body of the fluids spilled so carelessly into her precious place – a place prepared for love and motherhood by the secrets of the women in her clan, especially by her *kammammi*, her maternal grandmother. She held that dear face in her mind's eye, as she bathed in the cleansing sea.

Kakirra, the moon, had risen full and cast her shimmering light over Kirrila's body, helping her to feel beautiful again. Kirrila's name meant 'the shine of the full moon'. She had been given this name because she was born when the moon was fully pregnant. Kirrila grew up with a special affinity to Kakirra, and her knowledge of all her cycles was passed down to her from her *kammammi*. Men preparing to hunt would consult her about weather patterns the moon augured; a big ring around a ripe moon meant big rains – a small ring, light rains. Right now, this moon, the ring slipping a little to the side, suggested an occasionally blustery south wind. A tiny reflection of the silver orb glistened in the tears that welled in her eyes. Here, in the land of the dead, ruled by ignorant boorish white-skins, this special knowledge entrusted to her was useless.

Jeanette, sitting at her front window, watched the trio walk along Commercial Road. Just the oddest people she had ever seen. The man, an old-fashioned suit draping his thin frame, peered at her gate trying to discern a number. He heaved a cumbersome suitcase in front of him, the faded brown leather plastered with labels. The woman, strikingly pretty, stumbled behind with another suitcase. It was the little girl Jeanette was drawn to, even though she looked strange too. Instead of a normal dress, she wore long pants and lace-up boots. Her fair hair was braided in plaits just like Heidi on the front cover of the book Jeanette was reading. Jeanette was struck by the irresistible happiness that radiated from the girl's face. She wanted to be her friend. She stared ruefully down at the leg irons which rendered her an unwilling prisoner at her own window, and watched the family pass by. Jeanette knew where they were going. Miss Bressler next door needed someone to look after her frail, elderly mother, and had applied for Displaced Persons' help.

'There's lots of them coming over – refugees, or 'reffos', as they're called,' her father had explained at the dinner table. 'They are from Eastern Europe. Their homes and lives have been destroyed by the war. So they've nowhere else to go, poor bastards!' Jeanette's father, a veteran of the mammoth struggle against Rommel in the North African desert, was no stranger to the misery of war. He never could bring himself to talk about it. Although he managed to miraculously escape the bullets that killed his mates, he felt helpless in the face of the cruel polio virus that crippled his only child.

Jeanette wondered if Eastern Europe was anywhere near Switzerland, where her storybook heroine Heidi lived. She was intrigued that Heidi's real name was Adelheid, which became Adelaide in English. What could this foreign girl's name be?

Kua Murlawirra spied a sailing ship from a rocky outcrop up near Yurrebilla, the ears of the giant ancestor Ngano, who lay sleeping above the wide Tandanya plain. Many seasons had passed since that fateful day when his *pangkarra* was torn apart. He continuously berated himself for not spotting the boat that stole Kirrila. Why, he could see the tiniest movement of prey in the far distance, and spear it with deadly accuracy. He also berated himself for not protecting the tract of land, the *pangkarra*, passed down to him. Other male members of the clan had been hunting in the *wirra* that fateful day, while he recuperated from his circumcision, wearing his *yudna* for the first time. Since then he had undertaken three more initiations. He proudly fingered the tattoos, received during *wilyaru*, the final ceremony. These marked him as a fully-fledged warrior of the Tandanya, the Red Kangaroo people, or Kaurna as they would one day be called. As a fully initiated warrior, he hoped he could live up to the many secret lessons imparted to him. He officiated at the *banbabanbalya*, where he and neighbouring clans, particularly the Ngarrindjeri in the south and Ngadjuri and Narungga in the north and west, gathered to discuss important business. The current all-consuming topic was

7

the encroachment of the white-skins, and what should be done about them.

A central meeting place was at the Tandanya Rock, sacred site of the Red Kangaroo Dreaming, down by the Karrawirraparri. In view of the black swans, the *banbabanbalya* were volatile affairs and, interspersed with dancing and singing, often went on for weeks. Some men, especially the Ngarrindjeri, wanted to spear every white man they saw. The white-skins from Karta had stolen their women; '*kringal kop*', 'nose first', they called them disparagingly – who with their protruding white snouts sniffed after their women. The Ngarrindjeri were more warlike than the Tandanya people, who traditionally had the role of educators and advisors. Having undergone hunting initiation and proudly bearing the scars, Kua Murlawirra could wield a spear as skilfully as any Ngarrindjeri, but knew spearing white men was not the answer. The *banbabanbalya* also focussed on the terrible diseases that appeared at the same time as the whites. Smallpox, as the whites called it, and other alien scourges were decimating their numbers. There were so many new influences and big changes that had to be absorbed.

The ship Kua Murlawirra was watching anchored at the mouth of the Ngankaparinga, the women's river. Three white men came ashore and camped on a sandbank. The leader of the party was a kind looking man who seemed to carry no weapons, except perhaps for a strange round implement which flashed in the autumn sun. He kept looking at it and making marks on something that looked like a dried, pale piece of bark. Kua, spear in hand, approached cautiously. The white man surprised him by coming forward, smiling broadly and shaking his hand. He pointed to the river, indicating he wanted to know the name. Kua hesitated. He knew the women would be furious if he disclosed it. Its secret crevices had been their hiding place from unwelcome men, for generations.

'Burka-Paringa.' He improvised quickly. This meant 'Wise Man River'.

'Pooke-Parringa,' repeated the white man as he made marks on the pale piece of bark. Kua pointed at it quizzically.

'Paper,' he was informed.

'Pepa,' repeated the black man, marvelling at its smooth finish and wondering how white man could construct fibres so thin.

There were so many things he wanted to know. Why were they here? Where did they come from? How were the pelts they wore so fine? After exploring the foothills, the party packed up camp and went back to the ship. It seemed a harmless encounter.

Kua Murlawirra was puzzled. Others berated him, especially his young friend Ityamai-itpina, who grumbled, 'we should have speared the lot!' But discussions with elders confirmed the rightness of a peaceful way forward.

Stan Berwick walked home along Commercial Road from his job as hardware assistant on Unley Road. He lingered at number 48, peering over the high front hedge. He had heard unsettling news at the shop; Mrs Bressler's spinster daughter was engaging some foreign people to help her.

'Reffos!' he announced ominously to his wife and two children. 'Reffos have moved into the road. Can you believe it? I thought this a respectable neighbourhood.' He

banged the table. Forks clattered. Each evening, as soon as he
closed his front door, the mealy-mouthed shop assistant
metamorphosed into a bullying thug. His first task was to
mete out punishment to Billy, his eight-year-old, who was
always in trouble.

'You wait till your father gets home!' Molly Berwick
constantly admonished. Tonight, to Billy's relief, it was the
reffos down the road who incurred his father's pent up
wrath, not his beleaguered backside.

'If I had my way, I'd shoot the bastards!' growled
Stan darkly.

After tea Billy and his sister went outside and approached
her friends playing hopscotch on the pavement.

'Do you know there are some reffos at number 48?'

'Ooh yeah! We've seen'em. They're horrible. We godda
get rid of'em.'

—◦◦◦—

Captain Collet Barker was pleased with his successful
expedition. The fertile plain looked promising for future
settlement, which his military commanders in England had
asked him to investigate. They were a jot tetchy about the
French increasingly nosing around this southern part of
New Holland – 'Even devising dictionaries of the language
of the inhabitants, you know – awfully worrying, by Jove!'
Barker had seen very few of these inhabitants on his
exploration so far, but was pleased with the brief contact he
had made. The man he had shaken hands with by the river
had a good strong grip and friendly eyes. He was reminded
of Mokare, a Noongar man he had befriended in Western
Australia. But Barker's assignment was not yet over. He was

also charged with finding the mouth of the River Murray – a possible harbour for this potential colony. The inlet into the Pooke-Parringa was unsuitable, and another a few miles north looked swampy.

Anchoring his ship further down the coast, he and his party set out overland for the river. On reaching the Murray mouth, Barker noticed a high sand bar on the other side and decided to swim over to have a better vantage point. He ignored the remonstrations of his companions, 'The river is dangerously high!' and 'Surely this is taking duty too far.' Or 'Captain Sturt has warned that the natives are unfriendly!' Barker felt totally confident in his relations with natives, having befriended Mokare and many other black men during his last post at King George's Sound. He stripped, and jumped into the fast-flowing river, his trusty compass strapped to his head. His companions timed his crossing, nine minutes and fifty-eight seconds to be exact, and then watched him disappear over the sand bar. A couple of hours later they thought they heard a cry. Exceedingly anxious by now, they made a large fire and waited. Nightfall came, bringing with it the ominous sounds of a native dirge. A chain of small fires lit the sand hills.

'All night did those dismal sounds echo along that lonely shore,' wrote Barker's batman. What he did not yet know was that a trio of Ngarrindjeri had spotted Barker's tracks in the dunes. All three men had lost women to brutal white-skins who had shot their clansmen with their 'crack-a-backs'. And now here was a loathed white-skin on their territory! Naked. That was puzzling. Was he carrying a 'crack-a-back'? He held something round and suspicious which glistened in the sun. They approached cautiously. One threw a spear that went through the white man's thigh. Barker turned in horror, and staggered forward, shouting,

'No, no, stop. You don't understand. I am a friend! I have no gun. Stop!'

Another spear entered his left leg. Barker ran for the water.

'No, no! For the love of God, I implore you!'

The next spear went through his back.

—⁓—

Svitochka begged her mother to let her out the front gate to play. Tatiana, overwhelmed by all her new chores, snapped. 'Play out the back!' Svitochka, hearing the shouts and screams of the children, persisted. Tatiana relented and opened the front gate latch, which the child couldn't reach.

Blinking in the bright sunlight, Svitochka saw a pretty girl with ringlets coming towards her. She smiled shyly. The children stopped playing. Sudden silence. She pressed back uncertainly into the gate. It didn't budge. The girl with the ringlets approached threateningly. Svitochka's smile faded. A torrent of words rained upon her. She didn't understand them, but knew they were unkind. Her plaits hung heavily. She wished they would transform into ringlets. Then she caught the glint of metal at the other end of the street. Border guards on motorbikes flashed before her eyes. A big boy with guns strode menacingly towards her. A frozen scream rose in her throat. Chillingly, she knew this was her execution.

—⁓—

Kirrila ached to be back on her *pangkarra*; to laugh and squabble with the women; to gather *kangatta* berries; to dig for roots with her *katta*; to sing the songs associated with each fruit of the earth. Even the humble radish, the *kandara*, had its own special song. She missed her husband, who had been away hunting when she had been dragged off. Their joining had been a sparkling one. She remembered with fondness how she had to carry her own fire-stick from her family group, and join it with that of her intended. And what a 'kindling of fire' their marriage had been. All danced under a pregnant moon, happy faces flickering in the conflagration of the joint fire-sticks.

Enough was enough. She had to leave this bad place. She had swelled with child too many times, and had just strangled another at birth. She knew she couldn't do it again. She waited until the moon was full, weather signs favourable, and her captors full of rum. She made up the fire as usual and heated up stones for the evening meal. She wrapped the wallaby she'd caught in leaves and placed it in the freshly dug *kanyayappa* containing the hot stones. After feasting on the wallaby, the men stretched out and drank copious amounts of a new consignment of rum.

Kirrila slipped away to the water's edge. She trembled with exhilaration and fear; exhilaration that she was leaving this miserable existence, and fear of the arduous swim ahead. She doubted that anyone had ever made it, and moreover, she was not a sea person. Her people were of the land and that is where she longed to be more than anything else in the world, or at least die in the attempt. A light west wind nudged her gently as she struck out through the vast sea. The beautiful Kakirra was welling up in the east, her radiance flooding the waters. Kirrila swam slowly and steadily into her light.

—⁓—

Svitochka's screams pierced the leaden stillness of Adelaide suburbia. Tatiana rushed out the front gate, grabbed her child and unleashed a torrent of Slavic abuse. The children scampered. She guided the sobbing Svitochka into the house, not noticing the ravaged face at next-door's window. Jeanette, who had witnessed the whole scene, desperately attempted to stand on her leg irons, but had crashed forward on to the window ledge. Heidi, smiling in blonde plaits on the book cover, hurtled to the floor. Jeanette let out an agonised shriek as pain pierced her body. Tears rolled helplessly down her face.

Inside Number 48, Svitochka cried uncontrollably. Tatiana tried to shush her, as old Mrs Bressler was trying to rest. Svitochka sobbed as if her heart would break.

'Don't take any notice of them; they're just stupid kids,' pronounced Miss Bressler briskly, as she made a pot of tea.

There was a knock at the back door. It was Jeanette's mother. She held out a tray of cakes to the weeping child.

'These are from my daughter Jeanette. She invites you over to play.'

Svitochka didn't understand the words but was arrested mid-sob at the sight of the cakes. They were all in the shapes of frogs. Two green, two white and two pink. She was instantly enchanted, and let her hot face and injured heart be soothed.

'Zjaba,' said Svitochka, smiling through tears, pointing at one. 'Zjaba.'

'Frog,' corrected Miss Bressler, gently. 'Frog.'

'Flog,' copied Svitochka, trying to get her tongue around the word. 'Flog.'

1830, Newgate Prison, London

Edward Gibbon Wakefield was dreaming of a model British colony in Australia, where gentlemen capitalists would buy land at a good price even before they left Britain, and live in a 'paradise of dissent', freely practising whatever religion they pleased. Proceeds would pay for passages of labourers, thus not tarnishing the colony with the convict troubles plaguing other Australian settlements.

While most inmates were crammed together at the notorious Newgate Prison, Wakefield commanded a commodious cell, and even a serving maid. His habit of marrying or abducting a series of young heiresses had, as well as landing him in gaol, made him rather wealthy.

1830, Bedlam Lunatic Asylum, London

The Board of Governors were alerted to the fact that Apothecary Superintendent, Edward Wright MD, was found in the dark, in 'the female basement... in a very intoxicated state with his clothes dishevelled'. On investigation, it was discovered that as well as behaving improperly with female patients, he had also been removing the heads of dead inmates, illegally. He was dismissed. After not being able to find a position in either England or Syria, he actively sought a role in the Dissenters' Paradise of South Australia.

1833, Exeter, England

January 15th: John Jeffcott, Chief Justice of Sierra Leone was engaged to Flora Macdonald, grand-daughter of her namesake, the Jacobite heroine.

May 1: King William IV knighted John Jeffcott.

May 9: Sir John Jeffcott felt insulted by Dr Peter Hennis, over Flora Macdonald.

May 10: In a duel, Jeffcott fired prematurely and mortally wounded Hennis.

May 21: At the inquest, Sir John Jeffcott was found guilty of wilful murder.

This was a thorny problem!

What to do with a Chief Justice and Knight of the British Empire who was guilty of murder?

Well, the new colony being set up in South Australia needed a Chief Judge…

———

Wauwe Woman: So our usurpers included a planner who was a kidnapping criminal, a judge who was a murderer, and a doctor who was a philandering drunkard with a penchant for beheading corpses?

Author: Oh, that's just the beginning my dears. But I will be fair. There were some decent people too.

Wirra Woman: Hmmph! We are virtually extinct. Their decency didn't save us!

CHAPTER 2

White Sharks

Midlato looked out over the plain and the sea beyond as she wove string from roots she had gathered. She was perched at the front of her winter *wardli*, which nestled cosily among the gums high up in the gully.

'Bucha! Bucha!' The childish squeals caused a slight stirring among the shaggy koalas slumbering in their eucalypt nooks. Midlato and the children were engaged in their favourite pastime, watching out for ghost-skin boats in the gulf, and shouting, 'Bucha!' to each other. A dreaming story told by the Narungga who lived across the water, predicted the arrival of white man and his danger. It described how harmless brown fish had turned into white sharks with razor teeth roaring 'Bucha', the Narungga word for death. The first time Midlato heard the story around a campfire on the banks of the Karrawirraparri, she was petrified. The narrator had roared out a terrifying prophecy of doom through an imaginary shark's mouth, 'Bucha! Bucha!' It was the same night that there had been a shower of shooting stars, which augured bad tidings. A short time later her mother succumbed to an illness of suppurating sores and died in agony.

It was nearing the end of the cold season and Midlato was looking forward to *wiltutti*, the time to dismantle her cosy *wardli* and descend to the plain. The signs were promising;

the sun appeared earlier over the hulking shape of the sleeping giant Ngano behind her, and the air was warmer each morning. The Wardliparri, or Milky Way, gradually pointed to Ngarrindjeri country in the south, not towards the Wongayerlo as it did in cold season. She would soon throw off her possum pelt and run through the plain where blue and pink blossoms vied with fragrant wattle to scent the air. Midlato, like her totem creature the emu, hated being confined and yearned to roam free. She loved wandering through the *yarta* criss-crossed with the tracks of ancestral spirits; every hill, every creek, every group of trees associated with a Kaurna tradition and a totemic ancestor. She couldn't wait to get down to the Karrawirraparri to catch *kungurla*, and run through the red gums and silvery sheoaks that graced its banks. This river was a reflection of the Wardliparri above, whose stars mirrored the campfires that blazed at the large inter-tribal gatherings around Tandanya Rock, where her people would dance ecstatically and sing. The northern clans camped to the north of the rock, the southern clans to the south, and so on. The children ran and played in between, and shared discoveries. Midlato particularly liked inventing three-way string games with her best friends, Kartanya from Ngaltingga in the south and Kudnartu from the Nantuwarra, the northernmost Tandanya clan.

But a shadow had passed over the peoples of this land. There was considerable unease about the strange, pale people who had made various appearances, and more were expected, hence the children's vigils in looking out to sea. Around the fires after a meal of game, roots and fruits, animated discussions prevailed, often all night. Stories of the last thousand generations were resurrected and mulled over. Friendly neighbouring tribes, like the Narungga from over the Wongayerlo, shared their stories and prophecies. And sure enough the white peril had come. Kartanya's *kammammi*, Kirrila of Ngaltingga, was stolen, as were many other women. Magic sticks were pointed at the men who tried to defend their women, killing many. Some white-skins had even walked through the gully Midlato was sitting in. She shuddered at the thought.

There were endless discussions around the campfires about what to do.

'Spear the lot' growled Ityamai-itpina, Midlato's uncle.

'Set Karndo on to them,' muttered the Wirra, or Forest men, a northern Kaurna group who were renowned for sorcery. Kadlitpina, a respected Wirra warrior, tried to dissuade them. Kua Murlawirra from Ngaltingga, in the south, regarded by the elders as the most promising young male of the Tandanya plain, advocated caution. Midlato's *kammammi*, a female elder, a *ngangkiburka*, knew of the burden he carried, but also knew he was the best man for the job; strong, kind, and wise beyond his years; a capable elder or *burka*. She and the elders were already honouring him with the title, Murlawirrapurka.

The British were wary of the French and desperately wanted to stake their claim in the south of New Holland. They listened with interest to Edward Wakefield's colonisation theories, which were promoted vigorously by his secretary Robert Gouger. Gouger worked hard to bring Wakefield's ideas for an experimental colony to fruition. He managed to engineer the passing of the British Colonies Act in 1834 by courting the influential Duke of Wellington, promising him the new city would be named after him. But the Napoleonic hero was 'shabbily disappointed' when King William IV announced the honour would go to his Queen. Formerly Adelheid of Saxony, William had married her to strengthen his alliance with the Hapsburgs and produce a legitimate heir. However, this was not to be, as two infants died. The third infant, the new settlement of Adelaide, did survive, but only just and at great cost. The glaring problem in this proposed utopia was the gigantic imperialist blindspot that the land being dispensed with so freely was home to another people. For tens of thousands of years, the Kaurna had led a nomadic existence on their beloved *yarta*. The area where the city of Adelaide would eventually stand was, to them, Tandanya – the place of the Red Kangaroo.

However, there were a few enlightened imperialists, who, flushed with the victory of the recent abolition of slavery, raised the problem of the 'natives'. Lord Glenelg, secretary of State of the Colonies, insisted that a percentage of the land be put aside for their benefit and that they be appointed a protector. South Australia, as well as being convict free, would not be tarnished with the excesses suffered by the Aborigines in Sydney, Port Phillip Bay, and Van Diemen's Land, but stand as an example of enlightened colonialism. His was a noble vision.

In 1836 several ships set sail. Colonel Light, the Surveyor General, captained the *Rapid*. The colonial secretary, Robert Gouger, set sail in the *Africaine*, accompanied by his wife Harriet, emigration agent John Brown, and his servant James Cronk. Cronk, from Tottenham, was an enterprising young man who was taking advantage of free passage for labourers and the promise of wages. Gouger, himself a non-conformist, encouraged many other Dissenters to come to enjoy the religious freedom promised in South

Australia: this included Samuel Stephens, from a famous Methodist family, who was the South Australian Company's colonial manager; the non-conformist Bradshaw family; and a young Quaker, Albert Taplow, who all sailed on the *Duke of York*. Dr Edward Wright, disgraced of Bedlam, wangled a passage on the survey ship *Cygnet*, and proceeded to cause mayhem by quaffing endless tankards of rum and attacking people, including the captain. On the *Tam O'Shanter* sailed Captain Walter Bromley, who had been interviewed in London for the job of Protector of Aborigines by the future governor, Captain John Hindmarsh. Hindmarsh settled himself, his large family, his private secretary George Stevenson, the Resident Commissioner James Hurtle Fisher, and a huge array of livestock on the HMS *Buffalo*. Sir John Jeffcott, who had – amid controversy – been appointed Chief Judge of South Australia, was supposed to accompany the Governor. A long line of his creditors who waited on the Plymouth quay were irate when he failed to turn up. John Barton Hack, a wealthy Quaker, boarded the *Isabella* a few weeks later with his large family. He was surprised by the late and somewhat stealthy arrival of a Knight of the British Empire, none other than Sir John Jeffcott. Hack wondered what dark secrets this man was escaping.

'Yoko! Yoko!' Midlato was whipped out of her musings. The children were jumping up and down in a frenzy. 'Yoko! Yoko!' Shaggy koalas startled from their slumber, joined in the squealing.

Sure enough, there it was; a ship! Although fearful, Midlato marvelled at the *yoko's* great white pelts billowing out from three enormous sticks, which propelled it like a giant bleached swan up the gulf. Over the next few days the children reported the ship's whereabouts. It sailed around Mudlunnga, a nose shaped protuberance where Kaurna hunters trapped emus, and entered an inlet towards Yarta-bulti 'the marshy place where birds went to sleep'. This mangrove-lined swamp was where other bleached swans had also stopped. Why were they so interested in this place? It was so dank and full of dark spirits. The *yoko* then sailed out into the gulf again and went southwards. It stopped at Patawalonga Creek, or rather, it tried to stop. There had been a terrible storm that night. Perhaps the ancestors were angry that these ghost-skins were coming. Or were the Wirra sorcerers up to their magic? Kudnartu told Midlato that the people were calling on Karndo, a birdlike creature, to bring on the *worta bokarra*, the tempestuous north westerly winds, to stop white-skins from landing.

For the first time ever, Midlato was apprehensive of moving to the plains. She was glad of the stormy winds that delayed their descent. She blocked up the front of her *wardli* to keep out the *worta bokarra*, and peeked out the back. From here, she could just see the *jultiwirra*, the stringy bark trees at the top of the gully which marked Permangk territory. Her teeth chattered, the old enemy in front, and a new, sinister enemy behind.

The winds eventually calmed down. The *yoko* had billowed away for the time being, but all knew in their bones it would be back. They heard an intriguing story. The white captain of the ship had a Kaurna woman from Karta on board. Who could she be? Midlato fervently hoped it would be her friend Kartanya's grandmother. Ever since she had heard the story of her captured *kammammi* from her mother, who had so narrowly escaped, Kartanya would often sit at Ngaltingga and gaze wistfully out to sea.

Colonel Light was in a flat spin. He felt weighed down by his onerous task – to found the city Adelaide – the new Athens of the south, where the most enlightened ideals of the British Empire would flourish. After a delayed start, the *Rapid* arrived late. The South Australian Colonial Society from its Adelphi headquarters in London issued precise guidelines. The new city must sit on fertile land, have access to fresh water, and be near a good harbour. Light felt unwell, his phlegm spotted with blood. There was no sign of the *Cygnet*, which carried all his surveying equipment.

With the help of a Kaurna woman who lived on Kangaroo Island, Light explored the coast. She had lived with a sealer for several years who named her Sally, so spoke English well and could tell Light many details about the area. Light was impressed by her, and the Adelaide Aborigines, remarking on their friendliness and honesty.

It was springtime in the Southern Hemisphere but wintry squalls hampered travel. The *Rapid* was buffeted up to the place Sally called Yartabulti, soon to be dubbed Port Misery, and later Port Adelaide. It was a good harbour but too swampy for a city. The *Rapid* sailed south and anchored at Patawalonga Creek in wild winds, the stormiest weather yet. Light named the place Holdfast Bay, as the *Rapid* managed to stay put, despite the tempestuous waves. The bay was not suitable for a city, as it was reedy and marshy. 'Just what "patawalonga" means,' explained Sally in her musical voice, but then added that beyond the reedbeds was a larger river, the Karrawirraparri, or red gum forest river, which meandered down from the hills. Interested,

Light ascended a high sandy ridge and was enchanted by the vista which unfolded before him. Was he gazing upon the future new city? On the 3rd of October 1836, Light placed his flagstaff on the ridge to help him construct a chart of the gulf. Winds were still strong as the party sailed south and explored the mouth of the Pooke-paringa where Collet Barker had camped. Although fertile, the area lacked a good harbour. Further down the coast Light spotted a peaceful looking bay which abounded with pelicans, but on coming inland it proved treacherous. Deception Bay, he called it. Ironically, Kirrila had been abducted from there many years earlier.

Light kept coughing up blood. His lungs were being attacked by the onset of tuberculosis and his mind by anxiety, brought on by 'such repeated bad weather checking our work, and the dread of having a host of emigrants out before I knew where to land them.'

It seemed every time he tried to land, a vicious gale suddenly rose out of nowhere and nearly scuppered him.

—◊—

Light's Diary – October 12, 1836: *'Very fine weather... winter and gales being now over... At eight, we began sending things on shore; at ten the wind shifted to the NNW and WNW, at noon a sudden change of wind to the NNE with sultry and oppressive air; in a few minutes, thunder clouds appeared very near, from the westward; without any previous indications a sudden west wind sprang up, and a high sea... At half past one pm several severe flashes of lightning with thunder close to us, and the rain fell heavy; about two, this squall passed over but we found ourselves in now another gale... hard gales and a high sea throughout the night.'*

The Wirra sorcerers smiled in satisfaction. Karndo was doing her job, bringing on tempestuous north westerly winds every time the ship tried to land. The Wirra were determined to use everything in their power to stop the invaders arriving on their soil. Kadlitpina, who supported Murlawirrapurka's 'watch and wait' advice, scolded them.

'Why should we not use our magic?' they riposted. 'The white man uses his. Look at his exploding sticks.'

Wauwe Woman: What? You are suggesting that sorcery was stopping Light from landing? You can't possibly be serious!

Author: Yes, is this a problem?

Wauwe Woman: It is downright dangerous to accuse the Aborigines of dabbling in sorcery. Don't you know that's such inflammable tinder for white man to totally dismiss the black man's point of view? They will see us as a bunch of barbaric savages. I thought you were garnering sympathy for the Kaurna.

Author: Well I am. So, what do you want me to do? Suppress that information?

Wauwe Woman: Frankly, yes!

Murlawirrapurka, like Colonel Light, also felt weighed down by an onerous task. The future of the Tandanya people was in the balance, and he had been chosen to cope with the impending upheaval. What could he do? His people had lived in this area for thousands of years and had links with Aboriginal groups all over Terra Australis, as the Europeans called it. Each distinct group had its own language and culture and its particular strength to give to the whole: the

Ngarrindjeri were politicians and warriors; the Moorundie knew the secrets of the giant river; the Narungga, the tides of the Wongayerlo; and his own people were celebrated educators. Representatives from afar attended the famous *banbabanbalya* to seek advice from the Red Kangaroo people, renowned for their intellect and wise counsel. They brought disturbing tales of what ghost-skins were doing in other parts of the land. They also brought some good news, of extraordinary weapons and tools, and of a ghost-skin who had traversed the giant river from the east and given black men iron axes. The blacks were impressed – these axes were so sharp, so useful.

Moonlight flooded the sand bank at the mouth of the Ngankaparinga where Murlawirrapurka sat. He was spending time in solitude, accessing the spirits of the land and its deep wells of wisdom. He gazed at the moon shining overhead and thought of Kirrila. When he had first heard that the white captain of the *yoko* was accompanied by a Kaurna woman, he fervently hoped it was Kirrila. The whole clan had awaited her return. But Sally informed him that she had known Kirrila on Karta, and the last she heard was that Kirrila set out to swim back to the land of her ancestors. Murlawirrapurka looked out to sea and was sure he could see Kirrila's spirit shining in the shimmer of the moonlight on the water.

Another sadness that weighed upon him was the murder of Collet Barker, the white man whom he had spoken to by this very river. He had liked the feel of his hand, and had seen the spirit of understanding in his eyes. Sally had informed Murlawirrapurka about the circumstances surrounding his murder, as she had been called upon to act as interpreter in the case. The three young Ngarrindjeri explained it was not only revenge that drove them to kill this pale naked man. They were in awe and fear of all white men who seemed to have so much power over them. They knew that whole races in the east had been destroyed by them. White man loomed as a ghostly, invincible spectre. And that strange round weapon that this particular white man carried? How were they to know it wouldn't destroy them just as mysteriously as the exploding sticks? They wanted to know if a white-skin could actually die. Hence the frenzy with which they ran their spears through and through the hapless Barker; proving that a black man could vanquish a white man; that a black man did have some power over these white invaders, who showed no respect for their ancestral kingdom, let alone their women. While Murlawirrapurka had sympathy with this view, he knew the Ngarrindjeri had killed the wrong white man.

Barker's companions had explained to Sally what a good man Barker was, especially in his dealings with black men. In Western Australia, Barker had befriended Mokare. Unusually for a white man, he had let himself be guided through Mineng country, graciously accepting Mokare's authority as its custodian. The two men became close as they camped together under the stars, explaining to each other their different cultural histories and deciphering the meanings of each other's dreams. When Mokare heard about Barker's's demise he was distraught, and organised a group of Aboriginal men to travel the vast distance to the Murray mouth to avenge Barker's death. But before they could carry out their mission, Mokare died from influenza.

'Ah that such a good, white man was so cruelly murdered,' agonised Murlawirrapurka. He loved the hot-headed Ngarrindjeri, who had always helped protect the gentler

27

Kaurna from their common enemies. But he exhorted them to distinguish between good white men and bad white men. Murlawirrapurka knew it must work the other way around too. If white men were afraid of black men, they would be less likely to distinguish between good and bad black men. So far, most white men failed to distinguish between Aboriginal groups at all. They lumped them together as 'savages', refusing to recognise the rich variety of culture and hundreds of distinct languages that had resonated throughout this vast southern land for millennia.

Sally also informed Murlawirrapurka that many ships were now docked at Karta, all waiting for Colonel Light to find a place on the mainland for their occupants to live. She predicted that it would be somewhere on the Tandanya plain. Sally told him that these people were different to the sealers and whalers who came and went. It seemed they were here to stay. Her opinion of Light was that he was a good man, hard working and dedicated to his task.

Tindo, the sun, was sending up fingers of light over the sleeping ancestor in the east as Murlawirrapurka walked away from the sea. He surveyed the land, stirring in the splendid *wiltutti* dawn. Soon, white people would be watching this same dawn. Why were they here? What was his destiny with them? He was arrested by the sound of the crows in the tall eucalyptus trees. 'Kua, Kua, Kua!' His spirit guides called him. He was Kua Kertamerru; first born of the crow totem of Murlawirra at Ngaltingga. On completing his initiation ceremonies, he had inherited the totemic rites and songs of his ancestors.

He stretched up welcoming arms towards them. Within their cries he heard, 'We of the Crow totem are creatures of change. We are here to help you through the tumult that will sweep your ancestral lands. You, Kua Kertamerru Murlawirrapurka, a fine embodiment of the Crow Totem, are charged with the following, "Be mindful of your opinions and actions, and always speak your truth in your life's mission."

Your watchword is "Integrity". This will guide you for the immense task ahead.'

A sailor carried baby Elizabeth Beare from the 'Duke of York' on to Kangaroo Island and pressed her chubby feet into the sand; the first imprint of a white settler in South Australia. Samuel Stephens, bristling with importance as colonial manager, was a little peeved, and made sure he was the first adult. Albert Taplow and the Bradshaws, who had suffered Stephens' sermons for weeks on the high seas, watched wearily as he attempted to instil order laced with Methodist virtues on the hardened sealers of Kangaroo Island. He failed dismally. By the time Walter Bromley – a future Protector of the Aborigines – arrived, the place had degenerated into squabbling, rum-fuelled chaos. Stephens had failed to control not only the sealers but also many of the ship's crew and settlers who, in the arid, waterless environment, quenched their thirst with the demon rum. Stephens found solace by marrying Charlotte, Elizabeth Beare's ancient maiden aunt. Bromley, while awaiting the job of Protector of the Aborigines to materialise, started a school for white children under the shade of a large currant tree. The *Africaine* arrived with colonial secretary, Robert Gouger. He urgently pressed Light to decide where the new city was to be. He was concerned for his wife Harriet, who had discovered during the arduous voyage from England that the nausea she was experiencing before leaving was not only due to anxiety about travelling half way around the world, but also because she was pregnant. Light directed the *Africaine*, and the swollen-bellied woman to Holdfast Bay.

Midlato was dismantling her *wardli* at last. The women and children carried their possessions down to the plain as the men hunted game. The extensive freshwater swamps behind the dunes at Patawalonga Creek were rich pickings during *wiltutti.* Midlato gathered succulent roots of bulrushes and reeds, as well as the eggs of countless water birds. Her special job was to find emu eggs. Members of her totemic group were forbidden to kill emus, to ensure that these large meaty birds would always be plentiful. However, Midlato was free to gather some of their eggs. She crept up quietly behind the male emu who sat on about ten at a time, and deftly removed two or three. Mmmmm. These eggs were delicious and nutritious. In addition, there were many different varieties of grains to be gathered, ground, and baked. Midlato was digging for roots with her *katta*, when her older brother Milte-widlo shouted from the top of a sand dune, '*Yoko, yoko.*' Children scattered and screamed. 'White sharks! White sharks. They are here!'

Among the adults, heated discussions were afoot about the impending invasion. Wirra children hunted for a certain kind of bird dropping at Yartabulti so that Wirra sorcerers could make a special charm to keep white-skins out. Young warriors advocated war tactics but knew they were at a disadvantage – this was an unknown enemy who had already vanquished eastern peoples with their magic weapons. While some thought ghost-skins were long lost ancestors, others hoped that by ignoring them, they might go away. Murlawirrapurka reminded everyone that the traditional Kaurna role was as educators, and they would just have to teach these ghost-skins how to behave on their land, just as Mokare had taught Barker. Murlawirrapurka advocated that first, they watch and wait.

From the vantage point of a leafy gum, Midlato and Milte-widlo espied strange white people being rowed from the ship. They watched as sailors carried them through the surf on to the hard sand. Midlato was particularly struck by a girl with green eyes, who squealed as a wave swept up and drenched her. Midlato gazed with wonder and fear. She couldn't understand why this girl wore so many strange coverings all over her body. She was encased in them, with hardly any skin showing. A *wardli* type thing, which had spread out in the water, draped her body; black stuff encased her legs and pelt imprisoned her feet.

'Perhaps white skin is delicate,' Midlato said to Milte-widlo.

White-skins squinted in the hot sun as it bounced off the white sand. They began banging sticks into the ground and putting up strange *wardlis*. Midlato was intrigued that they didn't use bark or tree branches but thin white pelts, similar to those she saw billowing from the ships.

Harriet Gouger's birth was imminent and she was desperate to get on land after enduring days of rolling about on interminable waves. But even after the sea calmed down, landing still proved to be a nightmare. Small boats had to bring her and other passengers to the sand bar in Holdfast Bay. She then suffered more discomfort and indignity, as she was carried on the shoulders of sailors through choppy seas to the shore.

After weeks of cramped accommodation and being blown half way around the world, the new settlers looked at where they had landed. Holdfast Bay was as lush as Kangaroo

Island was arid. Majestic gums rose behind the rolling sand dunes dredged with flowers and sedge. Honey myrtle and golden wattle lined the creeks, infusing the air with sublime scent. Further inland, vast lagoons fed by fresh water springs gave way to dramatic gullies. Settlers struggled in the robust winds to put up makeshift shelters. Robert Gouger hastily constructed his tent near a couple of shady gums, while the goats and chickens he had imported foraged in the new terrain. Gouger's servants created as comfortable a space as possible for the impending birth. Harriet had to make do with sandy floors which crawled with insects, and canvas ceilings which dropped more. Fortunately, they had brought with them comfortable couches to sleep on, a godsend when Robert narrowly missed being bitten by a scorpion lurking on the floor. Then Harriet had to contend with the continual barking of bullfrogs in nearby lagoons and, worse still, being attacked by swarms of mosquitoes.

Floods of white cockatoos squawked an incessant cacophony, which sounded like, 'Go home. Go home!' *I wish I could,* thought Harriet, nursing her heavy abdomen, idealising the precious past and fearing the unknown future. As well as the impending birth, she was worried by spots of blood that were appearing when she coughed. But there were recompenses – the vegetation was alive with an array of exotic birds: laughing kookaburras; warbling magpies; bronze-winged pigeons; and green parrots. A flock of rainbow lorikeets fought noisily for a perch on top of a large printing press transported by Robert Thomas, the government printer. His daughter Helen gathered bunches of yellow flowers that smelt like new mown hay and strewed them over their tent floor, creating a fragrant carpet. Albert Taplow, the young

Quaker, helped construct a storehouse which was filled with surveying equipment, supplies and gunpowder.

On November 11th Gouger and Light walked inland along the Karrawirraparri, and were encouraged by the country before them. It was swathed in luxuriant grass reminiscent of an English park, studded by sheoaks, eucalypt and native pines, and framed by 'those enchanted hills'. Light became more and more convinced that this was where Adelaide should lie.

All around the Holdfast settlement tufts of kangaroo grass abounded with brown quail and ground parrots. Albert Taplow went exploring and chanced upon Milte-widlo making a fire in the nearby dunes. Terrified, the boy made to run away, but hesitated when Albert offered him biscuits. Albert's uncle had tirelessly campaigned for the end of slavery and Albert was keen to make friends with the natives. He beckoned Milte-widlo into the white camp and showed him the store house and his tent. Milte-widlo goggled at what he saw, especially the magical lucifer sticks which so easily started fires. He ran off excitedly to tell Midlato.

Camped at the edge of a sand dune, Ellen Bradshaw struggled to light a fire to boil water for tea. She had run out of lucifer sticks and was trying to use a flint. She saw some black children watching her unsuccessful efforts. Milte-widlo had brought back Midlato, who stared in wonder. Eventually her brother ventured over and very dexterously rubbed a stick into a stone and managed to get the fire alight. Her billy boiled and she gratefully made a nice cup of tea. Both children were amazed at the water boiling in the billy. The winds had died down and the sun beat fiercely onto the camp. With the heat came more insects and more ominous looking creatures. Ellen Bradshaw's daughter Lucy screamed when she saw what she thought was a dragon. Midlato recognised her as the girl with green eyes. She picked up the dragon and stroked its head, showing Lucy that it was a harmless *kalta* or sleepy lizard. As she did so a stunning butterfly with black, white, red and yellow markings fluttered past. '*Pilyabilya,*' pointed Midlato. '*Pilyabilya,*' repeated Lucy slowly, giving the black girl a big smile, 'What a beautiful word for butterfly.' Lucy was intrigued by Midlato's headband. It had what looked like teeth dangling from it.

Gouger tried to make his wife as comfortable as possible. He was relieved that initial encounters with the natives had been friendly. He wrote in his diary, 'I felt great anxiety respecting them and hoped our province would be unstained by native blood.'

The weather got hotter and hit 103 degrees as Christmas approached.

James Cronk proved his labouring skills by sinking the first well in the new colony. It went to fourteen feet and tapped a moderate supply of fresh water.

The number of settlers reached 300 as they waited patiently for Governor Hindmarsh to arrive on the *Buffalo*, and for a decision to be made about where the new city would be sited.

Christmas 1836 was 105 degrees. The settlers, stiflingly hot in their starched collars and stiff bonnets, insisted on a traditional Christmas dinner; roast beef and plum pudding, supplemented by pork and parrot pie. Fresh beef was courtesy of a cow, which having survived months on the deepest of oceans, drowned in a lagoon! A Christmas service was held in a large tent. Light, exhausted from all his hard work, was too ill to join in the festivities.

Midlato was intrigued by the clucking birds in cages near the white-skins' tents. She watched the girl with green eyes gather their eggs.

How easy to collect those, she thought. Midlato picked ground figs and quandong berries and gave them to Lucy Bradshaw. Lucy handed her a penny in return, grateful for some fruit after the long sea journey.

Midlato couldn't wait to find a hidey-hole so that she could look at her treasure. It felt round and warm in her hand. She nestled in the hollow of a gum tree hidden by tall grass, and gazed at her prize. She marvelled at its perfect roundness, like the sun or a full moon, and a bit like a smooth pebble in the river. She put the object between her teeth. It was hard. Must be made of *puri* or stone. The colour reminded her of the shiny brown back of a reed beetle.

'Ah!' she gasped at the image. The head of a man, perched on a fat neck, looked into the distance. Her heart leapt. Was this an ancestor of the ghost-skins? If so, how clever of them to etch his picture on this piece of brown *puri*. She marvelled to see tiny inscriptions around the edge of the disc. She turned it over and gasped again. A resplendent looking figure held a spear and a shield. Midlato was puzzled – the breasts showed it was female. A female ancestor who had a spear and a shield? Only the men of her people ever handled such weapons. It was a strange looking spear with three prongs. Looking more closely at the shield she saw a design on it – similar to what she had seen on sticks, flying in the breeze at Patawalonga Creek. The design reminded her of a simple spider web. There was something strange on top of the woman's head. What was it? It looked like a creature crawling over her head and down her back. A snake? Or perhaps some kind of possum? Or perhaps it was a large feather. *Or even cockatoo feathers,* she thought excitedly, just like her people wore in ceremonies. She would have to show this to her *kammammi* – what would she make of it?

Wauwe Woman: Oy, it pains me that you have Midlato looking at this penny with such wonder. The poor little mite. If she only knew what she was looking at.

Author: The man with the fat neck? It was William IV – a bit of a buffoon, ten illegitimate children; not quite as mad as his father, George IV, who kept a pet giraffe in his palace, but harmless enough.

Wauwe woman: Harmless! I'll have you know, this so-called common 'ancestor' was one of the most vociferous opponents to the abolition of slavery. Argued in Parliament that it would be the end of the British Empire.

Wirra Woman: How right he was.

Wauwe woman: He talked of his duty to keep the slaves 'happy' in Jamaica.

Author: Well Midlato didn't know any of that, did she?

The heatwave on the Tandanya plain pulsed relentlessly. The settlers, stuffed with Christmas pudding, scanned the sea anxiously for the arrival of the Governor and Resident Commissioner. Why the delay? Their world had been reduced to this camp, filled with blowflies by day, and blood-engorged mosquitoes by night. Then at long last – a sail!

The settlers, flushed with excitement, ran to the edge of the water and watched the portly Governor being carried ashore on the backs of several sailors. A marine guard of honour flanked Hindmarsh, as he stepped out onto his new domain. At his elbow strutted James Hurtle Fisher, wanting to assert his joint authority as Commissioner. Things had begun badly on the *Buffalo*, when both jostled interminably over which members of their large families should sit at the Governor's table. The ship was overcrowded, made worse by all the livestock Hindmarsh insisted on transporting, including dogs, cows, poultry, and mules.

The Proclamation was read by George Stevenson, Hindmarsh's secretary. The British flag was unfurled. Cannons fired a 21-gun royal salute.

The air rang with hurrahs as a lunch of cold pork and a ham was served. The Governor mounted a chair and announced the first toast, 'The King.' During the national anthem Lucy Bradshaw giggled as Osmond Gilles, the crown treasurer, already tanked with rum, gustily sang 'God save George our King', forgetting the salient fact that it was now a William who had been on the throne for six years.

'Rule, Britannia' was sung, and as evening descended more cannons were fired.

In all the excitement, only Albert Taplow took notice of the part in the Proclamation, which declared that the Governor 'would take every lawful means to secure to the Aborigines the rights of British subjects.'

The said 'Aborigines', who watched from various hiding points, ran away in terror every time they heard the deafening salutes. Even the Wirra sorcerers could not produce such thunder on demand. For Harriet Gouger, the reverberations heralded the start of labour. At dawn, she gave birth. Gouger happily wrote, 'My wife gave the new province a son! He is claimed by the Governor as his godson, as being the first child born in the colony, after the establishment of the Government.' The baby was aptly christened Henry Hindmarsh.

Governor Hindmarsh charged Robert Thomas to print the new proclamation, and ordered his marines to carry the printing press to a hut built for the purpose. The rainbow lorikeets quickly found a new perch on Mrs Hindmarsh's piano.

In his continued race against time, Light eschewed the formalities of the Governor's landing, and walked the six miles inland to check out his proposed site for Adelaide. He decided that's where it would be, writing, 'Nature has done so much that very little human labour and cost is requisite to make this one of the finest settlements in the whole world.'

Midlato and Milte-widlo wandered around the edge of the camps, gazing curiously at all the paraphernalia these white people possessed. Midlato saw Lucy carrying a strange long contraption that opened up into a beautiful picture over her head. 'Parasol.' said the white girl, laughing at the expression on Midlato's face. Midlato noticed this 'parasol' shaded her pale face. Charles Moon, a sailor from the *Buffalo*, beckoned Milte-widlo to come aboard his ship.

'No!' Midlato screamed in panic. 'Don't go, you will never come back. They will take you to the land of the dead.'

After a great deal of gesticulation, Milte-widlo was finally coaxed on board, leaving two bemused whites behind as hostages. Midlato watched and waited anxiously. It seemed an eternity before she saw him tottering back. His foolish grin convinced Midlato that white-skins had taken away his senses.

'Fire-water, we drank fire-water. It was so good and the food – excellent.' Milte-widlo rubbed his belly in great satisfaction.

Midlato's *kammammi* was not amused when her grandson came lurching back to the *wardli*. She shook her head sadly. She didn't like the way he smelt.

'They were nice, very nice. They have so many things; such wonderful food, such excellent fire-water. They are our long-lost brothers and together we will be so happy.'

His grandmother did not share his gushing enthusiasm. She knew Milte-widlo was young and impetuous and easily swayed. She didn't like the way his eyes rolled. She hadn't reckoned on this 'fire-water'. She recoiled from the notion and had a premonition that it would be very bad for the future of her people. She felt old and weary as she looked into the fire and sighed, 'Hmmph!'

Over the next few days, in relentless heat, Light had to endure opposition to his proposal for where Adelaide should lie. The corpulent Hindmarsh, puffing and huffing to the site, (no horse-drawn carriages here!) complained that it was too far from the sea. 'My good man, Britain is a maritime empire – unheard of to have a city so far from the sea.' Settlers meanwhile baked in their tents and waited while the worthies argued. Light attempted to compromise by suggesting they place the city closer to the coast, but after observing signs that the river flooded there, reverted to his original decision, much to Hindmarsh's annoyance. James Hurtle Fisher supported Light, if only to oppose Hindmarsh's authority. As resident commissioner, he appointed the South Australian Light and his surveyor Finniss to set up their camp at a spot by the river, just west of the Tandanya rock. More ships arrived. Flies and insects and exotic creepy-crawlies became even more bothersome. Of the flies, Gouger wrote, 'Nothing can equal their cruel perseverance.' Ann Finniss, after surviving gruelling months at sea and a sandy flyblown tent, graced the new colony with the first birth for the year of 1837. Wife and child were trundled six miles in a whicker boat on wheels, to where Finiss had set up his survey tent.

So, by natural increase as well as immigration, Wakefield's South Australia started to grow. But immediately ahead lay trouble.

Ityamai-itpina came back from hunting, and listened to Milte-widlo's excited babble. He decided to check things out for himself. He tentatively pushed open the door of the new storehouse and saw three white men. Albert Taplow was showing George Stevenson the huge stock of seeds he had organised. Albert spied the black man and beckoned him in. He was delighted to be in close proximity to such a fierce looking warrior, daubed with paint and except for his *yudna*, naked. Ityamai-itpina put down his spear and gazed around the store, agog with wonder. He espied a blue jacket with shiny buttons and yellow cuffs. Albert approached him, and much to his surprise started shaking his hand. After quite a lot of shaking Albert kept pointing at the black man's hand and it took a while for Ityamai-itpina to realise he wanted to know the Kaurna word for hand. Ityamai-itpina wasn't sure he should tell him. The metal buttons glinted so seductively that he finally uttered, '*marra*.'

'*Marra*,' repeated George Stevenson, who came forward and started shaking his '*marra*' vigorously. 'I'm George.' As well as being Hindmarsh's secretary he had also been appointed first interim Aboriginal Protector, so thought he'd better get acquainted with these 'savages', as he preferred to call them.

'Joj,' Ityamai-itpina smiled, displaying 'a mouthful of the finest teeth' Stevenson had ever seen.

'You?' George pointed at him.

'Ityamai-itpina.'

'It... what? I tell you what I'm going to call you Rodney. King Rodney.'

Ityamai-itpina looked blank and started touching the shiny buttons on the jacket in wonder. George coaxed him to put it on, and also some trousers.

'I'm going to introduce King Rodney to our civilised ways,' announced George. 'Now that he is decently dressed.' He led Ityamai-itpina out of the storehouse and guided him towards his ship, the *Buffalo*. Ityamai-itpina was wary – was this just a ploy? Was the white-skin trying to trap him? He signalled that he would only go to the ship if he could return. Albert, who was following, nodded that he understood and performed an elaborate mime to show how Ityamai-itpina could go on to the ship and then come back again. The black man liked Albert. He wasn't so sure about 'Joj.' Albert looked directly into his eyes, which he found reassuring. When they reached the ship, Ityamai-itpina jumped at the sight of a strange animal on the prow.

'A buffalo,' explained Albert, laughing, miming a buffalo with horns. The black man couldn't believe his eyes as he went on board. He had marvelled at these ships from afar, but now he could see the ropes, masts and sails in their intricate detail. He was in awe of the workmanship involved. The Kaurna were proud of their fibre culture, but these ropes and riggings were unbelievable. How did the ghost-skins do it? He entered a long low room where other white men were sitting at a wooden structure, piled with delicious smelling food. The men smiled and welcomed him, beckoning him to sit down and eat. Ityamai-itpina watched George, who picked up some finely wrought implements, and proceeded to cut and spear the food, then place it in his mouth. Ityamai-itpina carefully observed how the sharp bladed implement was held, and how the many-pronged spear worked. Soon he was able to slice some of the cooked meat and put it in his mouth. George was impressed by his dexterity. Milte-widlo had been right. This meat was extraordinarily good.

'Beef,' said George, pointing to the chunks of meat on the plate. Ityamai-itpina, smiling broadly, his white teeth glinting in the light of the lamps, went on to savour fish, tongue, and plum pudding. What tastes, sights and sounds! A ghost-skin seated himself at another wooden structure which supported a large array of large perfectly even teeth, and started pushing the teeth up and down. Ityamai-itpina couldn't believe the enchanting sound that issued forth, like the tinkling of a waterfall. Then to top it all, another ghost-skin blew into a shiny *winbirra*, as silvery as the moon. The resulting tune engendered in Ityamai-itpina a totally irresistible desire to dance. Like for all the Kaurna, dancing was deep in his blood, as was the spirit of exchange. These white-skins had graced him with food and beautiful music. In return, he wanted to offer them his dance. He eagerly mimed at George, 'I want to dance.' But George shook his head, (he must assert his white superiority and test this native's obedience!) The music continued. Ityamai-itpina mimed again, 'I want to dance.' Again, the white man shook his head. But the black man could not suppress the urge to dance that welled up within him. It was unbearable. Undeterred, he mimed again.

Albert who was watching all this burst out, 'Mr Stevenson, please sir, I beg you. Allow this man to dance!'

'Yes,' said Robert Cock, a Scotsman who had endured the interminable squabbles between Hindmarsh, Stevenson and Fisher on the gruelling sea journey. 'Let him dance.'

George, not looking too pleased, wiped his fingers slowly on a napkin, and at last deigned to nod. Ityamai-itpina leapt up ecstatically and 'began kicking and dancing with all his might.' The whites cheered and clapped.

George wrote in his diary that Ityamai-itpina possessed 'a degree of archness and quickness which places this race many degrees above the savage.'

Wirra Woman: What a condescending boor!

Ityamai-itpina was impressed by what he had seen, and was grinning happily as Albert and Robert Cock escorted him back to dry land. Ityamai-itpina returned to his countrymen, sporting his blue jacket with metal buttons. They took one look at his strange garb and ran away in fright. Only when he took the jacket off did they accept him back and listened to his stories, open-mouthed. Perhaps these people were old ancestors, who having learnt incredible skills and amassed great riches, had been resurrected and impelled back to their beloved land of birth; a deep pull every Kaurna knew intimately. Why else would these pale people come in such numbers? It didn't look like they were just setting up a trading post, like the Karta sealers. It must be that they were returning to share their good fortune with their black brothers.

Only the elders sighed and kept mum. *Let him believe for a while that all this is good,* they thought, as they stared into the camp fire embers. They will learn the truth soon enough.

CHAPTER 3

Aliens

Svitochka didn't know where in the world she had landed. A hair-raising escape through a scary forest, a long tedious journey over several oceans, sojourns in various migrant camps, a stint on a sheep farm, and now here; on the sun-baked streets of Adelaide, which harboured some decidedly unfriendly children. Her mother Tatiana, who loved partying and dancing and had disgraced herself by flirting outrageously with sailors and jackeroos, couldn't stand the quiet. The corner shop at the end of Commercial Road fell sadly short of the expectations engendered by the gaily-coloured Rosella Parrot painted on its side. Within the dingy interior lurked a few unpromising tins inscribed with writing Tatiana couldn't decipher, and no fresh produce whatsoever. A rather ancient proprietor regarded Svitochka's skipping about with great suspicion. Tatiana hastily bought a bottle of Rosella tomato sauce before escaping. She dragged Svitochka by tram into the city centre, looking for hustle and bustle and bright city lights. None were to be found.

Adelaide stood quiet, orderly and well defined. In one way, this was reassuring – Tatiana flashed back to Magdeburg, the city she had been transported to at the tender age of seventeen as a Nazi slave. For the next three years she witnessed Allied War planes pulverise this magnificent baroque city into a pile of rubble, killing most of the population, including thousands of her fellow slaves. Adelaide stood reassuringly calm and serene. In the shade of the Post Office tower, Tatiana looked out over the marigolds of Victoria Square, not knowing that they blanketed Adelaide's own war past, when they had been dug up for air raid shelters. The fact that Japanese bombers were extremely unlikely to fly so far south was irrelevant, the shelters reassured the South Australian citizens. Svitochka and her mother looked up at the statue of Queen Victoria, wondering who she was. Little did they know that in the name of the British Empire she had vanquished a far older race who, at full moon, danced ecstatically in this very square. But no one danced here now. Tatiana consoled herself by taking Svitochka to the nearby Adelaide Market, where German and Greek traders sold rather delicious produce. She filled her basket with sausage and olives, while Svitochka buried her face in a torte.

Tatiana was disappointed in Adelaide. In fact, that was putting it mildly. She had been induced into leaving the flattering attentions of numerous Jackeroos at a sheep farm near Wagga Wagga when Ivan had flown in to propose to her. Tatiana was impressed! Fresh from hard labour on a hydroelectric scheme in Tasmania, and fed up with loneliness and bad food in a cheap boarding house, Ivan wanted a wife. He had fallen in love with the tempestuous Tatiana on the journey to Australia. Now he had landed a job at the new General Motors Holden factory in Adelaide, and flew Tatiana and her daughter in. He was seduced by what would later be called Playfordism. The Premier of South Australia, Thomas Playford, attracted large numbers of refugees with promises of plenty of work, cheap housing, and cheap goods. Ivan was Tom Playford's perfect migrant; willing to work extremely long hours and help build the new industrial South Australia. Well, not quite so perfect – he was in fact a secret Jew, spoke a weird language, had weird customs, and could conceivably even be a commie. But these vagaries were to be smartly dealt with by the assimilation policies of both Commonwealth and State Government. Good Neighbour Councils sprang up all over Australia for this very task. Even new citizenship conventions were drawn up, to prepare for the influx of 'aliens', as the refugees were called. Of course, this did not extend to people with coloured skin. The White Australia Policy was a given in the 1950s, as surely as flies crawled up your nose.

Svitochka did not even know of the existence of Australia's original inhabitants. After all, the British had brought 'history', as well as their colourful spider-web flag, to *terra nullius*. Any inconvenient indigenous people were relegated to 'pre-history', and safely tucked away out of sight in far flung missions. But Svitochka did play on an old bent gumtree in Heywood Park, which was just around the corner from Commercial Road. Heywood Park was the last remnant of the Black Forest which covered the Adelaide Plain, in which the Kaurna once roamed, and in whose trees another little girl, Midlato, sat mesmerised by a British penny, over one hundred years earlier. Governor Robe razed South Australia's extensive Black Forest during the Crimean War.

Wirra Woman: Why?

Author: In case escaping Russians tried to hide there of course! Akin to the riddle of why marigolds were dug up from Victoria Square during World War Two.

47

Wauwe Woman: I want to comment. You think Svitochka had a bad time being a refugee? You try being a refugee in your own country! That's what happened to my people. At least Svitochka had more rights than us mob.

Tatiana and Ivan had a two-year compulsory contract to work out, in return for their passages to Australia. They stared at their incomprehensible 'Alien Registration Certificates' in dread. All they knew was that must obey these certificates and not lose them. Any migrants who broke the contract were jailed and deported. God knew where to! Giant graveyards were all that was left of the countries they came from.

While Ivan settled into his mind-numbing position on the assembly line at GM Holden, Tatiana was forced to work as a domestic. She hated it. She'd had enough of slave labour during the war. She soon fell out with Miss Bressler. Jeanette watched sadly as the trio trundled their cases past her window. They moved to a mansion in Springfield, from which Ivan cycled several miles to work on a bike rented from Super Elliots in town, and where Tatiana slaved as a domestic. But they soon moved again when Tatiana refused to wash off the excrement spread on the walls by the spoilt two-year-old of the household. Tatiana's friend Katherina, whom she had met on the ship, was fortunate to land an office job at Charles Birks, a large department store in the city. When Tatiana voiced her envy, Katherina replied,

'I tell you it's no picnic. The boss makes me come in an hour earlier than the Australian employees. I have to clean the offices. Of course, I don't get extra money for this. The rest of the time I'm a dogsbody, running around doing all the shit jobs that the Australians won't do.'

At the beginning of 1952 Svitochka turned five and went to school. She found this very unnerving, as she was the only child with a strange name. She envied the girls in their pretty pink angora jumpers, buckled shoes, and short bobbed hair. These contrasted painfully with her lace-up boots, heavy trousers, and long plaits, through which her mother wove brightly coloured ribbons. These ribboned braids, all the rage in some backwater village of the Soviet Union, at best attracted quizzical stares from these fluffy girls who sported easy hair styles. Their lunchboxes contained neat, white triangles of bread, encasing delicate slivers of Kraft cheese. They visibly moved away when Svitochka opened her lunchbox, liberating a pungent waft of garlic sausage bought from a new Polish stall in the market.

On the first morning, the class stood up and sang *God Save the King*. Svitochka didn't know who this king was. Two days later Adelaide was plunged into a deep gloom. When Tatiana took Svitochka into town to buy a straw hat, the stores were all draped in black. Pictures of George VI, resplendent with crown and sceptre, replaced the usual window displays. Flags hung at half mast. People shuffled about sadly, not raising their eyes from beneath the brims of their hats. Tatiana and Svitochka were puzzled. On the next schoolday, Svitochka discovered that the king was dead. In the big quadrangle, wearing her new straw hat with red cherries, she now had to sing *God Save the Queen*. This did not fill her with a lot of confidence in God.

She wasn't long at this school before the family moved again. On the first day at her next school, the headmistress asked to see her stomach. *Australia was very strange*, thought Svitochka, not really wanting to show this stranger her belly. Reluctantly she pulled up her jumper. 'Go home

49

immediately,' the headmistress pronounced. 'You have chicken pox!'

The chairs in the Returned Servicemen's League Hall on Tapleys Hill Road waited in neat rows for the afternoon Good Neighbour Council meeting. Miss Lynette Taplow, buck-toothed and squinting behind goggle glasses, sat at the front table. Her canary-yellow cardigan hung proudly from the back of her chair. She had just retrieved it from lay-by at Harris Scarfe in Rundle Street, having paid one shilling for several weeks from her scanty wage as a draper's assistant. Now she was annoyed that it was too hot to wear it. It was Wednesday half-closing day, and she was here for an important meeting of how local residents must handle the aliens who were filtering like germs into the area. She had already seen said aliens walk tentatively past the draper's shop, looking curiously at the materials and embroidery threads in the window. She held her breath and was enormously relieved when they walked on. Her shop was situated further along Tapley's Hill Road, dangerously close to the new Philips factory, where floods of aliens were being sent to work.

An imperceptible flush spread beneath Lynette's powder. She lightly swung the canary yellow cardie over her hot shoulders. Barry Guthrie had walked in, his brown shorts and gartered socks adorning his freckled legs.

'Good afternoon, Miss Taplow. Blimey it's hot today!' He immediately dismissed the uncharitable thought that her cardigan matched the colour of her teeth. His knees bulged out from in between his shorts and socks like awkward cauliflowers. His red flap ears sprang free as he took off his hat and liberated his sweaty head. Lynette didn't care

– he was her last hope as she sat on the dusty shelf of spinsterhood.

Recently widowed, Guthrie was a returned serviceman from World War One. He never tired of reminding people that 60,000 Australians were killed in that war, twice the number as in World War Two. He knew that soldiers suffered terribly in both wars, but he liked to think it was much harder for him. As a youngster, he had survived being blown apart by Turks at Gallipoli, been bombarded by Fritz in France, and endured having to watch his mates die in rat-infested trenches behind an elusive Western Front. He felt that this RSL Hall, built in dedication to servicemen returning from the Great War, was his stomping ground, and resented the new swathe of cocky soldiers who swashbuckled in from the recent war. The Government was bending over backwards to reward them with homes, work and education: much better than he'd had, when he returned from his war and was stuck out on a rocky barren farm.

The Second World War soldiers had been helped with payouts, water schemes, and bags of nutrients. Their farms were flourishing. Barry felt overlooked. An injury, courtesy of Fritz, had prevented him from enlisting again but he had worked bloody hard for the war effort. As supervisor at the Hendon Munitions factory he turned out guns and bullets galore, so those cocky whippersnappers could thrash the Japs. After the war, he felt as useless as the abandoned Hendon plant. But life moved on. A Dutchman bought the site at a bargain price, reincarnated it as the Philips factory, and Premier Playford bestowed his blessing with an official opening in 1947. Barry secured an important job supervising a growing migrant workforce. He was also in charge of the newly established local Good Neighbour Council. Today was the first meeting.

Displaced persons were trickling into the area. Fed up with being squeezed into hot iron huts, and travelling from far off immigration centres, many were setting up asbestos shacks in Royal Park, a suburb near the new factory on the other side of Tapley's Hill Road. The distinctly regal name belied the flat, uninviting, treeless wasteland that had once been the marshy reedbeds of the Port River, and was now scented by sewerage works. This alien invasion was not popular. Barry's job today at this Good Neighbour Council meeting was to help the good people of Hendon deal with the influx. The Labour Party under Prime Minister Chifley, which had been instrumental in bringing out these Displaced People, faced huge opposition. A 1947 countrywide poll showed that 83% of Australians were against accepting refugees from the Holocaust, and the government was accused of diluting the ethnic Anglo-Saxon balance. The immigration minister Arthur Calwell sought to pacify this opposition by dictating clearly,

'Our aim is to Australianise all our migrants … in as short a time as possible … only the local Australian people … can bring about the ultimate assimilation of any group of migrants in their midst.'

Barry braced himself with a glass of Woodies lemonade supplied by Lynette, and waited for the hall to fill. This particular section of 'local Australian people' grumbled fiercely at the impending destruction of their Anglo-Saxon way of life.

Barry sighed as he saw the biggest grumbler of all walk in and hand Lynette a tray of lamingtons for afternoon tea. It was Mildred Taplow, Lynette's sister-in-law. She was as large and imperious as the floral dress that draped over her expansive middle. The voluminous garment fell incongruously short, just below her stout knees, in the jauntier post-war style. Even though it was stiflingly hot she was determined to uphold British values and wore hat, gloves and shoes to match. As she took off her hat and waved the flies away, she exposed her hairstyle, a direct copy of her heroine Elizabeth, the wife of King George VI; as short and incongruous as her skirt.

Mildred had snapped up Albert Taplow, a diminutive, shy man, quite late in life, and to everyone's surprise produced Trevor, who trailed behind her.

'Say hello to Aunty Lynette,' she ordered the small boy, 'and go and sit down.' Trevor meekly did as he was told. He had disgraced himself already by getting shoe polish on his clean white socks. Mildred's attempts to make him to look like Prince Charles had failed miserably. The back of his head was suitably shaved but that was where the resemblance ended. Instead of a princely smooth top, a gingery unkempt frizz sprouted haphazardly to defy his mother.

'Why are these reffos coming to this neighbourhood?' was the burning question on all lips, as Guthrie started the meeting. All welcomed British migrants heartily. In fact, Mildred had enjoyed sending parcels to the beleaguered mother island during the war. She took pride in being a British subject, and in the fact that she and her husband were direct descendants of early settlers. Albert Taplow's great-grandfather and namesake had come over on one of the first ships, and Mildred's great aunt, Mildred Fowler, followed soon after. Mildred Taplow felt behoven to maintain South Australia's clean Anglo-Saxon heritage. These refugees from Eastern Europe were an entirely different prospect. It was fine to send them up to the Leigh Creek coalfields or to the army barracks at Woodside or even up to Mildred's hometown Gawler, to work on the little Para reservoir; the first lot of Displaced Persons had been sent to these places. And rightly so. Premier Playford was to be commended for bringing South Australia into the 20th century. But they were not wanted here; not in this bastion of Britishness. Not in Hendon. These Displaced Persons were well and truly aliens. They did not speak the language. They just would not fit in.

Barry Guthrie took a deep breath. Even though he went along with the mood in the room, his big task was to persuade his truculent audience that reffos were here to stay. The Phillips factory really needed them, as did the large new General Motors Holden Plant, just the other side of the Port Road.

'But why can't the British do these jobs?'

Barry didn't really like to say they wouldn't put up with the long hours and inferior accommodation; nor that it was easier to herd the aliens into the unskilled dirty jobs Brits and Aussies refused to do. Instead he explained that these reffos were among the lucky few to escape the bloodbath in Eastern Europe; they were homeless, rootless, and grateful to be working and to have food in their bellies. Mildred and the others shuffled and coughed. Tales of hardship did not move them. They had all been toughened by the Great Depression of the 1930s and the deprivation of the war years. Rations for petrol, tea, and butter had only recently ended. And anyway, there was still a war on. Australian forces were keeping back the commies in Korea.

'How do we know these reffos aren't a bunch of commies? How do we know who, or what, we are letting into our own backyards?' Murmurs of 'too right!' spread about the room. Lynette shooed the flies off the lamingtons.

'All foreigners are suspect,' was the underlying conviction. The goodly people of this area remembered their outrage when the giant 64-acre Hendon site had been bought by foreigners. Wasn't Tom Playford selling them out? Mildred had felt proud to contribute to the British war effort at the Hendon Munitions plant. For the first time in her life, she had received a wage to bolster the measly pounds her husband brought in from his job at Coles department store. The new Hendon railway station, built on the road at the back of her house in Pudney Street, had increased the value of their home. Big puffing trains spewed out workers for the munitions factory every morning and swallowed them up every evening. Now Mildred saw a different kind of people stuffing up the carriages. They wore ill-assorted clothes and gabbled in uncouth languages. She didn't like to enter the compartments with 'them'. They smelt awful and slurped soup out of filthy looking containers. She even saw one gnawing on a chicken leg! They were downright disgusting. At least they didn't live in this neighbourhood – yet! What would happen to the value of her house if they did?

In between swatting flies Lynette Taplow took notes. Barry Guthrie wearily fielded the barrage of questions and complaints and threw back the answers:

'No. These reffos are not commies. They're running away from commie regimes.'

'No, we aren't bringing in any enemies. No Nazis. A few Austrians and Germans maybe, but they all hated Hitler.'

'Jews? No, they are excluded from the Displaced Persons' programme.'

'No, there are no more Greeks or enemy Eyeties.'

Guthrie was tired. It was nearly four o'clock. Time for lamingtons and a nice cup of tea.

'No, you'll be pleased to know this influx of people mostly have fair skin and many have blue eyes. As Calwell has said, it is up to us to 'Australianise' them as quickly as possible.'

'And dark-skinned people?'

'Good God no!'

Barrie Guthrie and the RSL were 100% behind the White Australia Policy. As he gratefully pounced on the lamingtons Guthrie shuddered, remembering the dreadful incident when an Aborigine man, fresh back from fighting, tried to join the RSL.

'I am a returned serviceman. I defended my country. I dodged bullets alongside my white mates,' he argued, before being unceremoniously escorted from the hallowed chambers.

While Ivan was Playford's ideal migrant, Tatiana was Playford's worst. This was probably not surprising, since Playford's great-grandfather was a fiery Baptist minister who, in the early days of the colony, took it upon himself to stamp out wicked and frivolous behaviour. And Tatiana was wicked and frivolous. She wanted to have fun; to drink vodka; to dance; to paint her nails; to wear mink. She hated the drudgery of being a domestic. She also hated the prejudice she felt from ordinary Australians, especially every time they moved house. The Pleznowskis always seemed to be the first reffos in any new area but also the last to be served in shops. The neighbours of the semi they rented in the respectable suburb of Payneham were decidedly hostile.

Tatiana was close to blowing point. She was volatile already, but a past where she had always been the underdog weighed heavily on her pretty brow. One stifling afternoon when she and Svitochka had waited a long time to be served, Tatania exploded. To Svitochka's mortification, Tatiana started screaming at all the people in the shop. The trouble was she couldn't stop. It was like she had unleashed a bag of demons. She fell to the floor thrashing violently and sobbing hysterically. A doctor and then an ambulance were hastily called. Svitochka stood miserably in a corner as her mother was taken away.

A lady in a large hat covered in grapes took her by the hand and led her up Payneham Road to an imposing house, Wanslea Home, one of many philanthropic institutions in Adelaide. This one had been set up in 1941 to support the war effort, and was now dedicated to looking after children whose mothers were seriously ill or hospitalised. Svitochka was the first refugee girl they had ever seen. The ladies were kind enough, but Svitochka felt miserable as she pushed the baked beans around her plate. The taste reminded her of disgusting Rosella tomato sauce. She was worried about Tatiana, who seemed to flip alarmingly from being a laughing, sunny mother to a demonic, wicked mother. She would subject Svitochka to vicious beatings with seemingly little provocation. However, the demon you know is better than the one you don't, and Svitochka wiggled the cherries which adorned her straw hat to comfort herself. Tatiana, the good mother, had bought it for her, and she now refused to take it off. She didn't like this place. Not one bit. She didn't like the way ladies with forced smiles looked down at her as if she was an exhibit in a jar. She hoped she didn't have to stay here forever. Thankfully, she was saved by a very worried-looking Ivan; who took her home immediately. Tatiana was gobbling tablets, which seemed to calm her down.

Lady Norrie was arranging flowers in one of the upper bedrooms of Government House. She had just returned from accompanying her husband Sir Willoughby, the Governor of South Australia, on a visit to schools and mines in the outback. The Norries believed that their duty in the post-war years was to keep the 'empire spirit' alive. And they did so with gusto. Lady Norrie supported many charitable and patriotic causes, but there were limits. Like her husband, Lady Norrie criticised the 'misguided sentimentality' of Dr Charles Duguid. This goodly doctor kept harping on about Aborigine rights. He even had brought (would you believe!) Aborigines back from the missions, and allowed some to live in his house in the affluent suburb of Magill. She shuddered at the thought.

Lady Norrie preferred to direct her attention to worthier causes, like the 'Food for Britain Appeal', or assisted schemes to bring more British migrants over. The Norries stalwartly conceded that South Australia should accept Holocaust survivors, even though most of the population had voted against it. It was, after all, the Christian thing to do, and there were so many 'dirty' jobs they could usefully carry out: like excavating the brown coal up at Leigh Creek, so that South Australia did not have to rely on the eastern states for black coal. Or hacking at hard baked clay in the blinding heat, in order to assemble hundreds of miles of pipelines so precious water could keep the lawns of Adelaide green. She and Willoughby had examined the spartan Nissen hut up at Leigh Creek, where Hungarian refugee, Magdalena Leolkes, had made the best of a grim situation while her husband excavated coal. Magdalena felt honoured by the Governor's visit and spruced up her hut so it looked as immaculate as possible. Lady Norrie was spared seeing how the nappies that hung on makeshift lines immediately turned black with the coal dust that pervaded everything. But Magdalena wasn't complaining. At least she wasn't in a tent, nor forcibly separated from her husband, as was the lot of most other Displaced Persons.

But as Lady Norrie arranged her roses, she saw something far worse than three children crammed into a corner of a stinking hot hut while a pot simmered on a wood stove – so terrible she nearly dropped her vase. Horror of horrors – there were some people on the immaculately green front lawn of Government House. They looked like peasants. They certainly weren't British.

'Oh my God. It looks like they are spreading out a blanket for a picnic?'

With great urgency, she called for the servants.

Tatiana had at last persuaded Ivan to have a Sunday off and take her and Svitochka on a picnic. She wanted to go to the Botanic Gardens, which she heard were full of European trees. The trio entered what they thought was the Botanic Gardens – it was beautiful and green – full of the magnificent firs and oaks which Tatiana really missed. Choosing a charming spot surrounded by beds of flowers, she started to lay out the picnic: her homemade plaited bread dredged with poppy seeds; chunks of Polish sausage; dill cucumber; piroshki stuffed with cabbage. But scarcely had she taken out the flask of cold black tea from her basket, when she was startled by shouts. People were running towards them gesticulating wildly. Svitochka looked up in alarm. These people seemed very upset. Many unrecognisable words tumbled over the picnickers. Tatiana and Ivan looked to Svitochka to translate.

'Botanica Gah-den?' she carefully formed the difficult words.

'No, no, no, this is Government House! You must get out immediately. The Botanic Gardens are further up North Terrace.'

Tatiana, thinking this another attack on her being a New Australian, refused to budge.

'No, Mama,' implored Svitochka. 'This is where the Governor lives. We must leave now. This is not the Botanic Gardens.'

Again, she felt humiliated as they packed up their picnic and were hastily shooed out.

But not all outings were this fraught. John Martin's Christmas Pageant had been the highlight of Svitochka's life so far. John Martin's was the name of a large department store in Rundle Street, the main street in central Adelaide. Its owner, Edward Hayward, decided to start a pageant in 1933 as a pick-me-up during the Depression. For generations of South Australians, Christmas came to town on the day Santa waved from his pageant float and made his triumphant waddle into the Magic Cave, (conveniently located in the centre of John Martin's toy department). Every November an explosion of colour, music and magic was foisted onto the wide clean streets of Adelaide. Svitochka was in seventh heaven, squealing with delight as huge clowns swooped dramatically over her head, giant ladies floated serenely past and every conceivable fairytale unfolded upon mammoth floats before her very eyes.

March 1952 marked the end of two years that the alien family had landed on Australian soil. Tatiana and Ivan now received exemption certificates, which meant they were released from compulsory labour. Even though Tatiana didn't really love Ivan, she consented to marry him because he had promised to buy her a house. Their days of living in other people's houses to other people's rules were soon to be over. Tatiana bought a beautiful crepe dress and stunning hat and gloves from John Martin's. Svitochka, delighted to have her hair liberated into curls, wore a white lace dress. Katherina and her husband Kurt were the witnesses. Ivan, bothered that his beautiful betrothed thought money grew on trees, reluctantly shelled out his hard-earned cash. Playford's ideal immigrant had bust his gut working double shifts at Holden, and had scraped together enough overtime pay for a deposit on a house. It was at number 17 Pudney Street, Hendon, and only a ten-minute bike ride from the Holden factory.

Mrs Taplow donned her navy-blue gloves and hat, a stiff dark blue affair. *Must look smart,* she thought. She was on a mission. And dreaded it. But it was her duty to 'Australianise' these aliens as swiftly as possible.

'Brush your hair, Trevor,' she ordered. His frizzing hair did not take kindly to being brushed, insisting instead on forming little anarchic ridges that threatened the straightness of the side parting that his mother had so painstakingly instigated.

'We must set a good example for the New Australians who have moved in down the road.'

Sleepy lizards blinked as they walked along what was called 'the back road'. This road skirted the railway line to the gates of the former Hendon Munitions works, now the Philips Factory. A variety of houses in Pudney Street backed on to this road, interspersed with empty blocks and a few back-enders. Because of a shortage of building materials and cash, many families built the back half of their house first, like the Portman's at Number 19; next door to the aliens. Old Mrs Briggs had lived alone at Number 17 since Mr Briggs had died. Mildred bristled inside to think that reffos had bought this house.

'I thought they lived in tin shacks?' she spat at breakfast. 'And where did they get all that money from?' Albert quietly speared his bacon. Reffo rants were the norm these days. He didn't need to answer the rhetorical question.

'Up to no good, no doubt. Many decent Adelaide citizens can't possibly afford to buy a house.' The only reason Mildred had her own home was because she had snared Albert Taplow, who had lived with his cantankerous old mother and his spinster sister Lynette. Old Mrs Taplow died and Lynette moved out to live with a maiden aunt. Thankfully, Mildred now ruled the roost. She had to keep reminding herself of what was said at the last Good Neighbour Council meeting; these Displaced Persons were here to stay, whether she liked it or not. Premier Playford, she kept being told, was making South Australia great. And, as her special civic duty, she had taken on the responsibility of making sure this particular family was assimilated as quickly as possible.

Mildred and Trevor turned left through the yellow shed that served as Hendon Station, and walked up the little side road which flanked No 17. As Mrs Taplow opened the front gate to the 1920s bungalow-style house, she gasped at what had happened to Mrs Briggs' garden. The neatly laid lawn edged by rosebushes planted yonks ago by Mr Briggs was completely dug up. A man with a large nose was leaning on his shovel, his stained white singlet soaked with sweat. A little girl was jumping excitedly near where the man was digging, and shrieking in a strange language. They both looked up as the gate squeaked.

Mildred and Trevor stepped gingerly up the path in between clods of earth. The wire screen of the front door creaked open and a blonde woman in a spotted dress stepped out on to the large veranda. She looked quizzically at the visitors.

'Oh, how do you do? My name is Mrs Taplow, and this is Trevor. We live further up the road and would like to welcome you to Pudney Street.'

The sweaty man looked blank but came forward anyway.

'Helloia,' he said, hand outstretched. The neatly gloved hand stayed glued to the dark blue handbag. His hand hovered awkwardly for a few seconds, as if shaking away a fly. He enunciated slowly.

'Helloia. I pliz to mit you. Me Ivan,' he pointed. 'Zis Tatiana and zis Svitochka.' Both introductees gave beaming smiles. Trevor was mesmerised by Tatania's silver tooth as it flashed in the sun.

Svitochka jumped up and down again, and excitedly pointed to something in the freshly dug earth.

'Flog, flog!' Trevor saw a large green frog leap towards the wooden fence. Trevor liked Svitochka immediately and longed to take a closer look at the frog, but dutifully held on to his mother's other gloved hand.

Tatiana called out something unintelligible to Svitochka who stopped skipping about and joined her mother on the veranda. No one knew what to say next. Svitochka was fascinated by the stiff blue spikes that protruded from the side of Mrs Taplow's hat.

Finally, Mrs Taplow spoke. 'I believe that Swi-switokka starts tomorrow at Hendon Primary school. So does Trevor. We would like to pick her up and take her. We know a shortcut.'

Tatiana looked uncertainly at Ivan. She wasn't quite sure what this nice lady was saying. Svitochka gabbled something to her mother.

'Oh yes, tank you, tank you – vairy goode.' She rattled a question at Svitochka.

Svitochka looked up shyly, and pointing to the watch on Ivan's wrist, asked, 'What is time for shkool pliz?' Svitochka obviously did a lot of translating for her parents.

'We will pick you up at half past eight.'

'Huff pust eight,' repeated Svitochka slowly.

There then ensued a dramatic discussion between the trio. Mrs Taplow wondered how so much could be said about such a simple instruction, and why did they need to shout and gesticulate so much. She wasn't to know that in the Russian language half past eight was said differently. It was expressed as half of nine. So Tatiana wasn't sure if Mrs Taplow meant half of eight which would actually be half past seven! Finally, Ivan twiddled with his watch, put the hands to 8.30 and showed it to Mrs Taplow.

'Yes,' said Mrs Taplow.

'Yes,' chimed Tatiana and Svitochka triumphantly.

'We will meet you on the back road by the railway station at half past eight.'

'Yes, tank you, tank you.'

Perspiring beneath her stiff blue hat and with a 'come on Trevor,' Mrs Taplow pirouetted clumsily on her stout navy shoes and swept imperiously out the gate.

That evening at Number 17, over stuffed peppers and tomatoes, Tatiana said to Ivan, in their native Russian.

'Wasn't that lady nice – and that young boy? Very good manners.'

'Goody, goody, I have someone to play with,' piped up Svitochka. 'And he really liked the frog!' Svitochka shivered as she remembered the flash of bright green, leaping so high, from between the clods of earth.

'A frog is a very good sign,' said Tatiana. 'In my country, a frog in the garden means plenty of money and riches coming into the house.' Tatiana had seen an expensive raincoat in John Martin's for Svitochka, and a lovely dress for herself. She was just about to say this when Ivan interrupted.

'Ah good. We will need a lot more money coming in so that we can buy Svitochka's schoolbooks.' He was worried and felt a little out of his depth with this big new house. He was digging up the front lawn to plant potatoes. As a boy in Odessa his family had avoided starvation by growing their own food. This experience, the first of many such experiences, served to inculcate within him the injunction that he always had to prepare for the worst.

Tatiana felt deflated. Although she was pleased to have her own house, she wanted pretty clothes too. She had been through such an austere time in her young life. Here she was in the land of plenty and she wanted it all. Her heroines were Kim Novak and Marilyn Monroe. She wanted to be like them, and had dyed her hair blonde. She sighed as she dipped a piece of pepper and meat into the delicious sauce she had made from fresh tomatoes, onions, and garlic, purchased from the market. The Rosella tomato sauce which Svitochka had nearly vomited over stayed in the cupboard. They couldn't understand why Australians seemed to love something that looked like bright red glue.

Further up the road at Number 35 over lamb chops and boiled vegetables, Mrs Taplow said to Mr Taplow, 'Well we went and did our duty today and said hello to the New Australians down the road.'

'Very nice dear,' said Mr Taplow, lobbing dollops of Rosella tomato sauce all over his chops. He was tired. He had spent a large part of the day sorting out a big mess in the cold room at the back of the canteen. His head pounded.

'Very strange people though. Hardly know any English. The little girl, what's her name, Switokker or some such silly name, seems okay – a bit wild. But you know that wonderful lawn that old John Briggs watered so conscientiously – they've dug it all up. The cheek! And all those lovely roses. Mrs Briggs' pride and joy they were. Couldn't believe it. Just all gone. Disgraceful.'

Trevor sniggered.

'What are you laughing at? And eat up your cabbage.'

'That Witchky girl couldn't even say frog properly – she was saying "flog, flog".'

Tatiana was delighted that her new house had a bathroom. As she prepared a bath for her daughter, she told her about her girlhood where water had to be carried from the river and heated up on the wood stove. Baths were unheard of.

Svitochka sank into her first ever bath, luxuriating in the hot water and wondering about that cold northern country from which they had come. She was a bit afraid of going to a new school. Would the children like her? Would they shun her like the children in Commercial Road? She was glad that Trevor and his mother were taking her. But that Mrs Taplow did scare her. She felt uncomfortable when she thought of her. Her eyes were cold, dead even. She was ruminating for so long that the water became tepid. As she started to get out she looked at her hands and feet. They were all wrinkled.

'Mama, mama,' she screamed. 'I'm getting old.' Tatiana came in and teased her.

'Yes, you are. Old and wrinkled. Just like Baba Yaga.'

'Oh no,' cried Svitochka, recoiling at the thought of that wrinkled hag who was every Russian child's nightmare. 'I can't possibly go to school looking so old.'

Next morning, Svitochka, relieved that her hands looked young again, waited on the back road and saw Mrs Taplow and Trevor walking towards her. Tatiana had plaited coloured ribbons into her hair and insisted she wore boots and long trousers in case she caught cold.

'Good morning,' said Mrs Taplow, casting a disapproving glance over the clothes.

They'll have to go, she thought. *And as for that silly hair – makes her look like a peasant!*

Svitochka looked at Mrs Taplow's forced smile and saw something in her eyes that made her cringe. But she skipped ahead with Trevor, her plaits swinging from side to side. When they reached the Philips Factory gates, they turned left into a narrow lane that skirted its perimeter. Behind a barbed wire fence were untidy piles of pipes and rusting machinery; detritus of the lapsed munitions factory. On the other side of the lane were the back fences of the houses on the continuation of Pudney Street. Svitochka jumped in fright as a dozen bulldogs rushed at the fence, snarling and snapping.

'Oh, don't worry – they belong to old Mr Craxton. They won't escape.' They walked on past dilapidated asbestos chicken coops, a few more houses and empty blocks, until they reached Tapley's Hill Road. This was a main road that connected the south coastal area of Adelaide to Port Adelaide. And even in 1952 there was a steady stream of cars. Svitochka reluctantly held Mrs Taplow's hand as she crossed over. Down another small street, and there it was, her new school. Her heart was in her mouth as she went through the front gate.

CHAPTER 4

Pit Men

Midlato climbed into a tall gum tree and sucked a piece of wattle gum. From her vantage point she could just spy the sea in the distance, and the growing myriad of white-skin *wardlis*; so many different shapes; oblong, round, square, tapered at the top; alien forms draping over the pristine land as more ships disgorged passengers. She had never seen so many people. Why were they here? In discussions around the fires, it was suggested they must be long-lost ancestors returned from the pits of the dead. After all, she had noticed her dead grandfather taking on a whitish tinge after a few days. The name bandied around for these strangers was *pindi-meyunna*, pit men. She retrieved her penny from her possum pouch and gazed at the picture of the thick-necked man. He was brown, as was the strange woman on the back. Was the girl with green eyes giving her a message? Were these images common ancestors? The girl had pointed at it after she gave it to her and said 'penny'.

'Pen-ny,' repeated Midlato looking at it in wonder. She remembered how in awe she had been of the green-eyed girl, and encouraged when she had repeated 'pilyabilya' in such a friendly way. A word the girl and her mother used a lot was 'goode'. Midlato tried it out loud. 'Goode'. It seemed easy. But some of the other words were much harder; for example, the girl's name. She had heard her mother call her. "Was it Looty? Something like that. Not as easy as 'pen-ny." She had wanted to ask Looty if she was fifth-born like herself. 'Midlato' meant fifth-born girl. Her friend's name Kartanya meant first-born girl and Kudnartu was third-born girl. A favourite game at inter-tribal gatherings was to guess each other's birth order. She felt she could always tell and was convinced that Looty was fifth-born. There seemed to be a special connection between people of the same birth order. So many things she wanted to ask Looty. What was her totem? Did she play string games? Oh, the frustration of not being able to speak this 'penny' language.

As important people bickered over the site of the new city, James Cronk and his boss John Brown ventured over the hills to the south, to camp, hunt, and hopefully see natives in the wild. They got their wish. Several miles from Holdfast Bay they chanced upon Murlawirrapurka on a hunting trip. The meeting was friendly, with a lot of handshaking and repetition of the word 'goode'. After a feast of biscuits and sugar, Brown and Cronk continued on their way, encouraged by the bonanza of cockatoos and parrots that flooded the sky. A few days later, at sunset, the white men bumped into Murlawirrapurka again, but this time with a large party of natives. The women and children screamed in terror, having never seen white men before. The black men in a mock attempt at battle brandished spears. Murlawirrapurka, relishing any opportunity for a lark, did not throw his but grinned broadly instead. The women were soon pacified by Cronk's huge supply of sugar and biscuits but remained wary of the exploding stick he carried. Murlawirrapurka invited the white men to camp together that night. Cronk wrote,

'Not much sleep was had though, for one of the natives kept singing and beating 2 sticks until daybreak.'

Next day the men went hunting together. Murlawirrapurka and his friends were flabbergasted by the way the guns shot down birds. They picked up the dead birds, examined them, and had animated discussions. One bullet shot from 200 yards away lodged into a tree to a depth of finger length. The black men were in awe. This surprised the whites, who were blasé about the power of their own weaponry. In turn, the white men were impressed at the way the blacks nimbly climbed trees to dizzying heights, chipping a foothold at each step, and coming down with bags of possums. 'A foot long!' James wrote to his mother. 'And they were quite naked, as is their usual way here in the woods, for they could not climb trees with their clothes on.' Cronk, like all the prudish English, had to adjust to how free and easy the blacks were with their naked bodies.

A sumptuous feast of possums and birds was enjoyed by all. Cronk persuaded the women and children to come to his tent for more biscuits and sugar. As they walked over a rise, the women suddenly saw a sight they had never beheld before – several ships in the bay and more sailing in. They couldn't believe their eyes and stared in utter astonishment, but also great trepidation.

The bickering between Governor Hindmarsh and Commissioner Fisher continued unabated. Fisher would not lend Hindmarsh his bullock drays, and Hindmarsh refused to avail Fisher of his ship's tarpaulins. And so it continued. This did not augur well for the new colony. It was the blatant face of a mighty struggle for power between the Crown, represented by Hindmarsh, and the South Australian Commissioners, represented by Fisher. The seeds had been sown in the set up of the colony, when in the laudable attempt to create something new and more democratic, neither power had been clearly defined. A contest for the upper hand ensued, between a bluff, tactless naval man and a tough, calculating lawyer. The result was chaos. The quarrels were ugly, often in public, and of no credit to either. Both parties undermined anything the other tried to do. The unpleasantness was to boil over to horrendous proportions, and nearly scuppered the colony.

Into this arena of heated squabbles, more ships arrived. In January, the 'Coromandel' landed Samuel Stephen's brother Edward with his gold and safes, to set up the colony's first bank. In February, the 'Isabella' discharged the Quaker John Barton Hack, his large family, and a menagerie of livestock. Sir John Jeffcott, who had sneaked on board at the last moment, was conspicuous in his absence. He had jumped ship in Van Diemen's Land. Hack wasn't too impressed by such behaviour from a Knight of the British Empire, and had been shocked by his 'prodigious' quarrelling during the long voyage. Not surprisingly, he wondered how someone so hot-tempered and unreliable could hold such high office. The formative colony was sorely in need of a judge. Dr Wright had been charged with a drunken attack on the captain of the *Cygnet*, and Charles Moon who had so kindly invited Milte-widlo on board the *Buffalo* had, with his sailor mate Hoare, stolen his spears. Murlawirrapurka had to calm Ityamaitpinna down who was ready to attack the *Buffalo*.

'Is this how white man reciprocates!' he shouted, still smarting from Joj's condescension! But Murlawirrapurka explained that these were bad white men and that White Law could distinguish. However, they had to wait for three months for the trial, when the chief judge finally graced the colony with his presence.

Hack had brought with him two Manning cottages, which were examples of early flatpack technology devised by the resourceful Londoner, John Manning. After a preliminary scout around Holdfast Bay, Hack commandeered a picturesque spot by a lake to set up camp. On the other side of 'Hack's lagoon', as it came to be known, Midlato was collecting the fibrous parts of reeds to make string. She watched the teeming wildfowl flutter in panic as incessant banging and the excited squealing of little Hacks shattered the peace. A host of entirely new and strange animals were set to graze on the verdant grass. Midlato soon discovered that these few 'theep' and 'bullocky' were just small beginnings of what was to come. She was afraid of the 'bullocky', a few of which escaped and lumbered erratically through the bush, scattering ground parrots, wide eyed quoll, and inoffensive poteroos. And then there were huge animals with long hair on their heads which snorted and kicked. Terrified, Midlato ran off shouting, 'pindi-nanto', 'pindi-nanto', 'pit kangaroos'. She was even more awe-struck when Samuel Stephens mounted and rode one of these *pindi-nantos* along the banks of the Karrawirraparri.

While Light's big task was to convince Hindmarsh and the impatient landholders that the site for Adelaide was right, Murlawirrapurka's big task was to educate the various Kaurna groups about the *pindi* onslaught. They had stopped fearing being kidnapped, but now felt they were being invaded. They hated all the noise, especially the incessant 'boom-boom' of cannon. They would venture timidly from their hiding places to see what was happening, and more often than not their approach would coincide with outbursts of cannon. This seemed to be a favourite past time of the *pindi-meyunna* whenever a new ship arrived.

Don't they realise, thought Murlawirrapurka, *what they think is celebration strikes total terror into our people. We have only heard such explosions in times of terrible storms, when we believe that the ancestors are angry.*

Despite these assaults on the ears, Murlawirrapurka's interactions with white men so far had been very encouraging. He was heartened by the spirit of exchange when hunting with Cronk and Brown. Cronk, as well as teaching him many English words, was keen to learn Kaurna words. Robert Cock and Albert Taplow, who continued to be friendly after Ityamai-itpina's boat visit, were eager to learn their language too. Murlawirrapurka was taking the Crow's teaching to heart and acting with as much integrity as possible. One important task was to quell the fears of his own people. He could do this effectively through the *Ngunyawaietti* handed down to him from his ancestors. This was a form of Kaurna theatre entrusted to him to pass on Dreaming Songs by which ancient and modern lessons were taught.

The word *Ngunyawaietti* literally meant, 'a moving-with-joy event'. Whether by the light of the moon, stars or flickering fires, he and his people loved to dance and move their bodies vigorously to old and new rhythms. Throughout that first summer, during many gatherings by the Karrawirraparri, Murlawirrapurka performed numerous songs and *paltis,* or dances, specifically to teach his people the difference between good and bad white men and between good and bad ships; as well as the significance of the guns. These terrifying exploding sticks were incorporated into the *Ngunyawaietti* so that the Kaurna could begin to absorb the fact that these powerful *pindi* weapons would not necessarily kill them. Murlawirrapurka was impressed by the way white men's guns could bring down birds. What power! What certain death! He remembered with pain his old uncle, whose life had been blown apart by one of these weapons. How had the white men pulled off such a feat?

He sensed that the white man didn't treat this weapon with the reverence that he felt towards his spears. He loved his spears – he loved going to the Karraundongga, the red gum spear place not far from the Tandanya Rock, and gathering large branches to make the *winda*, the heavy fighting spears, shaping them, patiently hardening the wood in gentle flames, and delicately crafting the point. The finished spear was an extension of his body. Not only had the spear been finely honed, but so had the musculature which was needed to throw it. During every stage of preparation Murlawirrapurka felt the reverence of his ancestors. In *Ngunyawaietti*, there were countless songs and dances that celebrated the majesty and power of the spear and its potential to kill. He also thought that his spear was in some ways more efficient than the white man's gun with its flintlock. By the time the flint was lit, flashed, and banged, the prey had often gone. But ammunition was plentiful and whites seemed very trigger-happy.

Wirra Woman: What's changed?

Murlawirrapurka had already had to intervene when white men pointed guns at his people when they were burning off grass. Lack of language hindered him. How could he explain to these men it was custom to do this every *worltatti*, when the weather was clear and hot? How could he explain that they had carried this out for thousands of years, and that it encouraged new shoots to grow, which attracted game? How could he explain that by controlled burning and creation of havens for animals, his people were able to mitigate the effects of any uncontrolled bush-fires? He could already see the yawning chasm between these ancestors, if they were such, and the way his people did things. If they were indeed ancestors how could they forget the fundamental laws and customs?

The supposed ancestors had no understanding whatsoever of this seasonal firing of grass. When the 'John Renwick' arrived with Dr William Wyatt, a future Protector of the Aborigines, the ship's passengers were greeted with a terrifying sight. One of them wrote, 'The watchers on deck beheld a fire on one of the hills, which seemed to spread from hill to hill with amazing speed... it seemed as if the whole land was a mass of flame. We looked at each other, and the knowing ones declared that it was a signal for the native clans to gather for the purpose of destroying the white intruders.' The terrified passengers saw dark forms spreading the flames and were convinced that 'bands of naked savages' were about to descend upon them. Unfortunately, these sights filled many whites with a lasting dread of the natives. They were falling into the attitude that Murlawirrapurka feared – no discrimination between good and bad black men. As a settler wrote, 'for the first few months the whole settlement of Adelaide kept watch against a "black attack"'.

Fortunately, Robert Cock and Albert Taplow interceded in the first scrub burning fiasco, interpreted for Murla-wirrapurka, and helped calm both sides down.

Light was having his own battle with integrity. The attacks against him mounted, but he patiently and steadily defended his choice of site. The Governor, however, continued to undermine him and favoured the city to be at Port Misery or at the Murray mouth, where Barker had met his untimely end. As Fisher and his cronies backed Light, Hindmarsh was damned if he was going to give way. The site of the new city became a fraught bone of contention in the power struggle between the Crown and the Commissioners. Meanwhile, dissatisfied gentlemen clamoured loudly for the land that had been promised them. Light summoned a public debate to vote about the impasse.

The meeting took place on February 10th 1837 at Holdfast Bay. Hindmarsh's proposal was to move to the Murray mouth. He was backed by Samuel Stephens who, after being dumped as colonial manager, had set up a whaling station there. Light argued that his choice was the right one as it best fitted the original instructions. After a mélange of vigorous debate and astute lobbying, Light won the day.

But his problems were not over. Hindmarsh doggedly hindered Light as he began carrying out surveys with seriously few resources. Light's health deteriorated further. But despite all this the surveys of the new city were carried out meticulously and in a remarkably short space of time. Like a Zen gardener, Light walked up and down the river, contemplating the best way to lay out the city and to take advantage of the surrounding natural beauty, especially to capitalise on the Mount Lofty ranges, which he saw as 'these enchanted hills'. He often took Sally with him so she could explain the significance of aspects of the landscape. That he was open to the magic of the place is reflected in the design, built orthogonally around a central square, which Sally told him was the sacred Kaurna site Tartanyanggartu, and then weaving through the topography of various rises and falls of the land and the meander of the river. Modern day Aborigines delight in the fact that North Adelaide is shaped like an emu, while the city is in the shape of a kangaroo; the heart being present day Victoria Square. Light's plan that a cathedral be built on Tarndanyagga, or Victoria Square, never materialised. It would have sat on an energy grid which supposedly pulsates at exactly twice the harmonic of light.

As Light was busy surveying, coughing up blood, and resisting being undermined, the number of settlers had swelled to several hundred and many began the trek inland to towards the river where Light had set up his survey camp. It was quite a journey, during which people had to traverse several creeks through a 'boundless maze of strongly scented shrubs and magnificent gum-trees'. Many got lost in the Black Forest, George Stevenson's wife being one of them. As there was little transport everything had to be carried, rolled in barrels or pulled in makeshift contraptions. Some bullocks pulled drays, making huge tracks in the ground. Midlato and Milte-widlo gazed in awe. They had never seen a wheel before and were amazed at the marks it made – similar to snake tracks. In fact, Midlato's aunt forbade her children to walk on the track, fearing their feet would break out in little sores. Several journeys had to be made, and soon there were all manner of belongings strewn over the track. But as one settler proudly claimed, 'nothing was ever stolen'. This was not the expectation of Emma Stephens, wife of Edward, the treasurer of the new colony. He had left her alone at Hold-fast Bay in a tent piled with chests of gold and banknotes while he went to check the surveys. She was terrified that the natives would attack. Rumours of 'dark deeds', sorcery, and cannibalism brewed in every shadow that flickered in the candlelit tent. She threw herself over the precious chests, trembling, lest the evil black ones would slip in and rob her. She was an example of what Murlawirrapurka was afraid of – someone unable to distinguish between good black men and bad black men. To Emma Stephens, all black men were bad. How little she knew of the Kaurna who had virtually no concept of stealing. For them, the bounty of life was to be shared. It was deeply wrong, for example, to kill or take what was forbidden by Kaurna law. The central story of the Kaurna, as important to them as the crucifixion was to the Christians, was the story of Tjilbruke. Tjilbruke, the great Tandanya ancestor, liberally spilled tears of grief over the land because its laws, 'thou shalt not steal', and 'thou shalt not kill', were once tragically broken.

Makeshift camps were erected in the areas where Light planned to build the embryo city. Some who came out on the *Buffalo* set up shelters in Buffalo Row on the north-western corner of the proposed city, while others established Coromandel Row, a little to the east of it. These 'ship' settlements enabled friendships established on the voyage to continue. The inevitable taverns also sprouted up, including the Buffalo Tavern. The original figurehead of the ship, which had so frightened Ityamaiypinna, was removed from the prow and placed out front.

Dwellings were constructed out of wood, mud, grass and daub. Timber was lopped from a pine forest on the far side of the river and carried back. Black swans, which had shared this river with kangaroos grazing by day and people dancing by night, flew off in consternation as water barrels propped up on wheels were noisily trundled towards them. Women washed clothes in the deep pools and spread them out on the grass of the steep banks.

Lucy spotted Midlato and Milte-widlo fishing at the river's edge. They stretched out on half submerged tree trunks, holding out pieces of fat stuck on the end of small spears. She watched, fascinated, as Milte-widlo pulled the legs off black, crablike creatures and placed them on the bank in rows, waiting to be taken alive to that night's supper. When she pointed quizzically, Midlato explained they were 'kungurla'. Lucy would come to know them as 'yabbies'. She was intrigued by these black children; by their nakedness, their skill, and their agility. The only thing she didn't like was the way they smeared their bodies with wallaby fat, especially when it was colder. It made them stink terribly.

Wauwe woman: Didn't they do the same in winter in England?
Smear themselves with fat?

Midlato gave Lucy some emu oil that was soothing for the eye inflammations that she and other settlers suffered from. In return Lucy gave Midlato a billycan which, in great excitement, she took back to her *kammammi*. The old woman immediately put in various herbs and leaves, filled it with water and hung it over the fire. She could see how this simple pot of boiling water – one of white man's useful innovations – could extract the beneficial properties of plants and leaves more quickly than the traditional ways of long soaking in the sun.

Land sales were held from March 1837. Gentlemen capitalists within Adelaide, and from afar, purchased their segments. The Baptist preacher, Thomas Playford, who would start a dynasty of future prominent South Australian politicians bought a block at Mitcham, to which he would bring his family and a dollop of 'fire and brimstone' in 1844. Hack abandoned his lagoon and occupied a large section in North Adelaide. Here he built a substantial house with a veranda on which Ityamai-itpina loved to sit, especially when it rained. Albert Taplow and Robert Cock were constant visitors, and Ityamai-itpina grinned broadly when he saw them. The black man was intrigued by the strange iron implements with which Hack dug over the ground, but was distinctly less enamoured with the 400 'theep', which immediately started chomping the grass by the river. The same grass his people had so carefully prepared for their own game. Hack, in turn, watched with satisfaction as his livestock quickly grew fat on the verdure, marvelling how abundant it was. The settlers often remarked how like an English park the Adelaide environs looked, ignorant that it was the result of careful husbandry and deliberate fire burning, evolved over centuries.

Cronk encouraged the natives to bring firewood, skins and exotic birds to the white camps, in exchange for sugar, biscuits, and bread. Milte-widlo and his friends became bolder and did more work for the whites. They helped the surveyors carry their equipment or push the handcarts, never ceasing to marvel at the rotation of the wheels.

Milte-widlo was delighted to be given white man's 'baccy'. Pituri, a tobacco plant grown in the Northern deserts, was not easy to obtain. It was gathered and put in sand where the sun heated it up into a resin. A piece of this, to be put in the mouth and chewed, was bartered all over Australia. Milte-widlo was in awe of the abundance of this prized plant. Sailors seemed to be rolling in 'baccy'. They also rolled in fire-water, which they called grog. The teetotallers, of whom there were many, disapproved strongly. In fact, Hindmarsh had exhorted the colonists 'to prevent the Aborigines from imbibing from them a taste for that bane of humanity – spirituous liquors; I consider the most effective way the colonists can do this would be to form one vast temperance society.'

One gentleman who ignored Hindmarsh and got tippled regularly was Bedlam's Dr Wright who, while awaiting trial for attacking the captain of the *Cygnet*, dispensed morphine as liberally as he applied leeches. His habit of dispensing while drinking led eventually to a murder charge.

Adelaide was never to be 'one vast temperance society'. Taverns, like churches, sprang up everywhere. And Milte-widlo's eyes rolled foolishly as he traded lorikeets for grog.

Robert Gouger was having his own difficulties. Fellow passengers on the *Africaine*, suffering from mysterious eye inflammations, blamed him for this 'madheaded' project that had brought them to this far-flung part of the world. The constant jockeying for power between Fisher and Hindmarsh was also exhausting him. But the worst calamity of all was that tragically, in March, both Harriet and baby Henry died. His hopes for a wonderful new life in Utopia had crashed around him.

While the geographical quarrels continued to rumble, the political wrangling of who had the power in the colony, the Governor or the Commissioner, was getting out of hand. This wasn't helped by the fact that instead of being involved with the crucial setting up of the colony, Sir John Jeffcott was pursuing a romantic dalliance in Van Diemen's Land, which delayed him even further. He finally breezed into Adelaide to a veritable hornet's nest of intrigue and backbiting, but just in time to participate in naming the streets of Adelaide. Dignitaries who had set up the colony were duly honoured, but personal whims were also stamped indelibly on the future history of the city. Kermode Street was named after Jeffcott's fiancée, and O'Connell Street after the man who had helped Jeffcott escape from England. Local Kaurna names were never on the agenda.

There were many legal cases to pay attention to; many drunken assault charges, including that of Dr Wright and the case of the stolen spears. The two sailors, Hoare and Moon, stood trial in one of the first court sessions in South Australia. Jeffcott gave a very eloquent speech where he expounded the equal rights of Aborigines to be protected by British Law. Wearing a pair of itchy trousers Murlawirrapurka listened intently. With the help of Taplow interpreting, he thought the white legal system seemed fair, though exceedingly ponderous.

Wauwe Woman: – Fair! *She is nearly spitting.* Oh no, I forbid Murlawirrapurka to think that. The trial was just a big show. Jeffcott was an arch manipulator. Knew the right words to say to sound holier than the Pope. And besides, Hoare and Moon got off scot-free.

Wirra Woman: Yeah, but Jeffcott gave our boys back their spears and said some lovely things to them. That's pretty amazing in the early history of Australia!

Wauwe Woman: You know what I call that? Syrup on Shit. Oh, Jeffcott was a charmer and knew how to look good.

In Sierra Leone, he made his name catching slave traders and giving eloquent speeches. He knew that the British Empire wanted to look good in the eyes of the world by banning slavery. And this was his smarmy way of getting an early knighthood. Come on researcher extraordinaire! You must have dug up more dirt about him.

Author: Well yes, as a matter of fact. Jeffcott's coded journal has recently been deciphered in Exeter. According to that, he was an uncouth drunk who despised the poor and the blacks. For example, an entry from April 10th 1832 reads,

'Lack of progress with the Macdonald girl has caused me to apply for a post in Sierra Leone where I will enjoy flogging the natives.'

Wauwe Woman: Makes total sense. And besides, he was the only judge in history who had been tried for murder. To think he was shunted off secretly to Adelaide and dumped on us!

Wirra Woman: And even if he did, as you say, only give lip service to equality of our people, he was at least giving that doctrine credence. Whites had to start somewhere. Even though it was as thin as the 'pepa' it was so eloquently written on.

Wauwe Woman: Bah! All I know is that these so-called superior white-skins were a motley of maladjusted misfits. The one-eyed acidic naval captain pitted against the pig-headed, humourless lawyer; the supreme judge, a murdering hot-tempered debtor; the doctor, a drunkard and lecherer. And my people were supposed to give up their 'primitive' ways and be like them! Hmmph!

Cronk was delighted by his encounters with the natives. As well as learning their words and engaging in their affairs, they were making him money. His barter system, where they would exchange goods for sugar, was doing well. The trade in young cockatoos, lorikeets, and opossum skins was especially lucrative. Cronk sold these to ship merchants for three shillings each, making himself a princely profit of over one pound each week. That, plus his other wages, was much more than the six shillings he would have earned in England. 'And I eat meat every day and drink as much rum as I like,' he bragged in the Buffalo tavern. 'And I'll soon have enough to buy land like my boss.'

'Soon' came too quickly. Cronk was able to purchase an acre of prime land. This was contrary to the core of Wakefield's colonisation theory, in which the price of land had to be kept out of the reach of men like Cronk. It was intended that he stay at the level of a labourer, not be catapulted to landowning class. Consequently, it wasn't long before there was a labour shortage in the colony. Meanwhile, hundreds of native birds and animal pelts sailed to England where they were stuffed and placed in glass-fronted cabinets in homes and museums.

Wauwe Woman: Mad! And it wasn't long before they were putting our bones in museums as well!

Wirra Woman: Many of us are still there! Our mob in Tasmania are still fighting to bring their people home.

What did Ityamai-itpina make of all this? He was spitting angry. He felt Murlawirrapurka was handling this whole white-skin thing badly. Sure, he liked the food and the music he experienced on the *Buffalo*. But he hated being treated like some sort of lackey. His blood boiled every time he remembered having to ask permission to dance. Three times! What was that white-skin playing at? He could tell that Joj a thing or two. Most ghost-skins didn't seem to know anything about dancing and singing and were far too serious for his liking. Most only sang what sounded like a dirge. Every few days, it seemed, groups would walk to a tent or building, talk a lot, wail dirges and then come out again looking more miserable than before they went in. He and some other curious friends tried to join in one of these occasions but were turfed out by a white-skin with a stiff white band around his neck.

It was true that after a few tankards of grog the sailors would sing raucously but usually this led them to being thrown into the hold of the *Buffalo*, which served as a makeshift prison. Ityamai-itpina couldn't see what was so special about these white men anyway. Except for Robert Cock and Albert Taplow. They, unlike Joj, spent time with him. They called him by his name and he liked the way they looked into his eyes.

But what was really riling Ityamai-itpina was the way these people were walking all over his land as if THEY owned it. He had hoped fervently that, like the sealers on Karta, they would only be temporary. But it looked more and more like they were staying and interfering. Whites had run at him with exploding sticks just because he was burning off some scrubland. Why were they so angry? Didn't they know it would be impossible to trap game in the area if it was left?

Where did they think the succulent green grass their fat 'theep' gobbled up came from? And they were dessicating the red river gums and the silver sheoaks – lopping them down with their sharp axes, and scaring off small game with their unwieldy bullocky. And to top it all, the whites were running out of biscuits. The big white judge who had so kindly given back the spears had promised that whites would feed his people, but now they were getting less and less food. He never trusted the judge anyway – he had shifty eyes. All of them, black and white, would starve to death if this state of affairs continued.

Whites were spreading their stupid *wardlis* all over the sacred Tambawardli, where the Kaurna traditionally held interclan gatherings and contests. This raised, flat piece of ground to the west of Light's survey camp had been used by his people as a meeting place for generations. And his friends from the Ngarrindjeri were upset because white people kept stalking all over the mouth of the great river looking like they wanted to live there, too. The Ngarrindjeri were sharpening their spears! He might just join them. Ityamai-itpina was really looking forward to the *kudlilla* or cold season. He wanted to get right away from these strange white people who were infesting the land like fat white grubs in a tree. Every night he searched the sky for *Parna*. As this star became more visible it signified that the hot season *worltatti* was ending, and it was time for *wardliworngatti*, when the Kaurna left the plains and build winter *wardlis* in the shelter of the foothills.

Midlato was confused. This particular *worltatti* on the plains was so different to anything she had ever known, so many new impressions, some interesting, some frightening. There were more *palti* than usual. Murlawirrapurka was teaching his people how to cope with the white influx. White men came to watch the plays, laughing noisily around the edges of the group. She didn't like the way they smelt. 'Fire-water!' She knew this was bad. Her older sister was forbidden to attend *paltis* after a white man in a blue uniform had fondled her. He reeked of fire-water and touched her naked body. Midlato began to understand why white girls like Looty wore garments all over themselves. She looked up and was delighted to spot *Parna*. It was almost time to move to the foothills.

Ityamai-itpina continued to seethe about the further encroachment of the bleached skins on to all his favourite haunts. Darkly mumbling, he fashioned a new spear, utilising a sharp piece of glass for the point, rather than the usual flint – the ghost-skins had some uses after all. He looked out over a stretch of magnificent gums around his family's waterhole, wondering what would become of it. He hoped that the bleached skins who were prancing around as if they owned the place wouldn't poke their stupid noses into his sacred waterhole. Rather worryingly, he had seen a group of white men walking around it with strange instruments, and scratching something on their 'pepa'. His waterhole was on the bend in the river over a mile up from the Tandanya Rock, and held special significance for Ityamai-itpina's clan. Around it, the *kainkga wirra*, or gum scrub, had been a good hunting ground for generations because of careful management.

What was that? He noticed a lone white man with sticks stop on the other side of the waterhole. He then had the audacity to start erecting a pindi *wardli* right on the sacred site. The white man kept beckoning Ityamai-itpina and other members of his clan to come towards him. He enticed them with oatmeal biscuits. Some came readily, as they were hungry. But then he did a strange thing. He erected another *wardli* and tried to pull Ityamai-itpina towards it, pointing and saying – 'You go in there.' Ityamai-itpina had learnt a few pindi words – and was incensed that this man wanted him to enter this *wardli*. Ityamai-itpina knew the word, 'No,' which he started to say quite loudly. He pointed at the white man's tent reiterating 'No!' He tried to make the man understand he did not want him to put his tent there and pointed further down the river. The white man didn't understand, threw up his hands and went inside his tent. Ityamai-itpina rubbed his hand along the shaft of his spear, his blood boiling. As custodian, it was his responsibility to protect this sacred place. Murlawirrapurka's face came into his mind. Damn him. If he were here, he would probably just go and shake his hand! He was determined to challenge him in a council by the fire that night.

Unbeknownst to the Kaurna, the British government had specific designs for them. In a prestigious room in London, some worthy pronounced in June 1836 that 'asylums' should be set up for the natives where they would be protected, clothed and fed. George Stevenson, the very 'Joj' who insisted that Ityamai-itpina be deferential when he wanted to dance, had submitted a plan to Hindmarsh where natives would dwell in reserves containing homes and a schoolhouse, firmly believing that the natives would be happy to abandon their 'erratic habits' for the benefits of European civilisation. As he wrote in the colonial office records,

'The exchange we have to offer the poor savage for his fertile, but to him unproductive plains, is to instruct him in the Arts of Cultivation – to take away his waddy and his spear, and to put in his hands the hoe and the sickle – to bring him step by step within the range and influence of civilisation; but above all to arouse him from the brutish condition in which he now sleeps...'

What would the 'brutish' Ityamai-itpina make of that? He did see Joj from time to time but Joj was always too busy talking important business with other white men. Ityamai-itpina was right to surmise that Joj wasn't really interested in him at all. Stevenson was juggling many hats. As well as being Hindmarsh's Private Secretary and interim Protector of the Aborigines, he was also Clerk of the Court, a Justice of the Peace, Registrar of Shipping, Agent for Lloyds, Customs Officer, and Postmaster. But his real desire was to start a newspaper. He had worked for the *Empire and Globe* in London and, with Robert Thomas, had been appointed Government printer. The Aborigines, notwithstanding the dazzle of Ityamai-itpina's teeth, were of little importance to him. He resigned, and in April 1837 the job of Protector became available.

Walter Bromley, who had successfully civilised Indians in Nova Scotia using a similar method to Stevenson's plan, was patiently waiting on Kangaroo Island. He continued to give lessons to white children, but for a tiny fee, so was delighted when he was offered the position of Protector for £250 a year. When the wage of Light's assistant Finniss was a mere £100, this was a princely sum. Bromley abandoned his school under the currant tree and caught the next ship to the mainland.

For a few weeks nothing happened, and Bromley felt overlooked. Hindmarsh was having his own battles, and not just with Light and the survey team. He had finally been able to leave his ship and move ashore into a mud hut with a calico ceiling but Fisher, now his arch enemy, was putting all sorts of ridiculous obstacles in his way. One such instance was when Hindmarsh's marines cut some sticks and reeds to build the governor's residence, he was charged with committing 'an act of trespass and depredation'. George Stevenson was so exasperated by the childish power play, he wrote on the 8th May 1837, 'Take me away from this province I beseech you – I have seen enough of the new experiment in Colonisation.' Bromley and his harping on about the natives was the least of his concerns: the Aborigines were just a nuisance. Just to get the annoying Bromley off his back, Stevenson finally asked one of Light's surveyors to direct Bromley to a temporary site for his work with the natives. To Ityamai-itpina's present chagrin, this site was none other than a principal waterhole of his family. It was also a site earmarked for the future Botanical Gardens.

Walter Bromley felt very uneasy as he lit his oil lamp inside his tent that night in May 1837. He had been assured that this spot by the River Torrens was a good place to start his dream – to construct some huts and tents, and teach the natives about Christ and how to cultivate vegetables. The one they called King Rodney seemed very belligerent and uncooperative.

Further down the river in front of the Tandanya Rock, Ityamai-itpina was furious. He was shouting at Murlawirrapurka that white men were messing up the land; a stupid ghost-skin was pitching his *wardli* by his sacred waterhole; where his Spirit ancestors emerged, performed ceremonies, and entered again into the earth; where he and his clan danced *paltis* at moonlight; where his ancestors guarded the water for their descendants.

Ityamai-itpina yelled, roared, and stomped, saying he wished he had speared the ghost-skin on the spot. He was sure that this is what his ancestors would have wanted; moreover his move to the foothills was being delayed. But he was afraid to leave his sacred waterhole unguarded.

After he had calmed down, Murlawirrapurka explained to him that this white man was ignorant and needed to be persuaded to move. It would have helped enormously if Murlawirrapurka had been party to an important clause in a South Australian colonisation document, the Letters Patent, signed in early 1836 by King William. It recognised prior land rights of the Aborigines and guaranteed that 'any lands now actually occupied or enjoyed by natives would not be alienated'.

Unfortunately, the white men themselves were too blinded by greed to honour this clause.

Wirra Woman: And still are!

They were busy carving up the land for their own benefit. Murlawirrapurka explained to Ityamai-itpina that he must show the white man where to move to. But first he ordered the young man to dance off more of his rage.

Next morning, Bromley stacked up his fire on which to cook a slab of meat. A group of children skulked nearby. When he tried to persuade them into the second tent, they ran away, squealing. As he was eating his meat he noticed the one they called King Rodney come towards him. He had a spear and greasy red and white paint on his tattooed body. Sensing his belligerence, Bromley took a piece of meat and offered it. Ityamai-itpina came forward uncertainly, but took it. He ate it voraciously and then glared at Bromley.

He started gesticulating and pointing at where Bromley's tent was pitched.

'*Wakkinna, wakkinna,* bad, bad.' Then he pointed down the river. 'You go, you go.' He grabbed Bromley's arm and tried to pull him in that direction.

'I'm staying here,' insisted Bromley. 'And if you had any sense you and your tribe would join me.'

Ityamai-itpina, riled by this response, grabbed Bromley's arm and yanked him towards where he was pointing.

'*Kawai, kawai.* You come, you come. Tulya Wardli, Tulya Wardli.' He pointed down the river. *Tulya wardli* was the soldier's station about a mile away and near where settlers had set up Buffalo Row. Bromley was caught off guard and objected to being manhandled. He also abhorred the fact that this black man was touching him.

'Hey get your hands off me'- he stopped short of adding the words 'you filthy savage'.

He pushed Ityamai-itpina's hand away and, as he did so, he fell into the fire and upset his kettle. The boiling water scalded his leg. Ityamai-itpina immediately grabbed him and pulled him away. As Bromley bellowed in agony, Ityamai-itpina shouted an instruction to his daughter Iparrityi who disappeared. She reappeared with a kind of grease which she rubbed on to the scald. It was surprisingly soothing. The Kaurna knew a thing or two about fire injuries, and used a variety of oils and leaves to make their healing salves. Ityamai-itpina carried Bromley gently into his tent and laid him down, cursing himself for being so rough, and knew he would be reprimanded by Murlawirrapurka. Ignoring Bromley's protests, he instructed Iparrityi to tie a healing amulet to his leg.

'Goode, goode,' he assured Bromley.

Bromley lay on the bed, resting his leg. He removed the amulet muttering 'superstitious nonsense', but when his leg started throbbing again, put it back. To his surprise, the pain eased. He pondered his situation. This had been the spot he had been directed to: an ideal place to start the natives growing vegetables and loving Christ. He thought fondly of his success with the natives in Nova Scotia and how they had acquired civilised cultivation. He had learnt the Indians' language and used this vehicle to teach them all about the Lord. He felt miserable. It did not seem to be working here in this new settlement. When this opportunity arose to be Protector of the Aborigines in South Australia, Bromley felt the Lord wanted him to go, even though his family in England had begged him not to. He was over sixty, after all, and South Australia was at the ends of the earth. He fervently believed that Christianity was the perfect tool to extend the influence and control of the British Empire to the far-flung corners of the earth. Rodney didn't seem to be a bad chap – a bit aggressive at times but he had been so insistent that Bromley move. 'Tulya wardli'? Bromley was anxious to learn some of their words and he knew that 'wardli' meant hut so he must want him to move his tent. Anxious to get on the right side of the natives, he made up his mind as he blew out his lamp.

CHAPTER 5

Baba Yaga

'March, march, march! Left, right, left!' Every morning Svitochka marched around the asphalt yard of Hendon Primary School for what seemed an eternity. She preferred being in the shadow of the buildings, as being in the bright sunshine was hot, even at that time of day. A boy at the front banged a kettledrum. Svitochka quite liked the monotony of the rhythm, but was terrified of getting left and right mixed up, which she seemed to do with alarming regularity. Left was on the side where her heart was, she had to keep reminding herself. Left was where Western Australia was when she looked at a map. Fortunately, 'left' in Russian, was 'lyeva'. It took all her concentration to put all those concepts together. Turning at right angled corners always flummoxed her, often instigating a teacher to come over and order – 'LEFT, right, LEFT, right,' while jabbing her left leg with a ruler. Then all the kids had to stand in the schoolyard for assembly. After singing *God Save the Queen*, they all droned, 'I salute the Queen and promise to obey her lords.' This was really confusing for Svitochka and she took ages to get it right. When intoning 'sloot' she saw it was always accompanied by the headmaster pointing to his head. She did this too but was ordered to 'curtsey' by the teacher who seemed to enjoy prodding her with a ruler.

'Curt- what? Kurt was the name of Katherina's husband.' It took ages to understand that the girls must bob down while holding the edges of their dresses and the boys point their hands to their heads. Why? No one explained the rules. She surreptitiously copied the girls around her, holding on to her trousers, pretending she knew what was going on! When she finally thought she had got it right, it was only in adulthood that she realised that she had spent all her school years unnecessarily promising to obey the Queen's 'lords', whoever they were.

Assimilation. Svitochka didn't know what this meant but it was happening to her rapidly. No one could say her name. 'Witchy' they would snigger, those girls with simple names like Linda and Pam. They looked down at her long pants and boots. How could any girl possibly curtsey dressed like that?

'Witchy boy,' the girls would taunt, grimacing disdainfully at her trousers. Another problem was explaining all this to her mother. Tatiana refused to be assimilated. She had been irate when Mrs Taplow said Svitochka's plaits should be cut off. No way. Scooping the long tendrils of fair hair into ribboned plaits each morning was one slender connection she had to Tarasivka, the tiny village in which she had been born. Plaits and ribbons were an essential part of Russian girlhood. Tatiana loved her daughter's name, meaning flower in Russian, and the diminutive of Sveta, which meant light. Tatiana reluctantly agreed that Svitochka could be called Sveta, pronounced by Australians as Swetta. Sveta wasn't sure if 'Sweaty Swetta' was any better than 'Witchy boy'.

Tatiana did eventually buy her daughter some dresses, so at last she could curtsey properly, but this would provoke a row with Ivan. The worst time was when Tatiana bought Sveta a sumptuous red raincoat with a fur collar. Sveta couldn't wait to wear it to school. She had imagined showing it off to the Lindas and the Pams, proving that she was a real girl. But this was never to be. Ivan cycled home from a double shift at the Holden car factory, tired and fed up. The Australian foreman had ordered him to go and get a 'curenbun'. Thinking that this was a machine component, he had asked all over the factory floor for a 'curenbun'. It was only after virtually the whole workforce was roaring with laughter, he knew he had been set up, and sent on a wild goose chase looking for something more suited to munching along with a cup of tea than fashioning a new car. And this was not the first time. Previously he had been sent to look for a left-handed screwdriver. He felt profoundly humiliated. How dare they take advantage of his lack of English. He was Ivan Pleznowski, who had been about to study mathematics at a top university in Odessa when Hitler shattered his dreams with the biggest land invasion of all time. The Australian factory hands had him by the Russian equivalent of 'the short and curlies'. He really needed every hard-earned shilling from his pay packet. He would show them one day! So, when Sveta ran up excitedly and showed him her flash raincoat with its flash price tag, the usually mild-mannered man hit the roof. All his pent-up fury and humiliation of the workplace boiled over, and he ripped the beautiful red raincoat into tiny shreds.

At Number 19 Pudney Street, Bill Portman was planting lemon trees in his building site of a back yard. Broken concrete bricks lay higgledy-piggledy around a concrete mixer. Bill couldn't afford the sand and gravel to mix more concrete, nor to hire a brick-making machine to finish building his house. His wife Milly, pregnant with their third child, had been asking for a lemon tree ever since he had bought this block of land after securing a job at the nearby Sabco Brush Company. Bill's lined face and receding hairline belied the fact that he was not yet thirty. It was a friendly enough face but with slightly bulging blue eyes. Stationed up in Darwin during the war, he had been scared witless by the bombings. You could still see his fear of the unexpected, hovering in the reddish rims of his eyes. And those Plozidovskis, or whatever they were called, who had moved in next door, were absolutely unexpected. He rested momentarily under the shade of the almond trees from Number 17's garden. These two old trees offered the only shade in his yard on a hot afternoon. It was then that he heard the sound of an axe. Curiosity drew him to the tall fence that divided the two gardens and he craned his neck over. He saw Ivan chopping into the trunk of one of the almond trees. Portman's jaw dropped in disbelief. His sensibilities had already been disturbed by the transformation of demure roses-and-lawn-respectability to peasant-potato-uncouthness in the front garden. Now what was going to happen?

'God what the hell is he up to?' groaned Bill to Milly when she bought him a cup of tea.

'I hope it's not more potatoes!'

It wasn't long before the riddle was solved. In the middle of the night, it seemed, he was awoken by a deafening crowing.

Ivan felt really tired, and this was his first Saturday off in three weeks. Even though he was working double shifts, there was not enough money coming in. A shifty looking lodger had paid rent for a few weeks and Ivan hadn't liked the way he had looked at Svitochka. He understood why, when the police came to the door and arrested him on charges of child molestation.

What a close shave, thought Ivan. Tatiana had told him about the sheep hand who had sexually interfered with Svitochka when they had been stationed at Wagga Wagga. What was the matter with this new country? Was it full of perverts? In order to supplement their income, Ivan decided he would get several hens and a couple of roosters. In this way, they could occasionally eat the chooks, use the eggs, and sell the rest. The second almond tree had to go. He could then have a sizeable chicken run along the length of the side garden to the back road. He deftly swung the axe at different angles and cut a neat wedge into the gnarled old trunk. It was a mammoth job, and soon the sweat poured down his face. A gaggle of kids peeked in the side gate. Tatiana opened it and much to Svitochka's delight, she beckoned them in. Soon a wide circle of fascinated children watched as Ivan swung his axe. All screamed in excitement as the old tree crashed to the ground.

Tatiana missed her home country terribly. Often, she would take Sveta to the real Botanic Gardens where she would look longingly at the European trees. When they sat near the pond, little did they know it was once the sacred waterhole of dark skinned people who revered their ancestors at this very site. Tatiana was also delighted to discover Morialta Falls, a beautiful gulley in the foothills that was on the end of a bus ride from town. Here, waterfalls burst through a ravine and cascaded into the gorge below. It was so green and lush, unlike the hot dusty streets of Hendon. Sveta had no idea that the name Morialta was derived from the language of an ancient race which had named these falls, Mari Yartabulti, the Eastern Cascades. A little girl called Midlato used to assemble her winter camp nearby. Both Tatiana and Sveta felt soothed by the falls and rejuvenated, before they made their long bus journeys back to the heat of the Western suburbs.

At Number 15 Pudney Street, on the other side of the small road that led to Hendon Station, lived the Millers, in a yellow squat house. Peter, their son, was Sveta's age. The Millers hated the New Australians who were moving into the area, and especially the ones next door. They warned Peter to keep away. Peter would often peek through the fence to check out the strange new family. He saw a girl with long plaits singing to the chickens. He was fascinated. When Sveta espied him, he didn't move. Soon he and she would have chats over the gate, Peter always wary lest his mother catch him. Peter was intrigued about where Sveta came from, and soon was hearing about a distant northern country where snow lay thick on the ground, where wolves howled throughout the night and ate people whose sleds got stuck. He absorbed, wide-eyed, tales of Baba Yaga, an old Russian witch, who was used by parents all over the Soviet Union to keep children well behaved. Baba Yaga captured naughty children, fattened them up, and ate them. The next day a very irate Mrs Miller accosted Sveta in the street and warned her that she must stay away from Peter. He had suffered dreadful nightmares and was now too ill to come outside.

Sveta contented herself with reading her comics in the remaining almond tree. From her perch, she could spy on the Portmans. Their house intrigued her. It was literally half a house. The back was built from grey brick and abruptly stopped halfway, leaving an ugly slab of badly put together blocks that faced Pudney Street. The Portmans, like many other Australians, had been hit by wartime scarcities and a serious housing shortage, and couldn't yet afford to buy more materials to finish the front.

The Portmans' initial civility to their New Australian neighbours was severely tested when 200 chickens moved in and a chorus of noisy roosters greeted the dawn. Rosemary and David Portman, a little younger than Sveta, peered at her curiously through the fence. Soon Sveta started chatting to them. She seemed to be a born storyteller; she'd had a good teacher in Tatiana, who had passed down her culture's rich stories in the time-honoured Russian oral tradition. Sveta regaled the Portman children with tales of Baba Yaga. They were fascinated by this bone thin witch, with iron teeth, and a voracious appetite for small children. She lived in a hut, deep in the forest. This hut had a personality of its own and was perched on two giant chicken legs which propelled it through the forest, emitting blood-curdling screeches. Sveta provided sound effects, and aided by the chorus of chooks in the background, had Rosemary and David goggle-eyed in terror, especially when they heard that the hut was decorated by the skulls of eaten children, whose eye sockets illuminated the darkness.

That night Rosemary and David had nightmares. Giant chickens with iron teeth were chasing them and trying to eat them. The next day Mr Portman was at the fence yelling at Tatiana to keep Sveta away from his children. Tatiana yelled back. A few days later Rosemary and David crept up to the fence. They couldn't keep away from this strange girl who told them such electrifying stories. Suddenly Mr Portman swooped on them and ordered them to bed. Sveta was mortified to hear them screaming in their bedroom, forbidden to come out or have any tea. The miserable wailing lasted for hours, and Sveta felt keenly that she also was being punished with each heart-rending cry.

That night Sveta had a dream. Baba Yaga, the cause of all this suffering, was hovering above the house and amazingly she was smiling. Unbeknownst to Rosemary and David, to Sveta, to Tatiana, and in fact to most people who inhabited the vast northern lands where Baba Yaga wielded terror, there was a well-kept secret. Underneath Baba Yaga's black garments, withered skin, and iron teeth, beat a heart of gold. The people of the northern lands were not ready, nor able, to see it. Baba Yaga smiled a sad smile and just bided her time. She watched over the little girl who so avidly read comics in the almond tree. She knew that her trials were just beginning.

Sveta loved her comics. She found the strange English words easier to follow when describing a picture. Her favourites were Mickey Mouse, Donald Duck, Ginger Meggs, and Archie. Often, she would struggle with the meaning of the words. She was intrigued with one Archie comic, where Archie's friends were carrying a 'body' into a forest. She thought that 'body' meant 'bottom', and she puzzled endlessly why these children were carrying a 'bottom' into the wood. It seemed a very rude and strange thing to do. Sveta's favourite occupation was to take her huge pile of comics up into the almond tree, where, caroused by the chortling of the chickens below, she would devour each comic. Tatiana did not approve of her daughter reading these comics. The teachers at school did not approve of children reading comics either, and they were banned.

Sveta didn't really understand why. All she understood was that anything fun was usually disapproved of by that grim-faced band of adults that lived in the grown-up world. So she savoured her times up in the almond tree, pouring over the latest new comic avidly, before she heard the inevitable screech of her mother.

'Sveta. Sveta.' Then she would have to tear herself away from this exquisite past time and go and eat some silly food or do some stupid chore.

As Sveta wasn't allowed to take comics to school she would rush home eagerly at 4 o'clock and seek out her battered, well-read pile, and carry it lovingly up to her haven in the almond tree. One day the pile was not in its usual place. She searched around the house, in the garden, and in the garage. Where were they?

'Mama, where are my comics?' she finally asked Tatiana, who was chopping up boiled eggs for the new chicks which occupied a large box in the kitchen.

'Oh, I burnt them.'

'What!' the shock hit Sveta like an icy blast. 'But... but....' she stammered in disbelief!

'Yes. Comics very bad for you. Rottink for brain.' Tatiana threw some chopped egg into the box to a crescendo of excited cheeping.

'You burnt them? All of them?' Sveta felt a string tighten between her brain and her heart and a black hole engulf her belly. A strange whimpering noise emanated from her throat. 'oahhhh....'

'Stop it! Noww! Or I give you sometink to cry about! Go sweep yard!'

Sveta staggered out of the back door, the whimper threatening to explode into a demented howling. She froze it in her throat. She knew that Tatiana needed little excuse to get the strap off the hook behind the bathroom door. She clenched her stomach. She howled inwardly, the tears imploding into the soft tissues of her brain. Hatred. That's what she felt. It was a new feeling, and it shocked her. She stumbled around the side of the house. She stepped on to something soft and squishy. She looked down. A yellow bundle of feathers lay inert on the path. She had squashed a baby chick. The expected feelings of remorse did not come. She kicked the fluffy scrap into the dirt. She didn't care.

Even though school was regimented, and Sveta was still the only kid in the class with a funny name, she loved it. She found it far better than being at home with her increasingly unpredictable mother. She especially loved it when the rain drummed down on the tin roofs and all the kids drank their small bottles of free milk. On days like these the milk was warmed on the radiators, and cocoa and sugar added. Delicious!

Sveta was good at spelling, dictation, and sums. She was learning English very quickly. Some words she found curiously flat. The word 'pear' didn't capture the lusciousness of this fruit nearly as well as the Russian word 'groosha' did. 'Heart' was a poor substitution for 'sertsa', which denoted such profound love, warmth and livingness. However, she so badly wanted to be like the other kids she willingly took on the mantle of this new 'flat' language, and draped it over the core of her slavic being, counteracting the heady mixture of passion and drama that her native language expressed.

Mr Hussey, the headmaster, liked the New Australian girl. He saw how bright she was and wanted to put her up a class. He was very puzzled when Mrs Pleznowski marched defiantly to the school, and in broken English let him know she flatly refused. To her this was another example of assimilation that she didn't care about. Sveta had to translate to Mr Hussey that in the Soviet Union children did not start school until they were seven, and that Tatiana thought it unnatural and bad to learn too much at such a young age. Mr Hussey patiently explained that he understood that things were done differently in her country, but that in this case Sveta was far too bright to stay in her present class. Mrs Pleznowski was grateful for Mr Hussey's kindness. She felt listened to and understood. She consented to Sveta going up a class.

Sveta was now the youngest in her new class with a new teacher, Miss Bradshaw, who had a kindly face and grey hair tied back in a neat bun. However, the move meant that she left Trevor behind. Mrs Taplow did not like this latest development one little bit. It was great that her charge was learning English at such a fast rate, but it was another thing for her to be in a class above her own beloved Trevor.

Belinda Bradshaw drove out of the gates of Hendon Primary School and waved to Sveta. She had made sure that the New Australian girl was welcomed in her class. She was ashamed of the prejudice fellow Australians had against people who were different: especially against a whole group of people who were virtually invisible – the original inhabitants of Adelaide. Miss Bradshaw was an active member of the South Australian Aborigines Advancement League, and was leaving school early as she had a meeting at Dr Duguid's house. Charles Duguid had started up the League in the 1930s, and was one of the few voices reminding the worthy citizens of Adelaide of the existence of the original inhabitants. He was their tireless champion, and set up the Ernabella mission in the north of South Australia, widely regarded as one of the least oppressive and most culturally sensitive missions established. Here, he attempted to help the Pitjantjatjara people keep their cultural integrity. His home in Magill was open house for any Aboriginal person. Belinda Bradshaw fondly remembered the shining faces of all thirty-four children from the Ernabella mission who camped in his garden in the summer of 1934–5.

The meeting tonight was very exciting. The League was organising a rally in the Adelaide Town Hall, where Aboriginal speakers would address the public. Charles Duguid had made the hitherto revolutionary step of asking Aboriginal people what they themselves wanted.

Wauwe Woman: And still pretty revolutionary today I must say – whites still think they know what's best for us, and plan accordingly! Look at the current fiasco in the Northern Territory. Ignoring research that shows Aboriginal communities feel disempowered by compulsory income management and do NOT want it. Barging in like blundering wombats.

Wirra Woman: Yeah, they've always been so coercive – used us as slaves and whores – interned us in virtual concentration camps – regarding us as mindless savages.

In response to Duguid's question, Aboriginal members of the League had come up with several ideas, one of which was to build a hostel where they could hang out and meet each other when in Adelaide. Another crucial demand came from a group of Aboriginal nurses who had been turned away from the Royal Adelaide Hospital. The matron at the RAH had refused to even speak to Lowitja O'Donohue, and had told her and three other young trainee nurses that 'It would be much better if they went to Alice Springs and nursed their own people.' Belinda Bradshaw had been at Duguid's house the day these women had come to him in great agitation seeking help. She had never seen him in such a rage! It reminded her of her own great aunt Lucy's rage when Midlato, a Kaurna woman who had helped bring up her father and aunts and uncles, was treated with contempt by the white establishment of Adelaide.

'Hello Nancy!' said Belinda Bradshaw, as she walked briskly into the doctor's house. Nancy Brumby was Dr Duguid's efficient secretary. She had been brought up in Colebrook Mission.

Wirra Woman: Stolen from her parents, I dare say.

Wauwe Woma: No, she says her parents gave permission. And she regards herself as saved. She says she would never have had the opportunities to make it in white society if she had not been taken and educated by the Mission.

Wirra Woman: But thousands were stolen in the name of Assimilation. The State Authorities, in April 1937, resolved that 'the destiny of the natives of Aboriginal origin, but not of the full blood, lies in their ultimate absorption by the people of the Commonwealth, and it therefore recommends that all efforts be directed to that end.'

Wauwe Woman: Well, as Dr Duguid himself says – this was a policy of Absorption – trying to breed half-castes white.

Wirra Woman: Fuck'em white you mean?

Wauwe Woman: But Assimilation need not always be a dirty word. It was also an opportunity for those Aboriginals of mixed parentage who knew they couldn't go back to their old ways and wanted to have a half a chance in this new 'white world'.

Anyway, if Nancy had stayed out on the farms she would have been used as a slave and a whore by the white pastoralists! Instead, she has now become a hugely successful person in Australian society

Wirra Woman: Well I call it genocide. Anyway, Duguid was just another Dooguider! *She chortled at her own joke.*

Wawe Woman: No, he was part of a small progressive enlightened group of individuals keeping the fire burning for our people, who were being slapped down and made virtually extinct. Duguid was one of the very few whites who cared, when everyone else believed we were on the way to extinction, like poteroos.

Wirra Woman: Yes, but Duguid thought us inferior.

Wauwe Woman: At first, yes. But then he changed his mind. Especially when he saw people like Nancy Brumby and Lowitja O'Donohue excel. He was a product of his time and he changed his mind – which I think we should support.

Wirra Woman: Let's not have that argument now. Let's continue with the story!

Lunchtimes for Sveta were a nightmare. She hated going home, which Tatiana often insisted upon. Especially when she was plied with several cloves of raw garlic and returned to school to the taunts of, 'Pooh you smell!' When she was allowed to stay at school she had to undergo the humiliation of being fed soup at the school gate. Tatiana, donned in her Russian peasant scarf, cycled to the school with a hot soup on the back of her bike. As she gulped soup and humiliation, Sveta stared longingly at the Australian children who happily ate their fish and chips. It was at times like these that Sveta longed to be assimilated totally. She just wanted to be like the other children. She wanted a normal Australian mother who would give her a shilling for chips, or cut neat triangle sandwiches for her lunchbox. She would even eat Rosella tomato sauce.

As Sveta learnt to read, Ivan often bought *The News* home for her to explain what was going on in the country. Sveta was struck by a front-page story and picture that appeared on October 15th 1953. The headline read:

THE A-BOMB GOES UP

Beneath this headline was a large picture of a mushroom cloud with the caption:

The black mushroom-shaped cloud surges upward and begins to assume the shape of an Aborigine's profile.

Yes, Sveta could distinctly see a large face reproachfully gazing out of the plume into the sky. She couldn't fully understand the meaning of all this and was determined to show it to Miss Bradshaw. Miss Bradshaw had begun to tell them about history. Sveta thought 'history' was wonderful and sat entranced as Miss Bradshaw told them about the early days of South Australia. She was especially interested in the story of how Matthew Flinders circumnavigated Australia with the help of an Aboriginal boy. She didn't know what an Aboriginal boy was, and after putting up her hand was told that Aborigines were the original people of Australia. She took the front-page picture to school and showed her teacher. She pointed out the profile of the Aboriginal head in the cloud.

'Is that an Aborigine?'

Miss Bradshaw looked at the photo and then said a very strange thing.

'Yes, and I think that that Aborigine is an ancestor protesting against the atomic bomb.'

The picture depressed Belinda Bradshaw. She sadly remembered how hard Dr Duguid had campaigned at Federal level to stop atomic tests in the South Australian outback. He had argued that far from being empty it was the treasured storehouse of ancestral beings, and home to many nomadic peoples who wouldn't know what a nuclear test sign meant.

At the time of the first atomic test at Emu Fileds, a group of Pitjantjatjara people were terrified when they saw what looked like a dust storm moving towards them. Thinking it was a 'mamu', or evil spirit, they tried in vain to scare it away with sticks and woomeras. They soon developed skin rashes, watery eyes and diarrhoea.

It was getting close to the time of the John Martin's Christmas Pageant. Sveta begged her mother to take her. There was even a train put on for the event on the Saturday morning at Hendon station, to ferry eager children and their parents to the outstanding festive spectacle of the year.

'Yes yes, of course,' said Tatiana, laughing at the shiny, imploring eyes of her child. The night before the Christmas Pageant, Tatiana washed Sveta's hair. This was quite a job, as her hair was very long and took ages to dry. With her hair dried and plaited neatly for the big day, Sveta asked if she could go out and play.

'As long as you don't go too far. Dinner will be ready soon,' said her mother, putting potatoes on to boil.

At the back of Pudney Street was the railway line that brought the hundreds of workers to the Philips factory. Sveta loved balancing on the rails and leaping over the wooden sleepers. Nearby, she saw some workers who were digging up derelict ground.

'Very good,' they applauded as Sveta walked by, immaculately balanced on the railway line, like a circus girl on a tightrope. She loved the attention and started to show off, skipping along and even hopping.

'Excellent,' beamed the workers.

Then Sveta did a stupid thing that she lived to regret. She picked up a huge clod of earth that the workers had dug up, and placed it on her newly washed hair. She then walked on the rail line, balancing the earthen lump on her head. The men applauded. While she lapped up the applause, the ad hoc circus performer suddenly heard the familiar screech,

'Sveta! Sveta!'

She threw down the clod and ran home as fast as she could. Tatiana was in a terrible mood. She was brandishing a pot of burnt potatoes as Sveta ran in.

'Look what you have done,' she screamed. Where have you been? I was running around looking for you and dinner is burnt. Burnt!'

With that she threw the blackened pot at Sveta, narrowly missing her head.

That's when she noticed. The previously shiny and neat hair was dishevelled and covered in bits of dirt and grass.

Tatiana gave a demented screech and started pummelling the disgraced girl, lashing out and reigning blows on her head and arms.

'What have you done to your hair? You drive me crazy. I slave away all day cooking and cleaning, and look what you do. You are impossible.'

With this she got the dreaded strap and started beating Sveta mercilessly with it. The child screamed as she tried to evade the blows. She couldn't explain why she had got her hair so dirty. She just hadn't been thinking.

'You are not having any dinner and you are definitely not going to the pageant tomorrow.

'Oh, sorry Mama. Please oh please let me go to the pageant. Please.'

'Get to bed now!'

Sveta, with tears and dirt streaking her face, ran to the bedroom shaking and sobbing.

She lay on the bed. Her whole world had crashed around her. She couldn't bear the thought of not going to the pageant. She had been looking forward to it for a whole year, which to her six-year-old mind was an eternity. All the kids at school were going. All the neighbours were going. Oh no, this was worse than the strap. Worse than having to kneel on the coir mat in the toilet (a favourite punishment meted out by Tatiana). This was hell on earth. The only way she could get to sleep was with the thought that her mother had punished her enough, and would change her mind in the morning. Even though Sveta could see that Tatiana was acting more and more violently towards her, sometimes she could also be a good mother.

'Please God, let Mama take me to the Christmas Pageant. If she doesn't I will die.'

After crying herself miserably to sleep, Sveta got up next morning hoping her mother had changed her mind.

'Please Mama, I will be really good. Please let me go to the Christmas pageant.'

But Tatiana was intransigent.

Sveta clung to the hope that she would still change her mind. Life without going to the Christmas Pageant was empty, horrible and cruel.

She watched all the people walking past their house on the way to the special Christmas Pageant train. She watched all the happy children holding hands with their sweet-looking mothers, anticipation and joy bubbling out of their faces.

Sveta looked imploringly at her mother. Perhaps she would change her mind at the last minute. Panic started to rise like bile in her throat. Tatiana was chopping boiled eggs for the baby chicks. She was still in her nightdress.

The end of the world was nearly upon her. No more people were walking past. The train whistle blew. Sveta ran out the back. The engine was billowing steam. The wheels were beginning to make their slow, grinding noises. Then faster and faster. With a broken heart, Sveta watched as the train chugged out of the station – chugging to happy land, where children squealed with laughter and delight, where large papier-mache puppets swooped over the crowd, where the beautiful queen of the pageant graced the ecstatic throngs with her pearly smile.

Sveta stood watching the empty train-line for a long time. The train-line that had so unknowingly been her nemesis. She felt defeated. Darkness descended upon her. Life seemed utterly bleak.

Nearby, on the roof of the stationhouse, sat Baba Yaga. Her heart ached for the little girl. All she could do was to beam down as much love as she could. But she could see that Sveta was putting an icy ring around her heart. And it would be very difficult to ever melt it.

Sveta started to have breathing difficulties. She could never take a deep breath. It was partly because she didn't want to feel the deep anxiety that swished around her guts. She never knew when her mother would be a good mother or an evil mother. Sometimes when Tatiana's silver tooth glinted in the light, Sveta would become afraid and wonder if her mother was really Baba Yaga in disguise. She felt trapped in this chicken house; victim to a cruel witch. She was even force-fed like Baba Yaga force-fed her child prisoners. In fact, Tatiana was Baba Yaga, and she was eating Sveta alive. And there was no escape!

As fear gripped her, Sveta struggled to take a deep breath. Tatiana got sufficiently worried to take her to Adelaide Children's Hospital. Sveta quite liked it at this hospital, but unknowingly was to become victim of the latest fad that was gripping the hallowed children's hospitals of the Western world. 'Tonsils are evil.'

The tonsillectomy epidemic of the early 1950s was in full swing. Enlightened doctors believed that in order to save children from suffering tonsillitis, these dangerous appendages lurking at the back of the throat should be removed.

'Don't wait till they're infected, whip'em'out,' was the philosophy of the day.

There was nothing wrong with Sveta's tonsils. The doctor put a clean knife in front of her nostrils. It fogged up.

'See, she can breathe fine through her nose,' pronounced the doctor to the worried Tatiana. There was no way Sveta could explain to the nice doctor that she found it difficult to breathe because she thought her mother was Baba Yaga. After looking down her throat and seeing a healthy pair of tonsils that still dared to be there, the doctor booked Sveta in to have them taken out.

She felt very tiny and scared when Ivan took her in with her suitcase and deposited her on an iron bed. This was in a room designed to take three beds, but another six camp beds were brought in. Hundreds of children all over Adelaide were having their 'useless, will only get infected' tonsils out. At least Sveta felt she was one of the throng.

A starchy white matron entered the room and told all the unsuspecting victims that they were the luckiest children in the world. After the operation, they would be able eat ice cream and jelly for six weeks.

'Ooh,' squealed the children. 'Ice-cream and jelly!'

Sveta loved ice cream and jelly and couldn't wait. She even quite liked being in the hospital. For starters, she was away from Baba Yaga and she could breathe again. It felt safe and friendly and she had lots of children to talk to. She even liked being wheeled into the operation theatre by a team of nurses and doctors draped in green. She was going to be given a mysterious sounding gas called ether.

'I'd like you count backwards from 10,' said the nurse, placing something pungent over her face.

Feeling an urge to gag, Sveta started at 10. At 9 she saw a funny looking brick wall in her imagination and a mouse was trying to run up it. She was waiting for it to reach the top, when she woke up. Her throat felt terrible and she felt really sick. Something was badly wrong. She slowly opened her eyes expecting to be still in the operating theatre. Instead she was in a large room filled with prostrate children on camp beds who had just had their operations. The child next to her started to have convulsions. To her horror, blood started to spurt out of his nose and mouth in bright red arcs. Doctors and nurses rushed over from all directions and began administering to him. Sveta felt she was in a battle zone as the blood splashed on to the ceiling. What was this hell she had woken up to? The last thing she felt like was ice cream and jelly.

Sveta was surprised when Miss Bradshaw came to visit her in hospital. Miss Bradshaw said that she was at the hospital anyway, as she had come to speak to the management. The Aboriginal Advancement League was now championing the right of Aboriginal women to be trainee nurses in all the Adelaide hospitals, after Lowitja O'Donohue had finally been accepted into the Royal Adelaide.

Miss Bradshaw enthralled the convalescing girl (who still didn't feel like eating ice cream and jelly) with the story of the League's successful rally earlier that year. On a cold wet night at the end of August 1953, over a thousand people packed the Adelaide Town Hall to hear what the Aborigines had to say. After a film and some music, five Aboriginal people spoke eloquently and powerfully of the injustices they faced every day of their lives, such as being refused to sit with white passengers in the dining car of the train to Alice Springs. The audience was shocked. But according to the news reporter, what really shook their complacency was when Peter Tilmouth said, 'I am proud of my blood – both black and white. Through each I have inherited a certain intelligence and I am going to use it.'

On the question of a hostel in Adelaide, the audience were told,

'We want to feel we have your support for this project. But most of all we want your best wishes and, when we come to live with you, your neighbourliness.'

The disclosure at the meeting that Aboriginal girls were refused as nurses at the Royal Adelaide Hospital created such a stir that within a few days Lowitja O'Donohue and the others were invited to the hospital to start their training.

Belinda Bradshaw was delighted with the success of the meeting, as a result of which money poured in to the League's funds. But sadly, despite these small steps forward, most white Adelaideans, like their fellow Australians, ignored the 'Abos' and relegated them to the dusty edges of their consciences. There they sat, ignored, disowned and lost. Other shadowy figures joined them. There were the 'Chinks', or Chinese; the 'Eyties', or Italians, who had been interned during World War Two; and, of course, the Germans.

Thomas Playford's grandfather was elected to the House of Assembly for Onkaparinga in 1868, but was defeated in 1871 because he pointed at a German-born member, saying that the 'stinkwort was not the only weed that came from Germany'. This was hardly tactful, when his electorate included the German towns of Lobethal and Hahndorf in the Adelaide Hills. In 1888, Playford strongly supported moves to restrict Chinese immigration.

Albert Moir, a member of the present Playford government, was also hardly tactful when he commented on Italian migrants, who were beginning to flood into his constituency in 1953. 'These immigrants are of no use to us — a few of them are tradesmen but most of them have no skills at all. And when they intermarry we'll have all the colours of the rainbow.' A young lawyer named Don Dunstan, a member of the Aboriginal Advancement League, was appalled. An early proponent of multiculturalism, he let the Italians know what their government member thought of them, and consequently won the marginal seat of Norwood by 2,000 votes.

Belinda Bradshaw left Sveta's bedside to speak to the Children's Hospital matrons about taking Aboriginal trainees. She noticed the pursed lips of the starched white matron, which seemed to say, 'But I'm not sure of how CLEAN they are.' She had heard Lowitja O'Donohue report that at Royal Adelaide Hospital she had to make sure that her uniform was more spotless and her shoes more shiny than her white counterparts.

After a few days Sveta was sent home from hospital. From then on she always seemed to suffer from sore throats. But fortunately, her love for ice cream did return.

CHAPTER 6

The Curse

After spending a restless night, Walter Bromley dismantled his tent and followed Ityamai-itpina down the river to a place of the black man's choice. He was directed to a spot near the soldier's station. 'Here goode!' Ityamai-itpina grinned widely, showing his beautiful set of teeth.

Bromley set up anew and sent his servant Cooper to inform Governor Hindmarsh that he had moved, and to ask for a greater supply of biscuits, which the natives were rapidly devouring. Ityamai-itpina rewarded him with a large fish and some white grubs. Bromley happily accepted the fish but declined the wrigglers. Ityamai-itpina, Midlato, and their families abandoned their plans to move to the foothills. Murlawirrapurka had observed that this was the first time a white had offered to live amongst them. He appreciated the gesture and thought the Kaurna should reciprocate. Bromley's offer of blankets and food was an added incentive. As more ships disgorged settlers the kangaroos were keeping away and not drinking from the river, so it was getting harder to catch their meat and, subsequently, use their pelts to sew blankets. The green shoots of grass that these kangaroos usually ate were either trampled underfoot or gobbled up by hundreds of 'theep' and 'bullocky'. Any kangaroos that did venture near were chased and killed by white man's dogs. Ityamai-itpina hoped that the whites would go back to where they came from soon, so his people could get back to the practices that had sustained them for aeons. With a lot of sighing, Ityamai-itpina constructed a hut near Bromley, into which he moved his belongings. However, he preferred to sleep in one of the Aboriginal encampments that dotted the Karrawirraparri. He also preferred to wear his old kangaroo pelt than the ridiculous clothes that whites had tried to make him wear. His heart felt heavy, but at least he had succeeded in moving the ghost-skin away from his sacred waterhole.

Bromley asked Midlato and her friend Kartanya, to teach him some of their words. They ran to Midlato's *kammammi* who instructed them to go ahead, and also to learn as much of the white man's language as possible. Midlato showed Bromley her penny. Bromley pointed at the picture of the man with the thick neck and said he was the big 'King' of England, the country where the whites had come from. Her uncle Ityamai-itpina was often addressed as King Rodney and Murlawirrapurka as King John, which Midlato had found puzzling. This new information fed her vain hope that the ghost-skins were their ancestors. There was something about Bromley she couldn't fathom. She could see he was different from other white men in that he was living amongst them. But there was something desperate in his voice. He seemed kind in that he gave them food and blankets. But she didn't see any kindness in his eyes; in fact, the look in them gave her the shivers. In her tradition, looking deeply into the eyes was the way to sense the spirit of the person and understand them. She had liked the look in Looty's eyes. As well as being a lovely green, they were kind, and matched her voice and gestures.

However, Bromley was learning their language and, as her *kammammi* said, that was a good thing. Bromley told Midlato and Kartanya all about Jesus.

'Yee-tut.' They tried to say it. But there were no sounds like 'j' or 's' in the Kaurna language, and they and their people had difficulty pronouncing words with these letters in them. A particularly difficult word was 'soldiers' These were men in clothes with shiny buttons who often carried sticks which exploded. Midlato was afraid of them. She didn't like the way they looked at her, especially if they smelt of fire-water. The best approximation her people could manage was 'tulya'. And they lived at 'tulya wardli'.

Bromley doled out biscuits and oatmeal. The biscuits were snapped up, but the oatmeal was shunned. He tried to remonstrate, 'Perfectly good oatmeal – why don't you eat it?' They looked at it suspiciously and made vomiting noises. Bromley didn't know that flour and oatmeal had been laced with arsenic in other parts of Australia, and that this warning had been relayed throughout the Aboriginal groups. Bromley boiled up some oatmeal on the fire and made porridge.

'Boiled Oatmeal Porridge, BAP,' he said slowly, eating some of it to persuade them. 'Bap-py, bap-py. Very delicious!' He even added sugar from his own supply. 'Come try bappy; very, very good.' But the natives were reluctant. Some even spat it out in disgust.

'No good bappy!' they were insistent. 'Bappy gammon Ngaityerli.'

'Gammon' meant bad, and 'Ngaityerli' meant 'papa'. They had been told by Cronk that Bromley was their new 'father' or 'protector'. Besides, they would much prefer to eat what Bromley was eating. Midlato's stomach rumbled loudly as

Bromley roasted meat over his fire. That's what she wanted, not this disgusting 'bappy'.

'Ungrateful heathen sods,' muttered Bromley. Hindmarsh wasn't sending any more biscuits, and he was running out. He had to get these 'heathens' to eat oatmeal. Midlato came forward and tried some. The look on her face wasn't encouraging – and some of the other children tried too. But to no avail. Instead, they went down to the river and caught *kungurla* and cockles.

'They are so ungrateful and insolent, like spoilt children who would not eat their porridge,' wrote Bromley to Hindmarsh's secretary, George Stevenson.

Bit like all the white people here, thought Stevenson, remembering a recent, most ungentlemanly-like outburst in public between Commissioner Fisher and Governor Hindmarsh. The two continued their high-profile spatting without let up. Stevenson had finally started Adelaide's first newspaper, the *South Australian Gazette and Colonial Register,* and used it as a forum to attack what he saw as the abuse of power by the Commissioner and his cronies. He accused them of sabotaging the new utopia, and waged war against speculators who happily quoted Wakefield's high ideals but then used their resources to secure special privileges. The article caused furore. Fisher's henchmen regarded the publication of the *Register* as a declaration of war. Accusing Stevenson and the Governor of strangling free speech, they promptly proposed a rival paper. Stevenson rejoined, 'A few half-witted gentlemen have found their way hither, and not content with scribbling lying nonsense for the gratification of their private friends, are ambitious to see their lucubrations in print.' These 'lucubrations' eventually appeared in the rival *South Australian.* The war was on.

Robert Gouger, his heart heavy with the death of his family, became embroiled in a feud with Osmond Gilles, the Crown Treasurer, who could no more keep accounts than remember which king sat on the throne. Gilles felt insulted by Gouger, and threatened to 'Blow a hole in his carcase.' This led to a public brawl outside the new bank, much to the horror of its owner, Edward Stephens, who was obliged to take emergency snorts of snuff. The usually mild-mannered Gouger caned the foulmouthed Gilles with a walking stick which happened to belong to Charles Mann, the Advocate General. Cockatoos in the gum trees above screeched and ruffled at each crack of the cane. Top-hatted spectators scattered, tut-tutting at the scandal of it all. Edward Stephens ran puffing and blowing the few hundred yards to the Governor's residence. 'Come quick, your subjects are killing each other!' Hindmarsh despatched his marines who promptly arrested the said 'subjects', who by now were both bleeding profusely. At bayonet point, the miscreants were marched to Government Hut. Ityamai-itpina watched this high drama with some interest. He was puzzled by white men's haphazard way of fighting. In his tradition, the rules were well defined. But he did admire Gouger's use of the walking stick and thought it would make a fine *waddy.*

Hindmarsh, looking for any excuse to weaken his opponents, immediately sacked Gouger and proceeded to appoint his future son-in-law, Strangways, in his place. Being blessed with a clutch of marriageable daughters, Hindmarsh could continue this nifty nepotism by bestowing the position on yet another future son-in-law, George Milner

Stephen, when Strangways proved totally unsuitable. The idealistic dream of a new utopia had, in a remarkably short time, descended into a quagmire of intrigue, backbiting, mudslinging, and violence.

Back on the riverbank Bromley had his own problems. When Itya, Rodney's son, stole some rice, Bromley shouted at him and the boy ran off in fear. The next day Bromley smelt smoke and saw that a corner of his hut was on fire. As he threw water over it he spotted Itya skulking in the shadows.

In addition to the storms raging among the whites in June 1837, there were physical storms as well. The weather was wet, cold and violent. On the night of the 28th Ityamai-itpina and a clutch of others ran towards Bromley, crying out in fear, and insisted on coming into his hut. 'Ngaityerli, Ngaityerli! Karndo, karndo.'

Bromley had learnt from Midlato that this was the word for thunder, and refused.

'You all have a perfectly good tent of your own. Shoo!' But the next time the Karndo bird clapped six of them, including Midlato, Kartanya, and Milte-widlo piled in, terrified, and he couldn't keep them out. As he lay in his bed listening to the thunder and huge bursts of rain, he felt that things were going from bad to worse. His servant, Cooper, was unreliable and was drunk most nights. He hung out with Hindmarsh's marines, who had been nothing but trouble ever since they had landed. Hindmarsh forbade them entering the mushrooming taverns, but they didn't take any notice and Cooper loved getting merry with them. The worst thing was that Cooper would give some of his ale to King Rodney. Bromley felt that this was a bad development. Hindmarsh and the others were not supporting him at all.

They had the attitude that he was mad to be living among the natives, and didn't understand what he was trying to do.

When Bromley woke up next morning, not only had Rodney stolen the three-pound piece of meat that was to be his dinner that night, but he also had his hands in a bowl of rice. Bromley snapped. 'Get your filthy hands out of the rice, and where is my meat?'

Ityamai-itpina just shrugged his shoulders and said, 'I hungry,' and continued to shovel the *pindi pari*, or 'European maggots' as the Kaurna called it, into his mouth. He had sacrificed his usual winter hunting expeditions and was starving, and while the rice was nowhere as delicious as real maggots, it was better than disgusting bappy.

Midlato lay frightened in the corner of the tent. The voice and look of Bromley were now matching. She could pick up the hatred and disgust in Bromley's actions, especially when he spat, 'Get your filthy hands out of the rice!' The false smile was now well and truly gone. Ityamai-itpina blithely kept stuffing his face. He was of the opinion that he was owed the meat and rice. He was a hunter-gatherer. This is what hunter-gatherers did. If there was food, they ate it. When it ran out, they sharpened their spears and went out hunting. Simple. If these ghost-skins were the Kaurna's long-lost brothers and they were frightening away the game, they owed them food. This was the law as far as Ityamai-itpina was concerned. And how dare this ghost-skin keep meat for himself while giving him rubbish bappy! Didn't Bromley know the ancestor stories about not sharing food? Perhaps this was what was causing the thunder. Perhaps the ancestors were displeased with white man's behaviour. Ityamai-itpina was even more incensed when Bromley picked up the bowl of European maggots and threw it to the chickens.

'I was obliged to give what was left of the rice to the fowls after his dirty hands had been in it.' Bromley wrote in a letter to Stevenson.

Ityamai-itpina could see there was one law for the whites and another law for the blacks. He felt insecure. It seemed his way of life was being interfered with in a way he did not like. That night he danced furiously and sang many songs about the bad bappy and the dearth of tasty meat.

Hindmarsh and the commissioners, although on opposite sides in the white colonial wars, were in agreement about Bromley. They were not happy with the way he was setting out to be Protector. 'Why on earth does he want to mix so closely with the natives and learn their language?' they muttered privately to each other. They felt obliged to pay some attention, as there was a substantial clause in the South Australian charter to protect the natives. The gentlemen in London who had included this clause were the same liberal-minded people who had abolished slavery, and had been perturbed by the stories of terrible treatment of the Aborigines in the other colonies. They wanted South Australia to be a model of liberal humanity. Putting these principles into practise, however, was a totally different matter. To the land-hungry settlers, it was obvious that the natives owned no land and that they were just savages. 'Look at the way they cavorted about naked the whole night!' They couldn't see what possible purpose it served for Bromley to live right in the middle of them. Perhaps he was not quite right in the head, or too old and doddery.

They suggested to Bromley he might like to retire. Bromley was appalled. Relations with the natives had improved a little, especially since he had been able to make the oatmeal into cakes. Midlato could feel how much he wanted to help them. She, Kartanya and Milte-widlo had moved into his hut as it continued to be particularly cold and rainy. She missed her cosy *wardli* in the shelter of the foothills. It was unnatural to be sleeping on the plain this time of the year. Everything about it was wrong. But she was carrying out the important task of teaching Bromley her language. Bromley argued that he should stay in post, as he now knew 450 Kaurna words and was beginning to get the natives to cultivate the ground around the tents. He also argued that it was important to protect them from undesirable white riff-raff who were plying them with drink. But Hindmarsh and Stevenson were too engaged in their own continuing war to take any notice.

Robert Gouger, aggrieved about being suspended, prepared to return to England. He intended to acquaint the South Australian Commission with the tyrannical deeds of Hindmarsh, engender his dismissal, and return with his successor. Hindmarsh retaliated by trumping up a charge against Gouger that £2000 of public monies was unaccounted for. Charles Mann accused Hindmarsh of revenge, and hinted at the shady dealings of the treasurer Gilles. Hindmarsh turned a blind eye (the one he'd lost in the Battle of the Nile), to the fact that Gilles was running an illegal chandlery business under a false name, and stopped Gouger's salary. But the head rolling had only just begun. John Brown, Cronk's boss, was suspended, for among other things 'insolent malevolence'. Commissioner Fisher squealed loudly that Hindmarsh couldn't dismiss people like Gouger and Brown, who had been appointed by the commissioners, not the Crown. Stevenson called Fisher a 'pitiful blockhead'. The next head to roll was the Advocate General, Mann, who supported the 'blockhead'. His lethal walking stick and lofty position did not protect him from an angry Hindmarsh who was fed up with Mann's campaign to curtail his powers.

Stevenson enjoyed trumpeting all these disputes in the *Register*, and making what his enemies called 'vile, uncalled-for and disgustingly virulent attacks'. This led to the Perth Gazette commenting rather gleefully, 'The good folks in power in the free republic of South Australia appear to be a most unruly quarrelsome sort of gentry, each one trying who shall master.'

The other colonies, jaded by all the good press the saintly new colony had been getting, watched its fall into a quagmire of dissension with mounting satisfaction.

Judge Jeffcott threw his hands up in horror and escaped again to Van Diemen's Land.

Murlawirrapurka kept back, watching and waiting. The antics of the white men puzzled him. They never seemed at peace and always seemed to gather in plotting huddles or to gallivant about on their *pindi* kangaroos. He continued hunting the real kangaroos in his ancestral grounds to the south of Adelaide. He had grown in stature and respect among his own people and had attracted four wives. He was at the height of his powers but was alarmed at the rapid spread of the whites. His own continuing strategy was to be friendly. In July 1837 he joined a Doctor Leigh, who was out hunting with a friend. Murlawirrapurka helped them track down kangaroos, and impressed Leigh with his skills of living off the land, extracting large white grubs from roots, scaling tall gums for possums, and lighting Leigh's pipe by friction over dry grass. Leigh gave him some silver groats in return, which Murlawirrapurka regarded suspiciously. He had only been given brown money so far, and had discovered he could buy bread and tobacco with it. He didn't yet realise the value of these 'white boys'. Leigh was thirsty and noticed Murlawirrapurka seemed to be sipping something out of a tree through a straw. Fashioning his own straw, Leigh attempted to do the same, vainly sucking out of the trunk. Murlawirrapurka roared with laughter. Leigh was unaware that on the end of the black man's straw was small hook made out of fish bone, and what was being extracted from the tree was a large white juicy grub.

It was Leigh's turn to laugh the next day when he met Murlawirrapurka by the river, where he was searching for pignuts. 'Good marn Doctor,' greeted Murlawirrapurka, shaking the white man's hand. Leigh invited him to partake in some snuff. Thinking this the mark of a gentleman, Murlawirrapurka obliged. He took an enormous pinch out of the little silver box.

'He stared at me in great perplexity' wrote Leigh. 'Tears streamed out of his eyes; he could bear it no longer and spluttered it out all over me, exclaiming, "No goode: ah pooh!"' After a lot more choking, blowing, and laughing, Murlawirrapurka finally understood the mechanics of sniffing the snuff up his nostrils. In between violent attacks of sneezing he shouted, 'Goode, goode.'

He liked the light-headed feeling snuff temporarily gave him. A bit like fire-water or 'grog', which some marines had introduced him to in the Buffalo tavern. What he had liked most about 'grog' was the effect it had on white men.

They would loosen right up, begin to laugh, become more animated and stop looking so serious. They would put their arm around his shoulder and act like they really loved him; the physical contact made him feel good. But he wasn't sure of the effect of the fire-water on him. It blurred the edges, making him light-headed and less alert. Could he defend his land if the Permangk made an attack? He was a warrior, accountable to a long line of ancestors. The effect of 'grog' made his place in this line very wobbly indeed.

On the other hand, it dulled the nebulous anxiety he was feeling: a deep uneasiness at the sounds of banging and sawing, as alien buildings sprouted up on his beloved Tandanyangga, under his sky. The fire-water dulled the incipient realisation that life as he knew it was slipping rapidly from his grasp. He felt the fire in his belly and jiggled the coins he had been given. A poor exchange.

Doctor Leigh was impressed by Murlawirrapurka's stamina. After the day they had spent hunting and running together, Leigh wrote in his diary that Murlawirrapurka stayed up all that night dancing. It was full moon, and although Leigh was exhausted and had swollen feet, he decided to watch some of what he called the 'Corrobbaree'. He was treated to an energetic display of dancing by a band of warriors, moonlight bouncing off the striking red and white ochre designs on their naked bodies, in time to mesmerising chanting. He, like many observers of the time, was spellbound by the 'wild play of the natives', especially the spectacular leg-quivering dance movement that the young Kaurna men performed in front of the drumming women.

Leigh was witnessing one of the many *ngunyawaietta* that Murlawirrapurka performed that cold season, the first *kudlilla* his people had spent down on the plain. It was his way and his people's way to dance and act out the trials and tribulations they were enduring. Leigh noted that in this particular performance, Murlawirrapurka was wearing a straw hat and a soldier's coat, and proceeded to demonstrate his prowess at knee-straddling and spinning, and performing 'the most ridiculous antics'. Leigh's interpretation was that Murlawirrapurka was 'denouncing vengeance against enemies of the tribe' in such an energetic way that he 'literally tore the passion to rags as his coat flew in all directions.' Leigh was correct that Murlawirrapurka was teaching his people not to wreak vengeance against an enemy, but it did not occur to him to suspect that the enemy could possibly be him, the white man. Murlawirrapurka was also expressing his anger at having to wear white man's clothes, as represented by the soldier's coat and the straw hat. Many of the Kaurna were being forced to wear clothing after William Pearce, the colony tailor, was set the task to clothe the 'harmless and tractable' but 'shockingly naked' natives.

As well as violent storms that first winter, settlers were startled by a loud rumbling noise. The earth shook and trembled. The plain into which they had decided to sink their fortunes was on a fault line. Over twenty million years earlier, the rock below Adelaide had made a major shift. The settling down period was still continuing. The whites busily and greedily acquiring land were worried. Murlawirrapurka had to reassure them that in Kaurna tradition, earthquakes were part of the territory and were not usually very severe. Ityamai-itpina, on the other hand, was convinced the earthquake, like the unusually violent storms that marked that *kudlilla*, was an omen, and that the ancestors were furious with what was happening on the Tandanya plain. Kadlitpina suspected that the Wirra sorcerers were up to no good.

Bromley finally lost the job of Protector 'on grounds of physical and mental imbecility'. Even though he was promised he could start a school for the native children, he felt humiliated. He could not return to his family in England and admit he had failed. He had left his wife and daughters against their will, they being convinced something terrible would befall him. Midlato could feel his unhappiness but did not know how to communicate her concern.

Dr William Wyatt, the new 'ngaityerli', was appointed in August 1837. He had arrived six months earlier and bought some town lots at the land sale held in May 1837, which laid the foundation of a considerable fortune, and was busy building himself a house. He was also appointed town coroner. Due to his interest in ethnology, he was persuaded to take on the role of Protector of the Aborigines. Continued reminders from Britain about the rights of the original inhabitants meant that the whites in Adelaide had to pay lip service to 'protecting' the natives' interests. James Cronk, who had kept up his enterprising and friendly relations with the Aborigines, offered his help. He was joined by Albert Taplow and Robert Cock, who could also speak several Kaurna words.

The whites regarded the increasingly popular Murlawirrapurka as tribal chief, and called him King John. He played along with this, but in actuality wanted nothing to do with ideas of kingship. This was typical of the way white man thought – from crown down. How could he get across how black man thought – so differently, so non-linear, so raw, a mosaic way of viewing the world which was suffused in the reality of the land? White man seemed stuck in one-dimensional thinking – blinded and constrained by it.

Relationships between the whites and blacks remained friendly in these early days. The only serious troubles occurred over women. Murlawirrapurka was called upon to help. He accompanied Wyatt down to Encounter Bay where a white man, Driscoll, had been murdered for interfering with black women. A Ngarrindjeri man was arrested but escaped. Murlawirrapurka also helped Wyatt to establish the cause of death of Pegler, a white man found near the River Torrens. A rather ominous, thin pointed bone had been inserted into his back, piercing his heart. On investigation, it transpired that Pegler had shot some dogs belonging to natives, and on the night of his demise had intruded into a *palti* and accosted a black woman. Two Aborigines were arrested but escaped soon after. As in the case of Driscoll, little attempt was made to recapture them. Many settlers felt these men had got what they deserved. Murlawirrapurka felt relieved. It seemed that white men were continuing to distinguish between good and bad white men, as well as good and bad black men.

Wyatt set about to move the Aboriginal camp to the northern bank of the river to Piltawardli, or the possum place. Here he planned to build a schoolhouse, a storehouse, and proper huts for the natives; hoping to instil in them farming habits. 'The Location' was surrounded by a fence, which Midlato and Kartanya regarded with suspicion. As a settler observed, 'A sort of stockade has been formed for them about a mile from Adelaide, with huts ... the blacks would not enter the poundlike fence; they preferred sweet liberty and ease, rolling under the gum trees wrapped up in a rug or blanket.'

Another settler was neither so charitable nor so poetic. 'Their aversion to the huts which have benevolently been built for them is well known. In consequence, they are stripping trees, burning others, and peeling the bark off the finest to make roofs for their temporary huts. If this goes on much longer, the lovely spot reserved for the park will be deprived of its greatest ornaments, and we shall look in vain for a shady walk during the summer months.'

Wirra Woman: The audacity. See how quickly whites forgot whose trees and land this was!

Ityamai-itpina especially hated the confinement of the stockade. The only use he could find for his new hut was to store spears. That summer the heavens continued to burst forth, and he and his family preferred to shelter under the veranda of Hack's house. Here he would continue to interact with his friends Cock and Taplow. Ityamai-itpina's wife and Midlato liked to visit Bridget Hack who, unlike most other white women, was happy to see them. Midlato also noticed she was as affectionate to her children as Kaurna women were to their own. She loved watching Bridget, small children in tow, feeding the hens and pottering around in her garden. One afternoon, Bridget picked a long green plant and gave it to her. Midlato uncertainly started to put it in her mouth. Bridget laughed and showed her how to open it. Inside, Midlato was amazed to see some perfectly round green balls. 'These are peas – try some.' Midlato thought they were delicious.

James Backhouse, a Quaker preacher, visited Adelaide at the end of 1837 as part of an Australian tour to promote temperance, and kindness to the natives. Albert Taplow was delighted, as he was concerned with the dismissive attitude of most settlers towards the Kaurna. Backhouse stayed with the Hacks and was able to observe the Kaurna at close quarters, and was impressed. He wrote that the Adelaide native women did 'not appear to live in dread of their husbands', as he had noticed in the eastern colonies, and that they were 'very fond of their children, embracing and kissing them affectionately. One of them noticed Bridget Hack kissing her little son, and exclaimed, "very good" with evident satisfaction.'

Meanwhile, more settlers were swarming in to the colony, 2,000 by the end of 1837. Much of the land had not yet been surveyed so many squatted wherever they could, and a variety of tents and huts sprang up along the river banks, including a garden of watermelons planted by an enterprising Scotsman, Joseph Ind. Discomfited with this latest haphazard invasion, the Kaurna watched from their own camps. Whites, still awaiting a 'black attack', were wary. Summer sizzled and the grass yellowed; a tinder trap waiting for the inevitable explosion.

It came when a settler accidentally shot two black men while hunting quail in the long grass. Ityamai-itpina threatened to burn down the white man's hut if either of the two died of their wounds. Alarm spread. Settlers set up vigil. Protector Wyatt, with the aid of Taplow and Cock, intervened and tried to calm the situation. That night Itya carried a fire-stick down to the river to have a drink, as was his usual custom. A nervous settler, convinced the boy was about to set fire to his hut, shot at him. Ityamai-itpina was furious and ran for his cache of spears. It took Murlawirrapurka all his skill to calm him down enough and stop him from starting the 'black attack', which tetchy whites seemed determined to incite.

Likewise, Wyatt, Taplow and Cock had to allay the fears of the trigger-happy settlers. When some sanity was restored, Wyatt admonished the whites for taking the law into their own hands. Taplow helped diffuse the tensions by taking Ityamai-itpina and his kinsfolk to the Colonial Stores, where he handed out a generous proportion of extra food. The Quaker preacher, Backhouse, who witnessed this incident, had urgent talks with Wyatt in John Hack's house about what could be done to ease the rising tensions. A committee headed by Cock and Taplow was formed, which would assist Wyatt in protecting the black population. The committee agreed that 'The Location', where natives could always get food, shelter and protection, should be quickly completed.

However, despite the cordiality and valiant efforts of these worthy few, Backhouse observed that, 'The rights of the original Inhabitants of the country would be ultimately merged in the supposed interests of the Settlers.'

As well as their drinking habits, Backhouse did not approve of the land-grabbing greedy nature of the settlers as the land was surveyed. Prices were soaring. Acres originally bought for £3–12 were now fetching £40–65.

Backhouse, from a pulpit, urged a gathering of 200 Adelaide settlers to consider their rightful 'duty toward the black population, and the danger of bringing a curse upon themselves, if they neglected these things.'

Albert Taplow took what Backhouse said to heart. He was inspired to do his best for his black brothers. He did not want to invite a curse upon himself.

Judge Jeffcott returned briefly from Van Diemen's Land, and had to walk a tightrope between the bickering factions. Being Chief Justice in mosquito-infested Sierra Leone was child's play compared to being one in South Australia.

'Save me from these dissensions!' he exclaimed in a letter to England. He was desperate to return to Van Diemen's Land. He had heard rumours that his fiancée, Anne Kermode, was receiving the attentions of another suitor and that scurrilous gossip was being spread about him.

Wauwe Woman: It seems Jeffcott never could get away from scandal. He murdered poor Dr Hennis because the doctor had warned Flora MacDonald's family. What a scoundrel Jeffcott was. He brought his own little cauldron of trouble all the way over with him to the South Seas.

Wirra Woman: It just goes to show, you can never get away from your past. It seems Adelaide was full of people who were escaping from trouble, only to bring it with them and foist it on us.

Soon a legal matter arose which gave Jeffcott an excuse to leave again. Samuel Stephens, another white who could never stay out of trouble, was arrested for attempted murder after firing at a rival whaleboat, which was under the command of a Captain Blenkinsopp. As this was a crime committed on the High Seas, Jeffcott insisted that he had to consult with other judges about the legality of Stephens' arrest. Yes, and why was it not surprising that these judges happened to reside in Van Diemen's Land? The vessel on which he was trying to effect his mission, the *South Australian*, was wrecked at Encounter Bay and he found himself, oddly enough, in the company of the victim in question, Captain Blenkinsopp. While awaiting another ship, Jeffcott decided to explore the Murray Mouth to check its suitability as an alternative site for Adelaide. Hindmarsh doggedly continued to resist Light. Jeffcott sided with the Governor, pooh-poohing Light's argument that the mouth of the Murray was far too dangerous. To prove that it was navigable, Jeffcott and Captain Blenkinsopp attempted to sail out of it. Blenkinsopp's whaleboat fell foul to the unpredictable swells about which Light had warned. Both Jeffcott and Blenkinsopp drowned.

Wirra Woman: Serves Jeffcott right. Nothing but trouble, that man. Adelaide was well rid of him.

Author: But you should have seen the bloke who temporarily took his place. Jickling wore bright green spectacles and was as eccentric as he was shortsighted. Mistaking his lurid spectacles for a centipede, he smashed them to pieces and then blamed everyone else when he couldn't find them!

Wirra Woman: But at least he wasn't a philandering murderer!

Bromley cut a forlorn figure as he waded into the river every morning to fill up his tin kettle. Midlato and Kartanya continued to learn English and teach Bromley Kaurna words. Midlato noticed that he now often ate peas with his meat. She thought it hilarious that these little green balls seemed to have a mind of their own as he tried to pile them on his fork. Midlato taught Bromley the word the Kaurna had coined for this strange *pindi* vegetable; 'birki-birki', which literally meant, 'lots of little bits'. In turn Bromley showed her a picture of Yeetut, saying what a good man he was, and that he loved children. 'And me?' Midlato asked, wondering about this strange pale ancestor. 'Of course,' said Bromley. She was dubious. In the picture Yeetut was surrounded by a group of white children. If Yeetut loved her why were there were no black children?

'Is he king?' she asked, taking out her prized penny and pointing at it.

'Yes' said Bromley 'but not same king.' Then Bromley told her something which really puzzled her.

'This king,' Bromley pointed at the coin, 'is now dead. We now have a new queen. Her name is Victoria.'

Midlato and Kartanya heard the white-skins sing 'God Save the Queen' at an exceedingly bizarre event just north of the river. A group of *pindi* kangaroos were put in a line and then had to run extremely fast in the heat. White-skins stood on the side and acted the closest she had seen to a white man *palti* – yelling loudly, waving their arms, and stomping their feet. Midlato was witnessing the first horse race on her *yarta*. On the 1st and 2nd of January 1838, more than 800 settlers stopped their squabbling and joined together at Thebarton, just west of the river, to race horses, recently imported from Van Diemen's Land. Light and Fisher were the stewards. Samuel Stephens, no longer under arrest for attempted murder (as his accuser, Blenkinsopp, had conveniently drowned), enthusiastically shouted from the sidelines. A short time later he was thrown to his death from his own horse.

Wauwe Woman: Another troublemaker we were well rid of.

Another bizarre event intrigued Midlato, Kartanya and Milte-widlo during the second *worltatti* that white-skins had turned their life upside-down. Gubnor Hindmarsh laid a stone just south of the river and white-skins clapped enthusiastically. It was only later Midlato discovered the ominous significance of this ceremony. One hot morning she was startled by a mighty clap of thunder: the sound did not fit with the blue of the sky. Then another! Terribly frightened she rushed over to Bromley's hut, 'Ngaityerli, Ngaityerli!' Bromley explained as best as he could that white men were putting gunpowder into the limestone escarpment on the side of the river and blowing it up. Why? So, they could get stone to build giant *wardlis*. Midlato ran to her *kammammi* and clung to her every time there was an intermittent blast. This caused great consternation among her people. Ityamai-itpina couldn't believe that white man could create such earthquake and thunder.

'How can white man turn on this thunder magic? How can he gouge out the rocks imbued with our ancestor's spirits with such irreverence?'

Ityamai-itpina was now convinced that whites were performing very bad magic and absolutely no good would ever come of it.

Whatever the authorities thought of Bromley, his command of the language was invaluable, and in March 1838 he was officially appointed Superintendent of the Young Natives. However, his relief was short-lived. A few weeks later he waded into the river to fill his kettle as usual. He suddenly felt his foot being snagged. He lost balance and fell. It seemed he was being dragged under. Somewhere a kookaburra laughed. His head submerged as he gulped for air. His billy floated away, and it took a few seconds for the bubbles to stop coming to the surface.

Wirra Woman: Well, was he murdered?

Wauwe Woman: Nobody knows, and frankly nobody seemed to care.

Wirra Woman. Well it sounds pretty fishy to me. *Wirra Woman laughs uproariously.*

At the inquest, his death was not regarded as suspicious.

Wauwe Woman: Mr Bromley epitomised the kind of ghost-skin summed up in the adage, 'The road to hell is paved with good intentions.'

The blasts continued on the banks of the river, changing its shape. Midlato, Kartanya and Milte-widlo stared hollow-eyed as Hindmarsh's foundation stone grew into the Holy Trinity Church, and then as other giant stones were gouged from the earth and turned into monstrous edifices. The miserable truth seemed that white man was here to stay, and he was changing the very structure of the landscape.

The committee formed by Quakers, Backhouse, Taplow and Cock to protect the natives advised Protector Wyatt to engage Kaurna men to deal with thefts and minor disputes between Aborigines and settlers. Albert Taplow was set up as the police officer in charge, and he promptly appointed Murlawirrapurka and Kadlitpina as honorary police constables to help the Protector. The black men were amused and honoured. Cronk took them to the Buffalo's Head to celebrate. There he renamed Kadlitpina 'Captain Jack'. Murlawirrapurka and Kadlitpina were playing along with white man's rules. Cooperation seemed to be working, even though they found their customs exceedingly strange.

For a start, King John had a problem wearing trousers, which always seemed to fall down every time he stood up. And as for gloves! What ridiculous pieces of attire they were! However, it seemed the white man was definitely here to stay, and unfortunately much longer than previously believed. Murlawirrapurka was happy that he would now be called upon in disputes between whites and blacks. However, he was soon to witness a shocking aspect of white man's law when a bad white man was gruesomely hanged.

There had never been an official police force in South Australia; that role had been taken by Hindmarsh's drunken marines. The first settlers were mostly a hardworking lot, fully occupied in carving out a living from the bush. However, escaped convicts from Van Diemen's Land infiltrated the colony, and Samuel Smart was appointed the first sheriff. The Van Demonians, as they were called, teamed up with bushrangers and other outlaws and hid up in the Mount Lofty Ranges. Sheriff Smart assembled a police force.

Sheriff Smart was attacked and shot at one night by three Van Demonians. One Michael Magee was captured, tried and sentenced to death. He was to be the first man hanged in Adelaide, and his public execution was set for May 2nd 1838. Ityamai-itpina and his son Itya were curious about white man's form of revenge. Accompanied by Murlawirrapurka they followed the thousand or so settlers who thronged thirstily to their first public execution. Unfortunately, this hanging was totally botched. The reluctant hangman placed the noose too loosely, and as the cart was drawn away Magee swung in terrible agony yelling, 'Oh God Oh Christ save me.' The hangman, who bolted in terror, had to be chased and brought back to finish the job.

The *Register* reported, 'Some spectators cried out "Cut him down"' whilst others, with a different kind of consideration, urged the marines to shoot him with their muskets. It was a horrible sight to witness. The twisting of the rope and the man turning around like a joint of meat before the fire, while women were fainting, and the Sheriff attempting to address the crowd amidst fierce cries of "Shame! Shame!" Finally, the hangman made a fiendish leap upon the body of the dying man and all was hushed; Magee's hands could cling no longer to the rope, and his agonised cries were heard no more.'

Mildred Fowler, a newly arrived immigrant, was one of the women who fainted and had to be given a dose of smelling salts by Dr Wright.

Murlawirrapurka, Ityamai-itpina, and Itya were appalled. They hoped they would never have to suffer white man's justice.

Light continued to be harassed by Hindmarsh as he continued his surveys. In June 1838 he resigned and formed his own surveying company, which completed surveys of over 150,000 acres, including the Port Adelaide area and the proposed northern town of Gawler. With equal alacrity, settlers moved in. Mildred Fowler and her staunchly Methodist family from Cornwall acquired a modest plot in the future Gawler.

Preacher Backhouse had been right. Greed was taking over, and white man gave little heed to the rights of the original inhabitants. The South Australian Colonisation Act, although giving lip service to Aboriginal rights, provided no legislative mechanism to honour those rights. South Australia was described therein as 'certain waste and unoccupied lands.'

Hindmarsh, who had been amenable to the plan of setting aside some land for the benefit of the Aborigines, was swamped by his own problems, and had the threat of recall hanging over him. Aboriginal Protector Wyatt, who had been influenced by the exhortations of James Backhouse, Albert Taplow, and Robert Cock, approached Commissioner Fisher about reserving land for the Kaurna but was told that his application was 'useless'.

In September 1838 Cock, frustrated at the attempts to exhort the commissioners to honour their earlier promises to the original inhabitants, sent Fisher the sum of £3 16s. 6d. with an accompanying note stating that, 'being the interest, at the rate of 10 per cent, on the one-fifth of the purchase-money of the town land, purchased by me, on the 27th March, 1837... I feel it my duty to pay to the proper authorities for the use of the natives, this yearly rent... I disclaim this to be either donation, grant or gift, but a just claim the natives of this district have on me, as an occupier of those lands.'

Speculation was still rife as people bought and sold. The black man, not understanding white man's ways, and trusting in the fundamental law of decency and reciprocation, was victim to daylight robbery.

Cock's gesture was the only one that came even slightly close to what the ideal could have been – to acknowledge the Kaurna and their land, and to mutually decide what would be compensation, if there could be any, for losing their entire way of life.

Murlawirrapurka had made good progress with the Ngarrindjeri to quell their warlike ways. When Jeffcott had drowned at the Murray Mouth three of the survivors had been pulled from the frothing water by the Ngarrindjeri, who 'generously risked their own lives to save ours, thus shewing an example of magnanimous humanity to the disdainful, civilized white man.'

They had even kindly buried the body of Blenkinsopp when it was washed up a few hours later. Jeffcott's body was never found. Another ship, the *Fanny*, was wrecked on the Coorong in June 1838. As her survivors lay wet and freezing on the sand, a group of Milmenrura, one of the Ngarrindjeri clans, had lit a fire for them, brought them water, and cared for them for several weeks. The captain of the *Fanny* and William Longbottom, a future pastor in Adelaide, had nothing but praise for them, saying, 'They were well disposed, and the most inoffensive race that we had ever met.'

Murlawirrapurka was satisfied that the Ngarrindjeri had learned their lesson after murdering Collet Barker, and could now distinguish between good and bad white men.

While Murlawirrapurka continued to persuade his fellow blacks to absorb strange new ways, he himself was most happy when he could shed the accoutrements of supposed civilisation and run naked through the kangaroo grass, the wind caressing his lean muscular body; or daub himself with red and white ochre and dance in the moonlight. However, not long after Magee's botched hanging, he was sorely tested. In his capacity as native constable, he was informed that a fowl belonging to a settler had been killed by a native's dog. The settler demanded that the dog be shot. Murlawirrapurka was horrified to discover that the dog in question was a favourite of his youngest wife. Murlawirrapurka, his wife crying on one side and the settler demanding retribution on the other, wondered what to do.

This is what dingoes do, he thought. *They hunt birds for food – and* pindi *birds are no exception!* He deliberated deeply and decided that he must sacrifice his wife's dog to please the white man. He retained some sense of control by slicing off the dog's head rather than have it shot, and delivered it to George Milner Stephen who, as well as marrying Hindmarsh's daughter had taken over from George Stevenson as colonial secretary. The sacrifice did not go unnoticed. The colonial secretary noted on receipt of the dog's head, 'knowing their strong affection for their dogs this speaks much for their innate sense of justice, for this Aborigine was well aware that similar depredations had gone unpunished.'

That night Murlawirrapurka performed a strong dance, beating into the earth his frustration and heartache over the invidious position he had been thrown into by the advent of the white man. He also knew his trials were only just beginning.

CHAPTER 7

Hill's Hoist

Just as settlers had expanded into Adelaide in the late 1830s, the South Australia of the 1950s was also expanding rapidly. Much to Mildred Taplow's horror, more migrants were flooding in. Dark swarthy creatures swarmed onto tomato farms up Tapley's Hill Road. Like the racist politician Albert Moir, she shuddered to think what would become of Adelaide's Anglo-Saxon heritage. She fervently hoped 'Eyties' would not move into Pudney Street.

Tatiana took Sveta to the beach on the train and mingled with migrants from Italy and Greece who enjoyed the Mediterranean climate. Tatiania loved these happy people who brought their warm vibrant spirits with them and brightened up life in Adelaide. One day, Tatiania was overjoyed to bump into Kirov and Vlada on the jetty at Henley Beach. They were Bulgarian friends she thought she had left behind forever when she had escaped from Czechoslovakia. The reunion consisted of a lot of shrieking, sobbing, and laughing.

Sveta was horrified to see where Kirov and Vlada lived, a hot tin shed among glasshouses not far from the beach. Their two baby daughters lay in tomato boxes smothered in flies. But love and laughter rang out from that humble shed as Tatiana and her friends caught up with each other. Sveta was glad to see her mother happy again. In fact, Tatiana decided there and then to throw a party. She just loved parties, having fun, getting drunk, and dancing. She came from people who would guzzle vodka and think nothing of staying up all night, eating, laughing, and singing at the top of their voices. Unfortunately, in Playford's Adelaide, there was little emphasis on the word 'play'. Thomas Playford, who had been Premier since 1937, had been nurtured in a puritanical nest that harked back to his Baptist namesake great grandfather, who, appalled by the frivolity he found in 1846 Adelaide, spent his life stamping it down. His great grandson, Tom, had enjoyed his very long term in office, partly because of the blatant bias in the voting system towards the rural population. 'Playmandering' it was called. Playford represented country people, as did his grandfather who, in 1899, during a vigorous debate on the electoral system, expressed his influential prejudice against townspeople.

'Good-for-nothings, ne'er-do-wells, rogues, prostitutes and vagabonds are found in the big centres of population, and if they were wise in their generation, they would not give them the same representation as perhaps the more wealthy, the more intelligent, and honourable people who live in the country.'

Tom Playford came from a long line of industrious farmers and country folk who went to bed early and woke up early. When people complained that nothing happened in Adelaide after ten pm, his riposte was, 'who in their right mind is still awake after ten pm?'

Pubs shut at six pm and even then 'were joyless oases where the sexes were segregated and entertainment forbidden'. Pleasure loving Italians opened up eateries in salubrious Hindley Street, but had to serve wine in teacups not to fall foul of licensing laws. To Sveta's delight they also opened up ice cream parlours. Their homemade cassatas licked South Australia's Amscol ice cream into a cocked cornet. Frivolities such as dancing after dinner were frowned upon, and even considered illegal. It was not without reason that Adelaide was known as the city of churchgoers, a 'conservative backwater', 'and a 'far flung outpost of wow-serism, prim and proper, asleep in the sun'.

The period of intense industrialisation that Playford fostered in the 1950s was at the expense of personal freedom and the pursuit of happiness. Tatiana was a night owl and ready to party. However, Playford was not her only obstacle. Ivan was not Playford's perfect migrant for nothing. As well as liking to get up early and work hard, he hated partying and socialising. When Tatiana begged him for a party, he reluctantly agreed, thinking it might get her off his back. He was horrified when she dug up a Ukrainian band, complete with accordion and violin, in Royal Park, whose motley members were willing to walk up the lane behind the Philips Factory to the house at Number 17.

Tatiana invited Katherina and Kurt, Vlada and Kirov, and some of their other New Australian friends. She bought herself a glamorous new dress, dyed her hair platinum blonde like Marilyn Monroe, and put on shiny red lipstick. Sveta, with great excitement, helped her get everything ready. The front bedroom was cleared out and the band set up by the fireplace. Sveta was allowed to stay up very late, and entertained everybody by swigging down tots of vodka, neat. She got quite tipsy quite quickly. The evening was a blur; flashes of her mother dancing about gaily to the poignantly romantic blend of accordion and violin; Ivan sitting morosely in a corner, hating very minute; and the screaming row next day when Tatiana accused Ivan of wearing his 'I'm going to be hanged tomorrow' face.

Mrs Taplow felt her assimilation of Sveta's family was going too slowly for her liking. She tut-tutted when she heard from the Portmans and Millers about foreign accordion music coming from Number 17 until all hours.

'Disgraceful.'

She didn't know if this was better or worse than the screaming fights that the neighbours also reported.

'Dreadful.'

They had even seen a grim looking Ivan bearing a gash across his head after what sounded like the smashing of plates.

'Appalling.'

Mrs Taplow continued to be irked by Sveta's plaits, and didn't fail to remind her every time she saw her. She tried different tactics, like telling Sveta that it was very unhealthy, that the hair was taking all the nutrients from her body and this is why she was so thin. This worried Sveta terribly and added to her growing list of '*Things to worry about.*'

Sveta felt totally unaccepted by Mrs Taplow, and so badly wanted to be. But she did not know that assimilation was the name of Mrs Taplow's game. She did not know that Mildred was coming from what Mildred thought were very good motivations – to make her Australian as quickly as possible. Instead, she felt very inferior, deeply hurt, and always not good enough.

Mildred particularly despised the fact that Tatiana and Sveta still spoke in their silly language in the street. And she winced when they accompanied this dreadful gabbling with what Mildred judged to be histrionic and unnecessary gesticulations.

But something was about to blow up on the national level that would be of unexpected assistance to Mildred in her task. It would put a stop to Tatiana and Sveta speaking their own language in public. It was the infamous Petrov affair.

Joseph Stalin had died in May 1953. This caused mixed reactions at 17 Pudney Street. Tatiana was relieved the dictator with the 'cockroach eyes', had gone. Ivan, once a proud Communist, was pulled by the love he still had for the heroic leader, and felt sad. But there was as yet no evidence of any thaw from behind the Iron Curtain. Khrushchev, the rising new Soviet star, was very suspicious of the West. Resounding in his ears was Stalin's remark that after his death, 'the capitalists would wring the necks of his successors like chickens'. So, with wary hands to his throat, Khrushchev continued the Cold War and the military build up.

The Petrovs, spies for the Russian secret service, the KGB, had come to Australia in 1951 as members of the Soviet Embassy in Canberra. After Stalin's death, Beria, the head of the KGB, was tried and shot. As a result, the Petrovs were now in danger if they returned to the Soviet Union. In early 1954 Petrov, without telling his wife, defected and asked for asylum. Prime Minister Menzies informed a shocked nation. Mrs Petrov had no idea what was going on. She thought her husband had been kidnapped by ASIO, the Australian security services. She was perplexed when two KGB henchmen arrived in Canberra to escort her back to the USSR. Anti-Communist demonstrators surged onto the airfield where Mrs Petrov was being manhandled on to a plane, objecting to what they saw as a forcible removal. As the plane flew to Darwin, Menzies intervened. On landing in Darwin, Mrs Petrov was snatched back from the KGB, and kidnapped by ASIO. These dramatic events hit Australia forcefully. The front page of the *News* carried the picture of Mrs Petrov, looking frightened and in stockinged feet, being forced on to a plane by grim-faced KGB thugs. Good was fighting evil on a grand scale. Hand in hand with Senator McCarthy in America, Robert Menzies was fighting the good fight. The 'Free World' was grappling 'Communist Evil'. Pudney Street was up in arms.

At morning recess, a teacher came up to Sveta and asked her from which country she came. Sveta was never really sure, as her mother always seemed to have something to hide. 'Russia,' she answered brightly. 'We speak Russian at home' The teacher was very interested and asked her many questions. Sveta liked the attention. That evening Sveta gabbled excitedly at dinner, telling Tatiana what had transpired. Tatiana went pale and gripped the side of the table.

'What's the matter, Mama?' Sveta was frightened.

Tatiana grabbed her daughter by the shoulders,

'You must never tell anyone we are Russian. Never! When we are outside this house we must never speak Russian. Only inside these four walls. Do you understand?' She was almost screaming, and her tight grip hurt Sveta's thin arms.

'But I don't understand. The teacher was so nice, so interested!'

'Just do as I say.'

After dinner Sveta went out on to the front veranda. She was puzzled by her mother's pronouncement but was also very absorbed in a book she was reading. Books had taken over from comics. Mrs Taplow called her a bookworm, in a disapproving tone. She was in the middle of an Enid Blyton adventure Trevor had lent her. Suddenly the book was snatched from behind. It was Trevor.

'Mum said I have to come and get all my books and that I am not allowed to play with you any more.'

Sveta was shocked,

'Why?'

'Because Mum said you're a commie!'

Petrov fever gripped the country and influenced the next general election. Anti-Communist fervour fuelled an Australian version of McCarthyism. The Labour Government, tipped to win the 1954 election, lost to the 'Aussie Superman of the Free World', Robert Menzies. Sveta was confused by all the incessant discussions about the Petrovs and Menzies. She thought Menzies was the name of biscuits. The Menz family, early German settlers in South Australia, had created a successful business selling delicious Menz's biscuits.

Tatiana did not speak Russian in public any more. She was haunted by the picture of the henchmen who had come for Mrs Petrov, which had been splashed all over the newspapers. She saw the look of terror on Evdokia Petrov's face. She knew that look. She had seen it too many times on the faces of her own family, who had been constantly hounded by the NKVD, the equally unpleasant precursors to the KGB. She was convinced that they would now come for her. She had heard how the NKVD had spared no expense in outfitting their death squad when they were hunting for Trotsky in Mexico. Assassins were equipped with bogus police uniforms, submachine guns, dynamite bombs, a power saw, and grappling hooks. Trotsky was eventually felled with an ice axe. Tatiana looked around the quiet, ordered streets of Adelaide fearfully. She was sure that the Rosella parrots, painted on the sides of corner stores, were piercing her with evil looks.

Only two weeks after the Petrov affair even the safe streets of Adelaide were in for a seismic shock. Unbeknownst to Tatiana and most residents, Adelaide lay on what is called the Eden Hills Fault Line. Other shocks in 1837, 1897 and 1902 had created plenty of disturbance.

Katherina and Kurt had bought a house in the open countryside of Marion, to the south of Adelaide. They both remarked how still the air was when they went to bed on the evening of February 28th. Little did they know that their house was built virtually on top of the fault line, which continued down Tapleys Hill Road, skirted Pudney Street and extended to the Port River. At four am they woke to a terrifying rumble and the sound of loud crashing. Reverberations continued down the fault line. By the time it reached 17 Pudney Street the rumble was weaker, but still loud enough to wake all the inhabitants and have Tatiana screaming in terror. Convinced that the sound was the dreaded knock of the KGB, she ran out into the backyard in her nightdress. Apart from lots of squawking in the henhouse, not much damage was sustained. For Katherina and Kurt things were more serious; a chimney had fallen and caused damage to the front living room. They didn't have insurance, and it was with a heavy heart that Katherina took the train to work in the city the next morning. The centre of Adelaide was in chaos. When she arrived at Charles Birks, an hour earlier than the rest of the staff so that she could clean the office, there was a huge mess. Katherina choked in the fine dust as she picked her way through the rubble. Windows had been shattered and large fragments of glass reminded her of the war she had recently endured. In nearby Pirie Street, the three-storied Commercial Union Building survived the force of its third earthquake in 57 years, but the statue of Britannia on top did not.

The imposing symbol of a crumbling empire had finally collapsed. Britannia, regal-helmeted effigy of mighty British imperialism, had been severely shaken many times before, but this was her death knell. Britannia crashed down from her lofty place of vantage over Adelaide, never to be replaced.

Wirra Woman: Well you know what I say – my ancestral spirits demolished her.

Author: Oh, your Wirra sorcerers?

Wirra Woman: But of course. I don't agree with Wauwe Woman about sorcery. I am proud of it. It is our magic. Our ancestors were determined to bring down Britannia, the symbol of power that Midlato first espied on the back of her penny. They sent an earthquake in 1897 where an arm came off. Then bingo! In 1902, off came her head. Mind you, that was replaced. But in 1954 she finally gave up the ghost.

Author: But this might have been nothing to do with the Wirra. Just a coincidence. And anyway, the British Empire was nearly over. British Empire Day was renamed British Commonwealth Day in 1958. It was the end of an era.

Wirra Woman: Oh, you and you rationalising. How do you explain a boomerang shaped earth crack during an earthquake in the north of South Australia? Or the Aborigine's head in the nuclear cloud?

Author: Coincidences?

Wirra Woman: No, they are signs. We are still around. You can't push us down. Look at the timing of the 1954 earthquake. The new Queen was already in Australia and on her way to Adelaide. Don't you think that is significant?

Author: Oh, just another coincidence

Wirra Woman: You and your coincidences – how long is it going to take you to realise there are no such things!

The earthquake was sizeable, 5.4 on the Richter scale. Adelaide was the earthquake capital of Australia. Fortunately, no one – other than Britannia – was killed, although several people had narrow escapes. Monkeys chattering in fright at the Adelaide Zoo caused other animals to stampede. Mrs Taplow was in a frenzy. Not only Britannia, but also her Methodist church in Lockleys had been damaged. And the spire on the main Methodist Church in Adelaide had toppled down. All the Methodists, the largest religious group in South Australia after the Anglicans, were called upon to help. But Mildred decided that raising money for that would have to wait.

Something much more important was looming up. Mildred was preparing for the arrival of the new young Queen of England. Princess Elizabeth had been sailing to Australia in 1952 and Mildred had been beside herself then, but the King died and the young princess was obliged to return. Mildred contented herself by collecting memorabilia of the Coronation. But now the Queen herself was coming to Adelaide. Mildred was feverish with excitement. It was the first time that a reigning head of state had come to Australia, let alone to the backwater of Adelaide. Mildred was hyperventilating in rapture, and bought herself (on lay-by) a brand new feathered beige hat with gloves to match.

The Queen visited the eastern states first, where a giant welcoming boomerang arched over the calvacade as she passed through. This was little to do with recognising Australia's Aboriginal past, but a cute ethnic way of letting the head of Australia know that her subjects hoped for a speedy return.

In Adelaide, Charles Duguid sent a letter to Playford, pleading for a select group of well-behaved Aborigines from the Ernabella mission to travel down and see Her Majesty. Adelaide buildings were festooned with decorations. Sveta went with her mother to town to see a film at the Metro theatre in Hindley Street. Slurping up a delicious cassata afterwards, Sveta was enchanted by a giant lighted crown, lit up and sparkling from the top of the skyline.

Such a young beautiful queen, and Sveta couldn't wait to see her. Her school was preparing to descend on the Wayville Showground to see the Queen and Prince Philip drive past in their motorcade. Girls had been chosen to wear yellow and green dresses and perform a wattle dance. She saw them practising and wondered why she hadn't been asked. She also envied Rosemary Redman, who had been picked from thousands of hopeful Adelaide girls sporting shiny patent shoes and short hairdos, to give the Queen a bouquet. If only she, Sveta, had such a lovely name, such a lovely hairstyle, and such an honoured task. Mayawara Minutjukur was part of a group of excited Aborigines from the Ernabella Mission who travelled 1,600 hot dusty miles to sing for the Queen.

When her school arrived at the Wayville Showground it was heaving with humanity, and Sveta couldn't see a thing.

She was right at the back of an eight-deep crowd. This wouldn't do. All she could see was a bunch of backs. She told Miss Bradshaw she felt faint. This did the trick, and she was put right in front to sit on the grass. She had a beautiful view of the Queen. So close she could see her lipstick and powder, and the stunning green-feathered hat that set off her striking prettiness. It was so good to see this queen, whose salvation she had sung for with such gusto.

Gradually Queen Elizabeth and Petrov fever calmed down. The Queen, well boomeranged, well saluted, and well didgeridoo-ed, returned to the mother country. Menzies, nothing to do with biscuits, was re-elected Prime Minister. It looked like order was returning to the land. Trevor was allowed to play with Sveta again, and Mildred Taplow made and sold toffee apples to raise money for the Methodist Church fund. Tatiana got a job looking after a pleasant wealthy widow, Mrs Fricker, on the Port Road, as well as making a little money from selling eggs and almonds. Ivan felt happier that more money was coming in. South Australia was prospering. World wool prices soared. More migrants flooded on to the beaches, marvelling at the spectacular sunsets that exploded in the western sky. The Petrovs eventually slipped into quiet anonymity and became the Melbourne suburbanites Sven and Maria Allyson.

Mr Portman was watering his lemon trees, now a couple of feet high. He hoped they would be able to give Milly lemons soon. He also looked forward to a bit of shade, so he could sit and have a nice cold beer out of the ice-box. He was distracted from his thoughts by the sound of shovelling from next door. He peered over and saw Ivan digging a large hole in the middle of his backyard.

'What the hell is that sonofabitch up to now?'

He had only just got used to the cacophony of squawking, clucking and scratching from the full-blown chicken farm on his back doorstep. Now he wondered what new horror would be visited upon the backwaters of Hendon. A large truck pulled up to the side fence and Mr Portman soon saw what was to go in the hole.

'Well I'll be damned! A Hills Hoist clothesline,' he marvelled. Milly, holding her baby, came out to peek over the fence.

'How the bloody hell could he afford that? It costs at least two weeks' wages.'

'It's all the eggs,' said Milly, 'they must be bringin' in a lotta dough.'

They both stood in silent reverence as the Hills Hoist was placed in the hole. Lance Hill had returned to Adelaide after the war and grew fruit trees in his backyard, to supplement his meagre income. The only problem was there was nowhere for his wife to hang out the washing. So he devised a rotary clothesline, which, as well as taking up a lot less space, had the added advantage of a handle that could raise and lower the line. These Hoists became all the rage for the select few housewives who could afford them. Milly, wife of a mop maker, did not qualify. She would have loved one of these Hills Hoists right by the back door, where she could hang her nappies and then winch them up to dry in the wind. Instead she had to traipse over piles of debris with a heavy wash basket and hang out sheets, dungarees, kids' clothes, and nappies on long untidy strings, which more often than not would sag into the cement mixer or over the piles of dusty bricks. But she knew it was out of the question. Bill didn't earn a huge wage fashioning mops at the South Australian Brush Company. And besides, any extra money was needed to make bricks, so that one day the concrete shoe-box she lived in would be expanded, and the front eyesore of the house transformed.

Milly secretly admired Ivan – the way he worked so hard for his family. Bill, on the other hand, resented Ivan bitterly. He liked to go down to the Philips oval on a Saturday with some beers, and watch his SABCO work team play footy against Philips. He did not want to work overtime, and besides, he had to continue making bricks so that eventually he could finish building the house. He ignored his wife's strained breathing as she bumped the heavy wash-basket down the cracked concrete steps and heaved it over piles of bricks. He was grateful that Milly never complained and never mentioned that she was ashamed that the front of the house looked like a bomb crater.

Milly knew to stay quiet. Bill had a foul temper, as had her own father, and she was loath to do anything to rouse it. All the unspoken complaints and broken dreams steadily etched themselves into her face, and were baked into permanent lines by the harsh Australian sun. She also secretly liked Tatiana, who often came around during the day, and would give her a dozen freshly laid eggs. Tatiana had confided to her that she was expecting a baby and that it would be born in June. Milly didn't tell Bill of these visits, nor that the eggs were given freely. Instead, she secreted away the 1/6d they would have cost,in her underwear drawer.

Mrs Taplow was furious about the Pleznowski's Hills Hoist, and didn't fail to let Mr Taplow know that New Australians were destroying the country. She was horrified that Italians and Greeks were now everywhere. One had even dared come to her front door with a box of tomatoes to sell. Awful looking man with curly black hair sprouting from his open shirt. She slammed the door in disgust. How would such creatures ever be assimilated? To make things worse, all the nice British migrants were being siphoned off to Elizabeth, a new town north of Adelaide. She envisaged the Italian with black curly chest hair moving into one of the empty blocks in Pudney Street, and shuddered.

Albert Taplow couldn't be bothered to argue that rather than ruining the country, the opposite was the case. New Australians were helping to dramatically transform South Australia from an agricultural society to an industrial society. Playford, whom he admired enormously, was nationalising the electricity and water industries. This in itself needed huge swathes of manpower. Immigration agreements with Italy and Greece meant a continual supply of labour from these countries. But he knew what was really bothering Mildred. She desperately wanted a Hills Hoist herself. He would have dearly loved to buy her one. He had hoped to get enough money from the orchard on their large corner block. But fruit fly had destroyed his last year's crop. He was beset with worry. He had to spend large parts of each day in the cold room in Coles basement sorting out the pressed meats. The cold was eating into him, and the migraines he had always suffered from were getting worse. Mildred's continued nagging didn't help, especially on a Saturday when he couldn't escape. He was pleased when Mildred would go off on Sundays to visit her family, the Fowlers. It gave him much-appreciated peace and quiet. At least Mildred had stopped reproaching him for not joining her in worshipping at Lockleys Methodist Church. Albert came from a long line of Quakers and preferred communing with God in silence.

Tatiana gave birth to Sonia at the Queen Victoria hospital. She looked at the baby but felt little joy. Sveta looked at the baby and felt great love. A sister at last, with whom to share this crazy household and perhaps to stop her mother being so obsessed with her. Sveta was packed off to the Taplows. She began to accompany them every Sunday to the Fowlers. Mrs Taplow had a brother, two sisters, and her father. They once had a farm outside Gawler but had been forced to come into the city after a succession of dreadful droughts and the severe depression of the 1930s. Mildred's mother had died of stomach cancer soon after. Mildred's father, Sid, was looked after by his unmarried daughter and son.

Sveta thought they were the weirdest people she had ever seen. Meg Fowler was a large-boned spinster with goggle glasses perched on a broad flat nose, who was, according to Mildred, devout and holy. Uncle Ron was a bit simple and never spoke. He always wore a thick white singlet that hung baggily over his brown trousers. The Fowlers probably had more skeletons in their cupboard than most families. Mildred shuddered when she heard them rattling. Her great grandmother, Mildred Fowler, was about to marry when her intended was speared by an Aborigine. He was working as a shepherd with Mildred's two brothers on a sheep run near Gawler. Shamefully, she was pregnant at the time and gave birth to an illegitimate daughter, Fanny Fowler, Mildred's grandmother. Both she and Mildred's mother married first cousins, so had retained the family name. Some people had even suggested that Meg and Ron were odd because of what they called 'yokel inbreeding'. Mildred always hotly defended these unions by giving the example of the great Queen Victoria, who had married her first cousin.

'And look how normal her family has been,' she concluded with a flourish.

Sveta accompanied Trevor to the Methodist Sunday school and continued to be criticised mercilessly by Mrs Taplow for her hair and clothes. Since the arrival of the new baby, Tatiana had been more morose than usual, and Sveta felt she couldn't ask for a pretty dress. The Methodist young ladies in their best flouncy dresses smirked at her green striped pinafore and green ribbons that laced so strangely through her plaits. Sveta continued effortlessly to feel inferior. But the worst thing about these Sunday visits was old Sid Fowler, who was well into his eighties. On seeing her he would leer and wheedle,

'Hello sweety, come and sit on grandpa's lap.'

But she knew what would happen when she did. Inevitably, his gnarled fingers wormed their way under the green striped skirt and found their way through the elastic into her pants. She would try and squirm away, playing along with his pretend tickling game. If she shrieked too loudly Mildred would snap,

'Shoosh! This is the Lord's day, and you'll upset Aunty Meg.'

If she declined to sit on the old boy's lap, Mildred would cajole,

'Go and keep Grandpa happy Swetta, there's a good girl.'

Easter was worst. Aunty Meg would walk about slowly, mourning her dying saviour. A stifling heaviness enveloped the house. Sveta couldn't wait to go home and gorge herself on the chocolate eggs Tatiana bought in abundance. Fortunately, Grandpa soon died, and all Sveta had to do then was steer clear of Uncle Ron. He had an unnerving habit of skulking in dark corners, staring at her and fiddling with the bottom of his white singlet. This made her feel very uncomfortable, especially since he had a severe walleye and she didn't know which eye to look at.

Dreadful bushfires raged through the Adelaide Hills in early 1955. The Governor and his wife, staying in their Hills residence, made a narrow escape. Sveta's class at school swelled in size. Adelaide was going through a population explosion. Not only were there more immigrants, but post-war baby boomers were flooding the schools. In Sveta's class, the number reached fifty. In other schools, it was often seventy. There were not enough desks, chairs, or rooms, let alone teachers. Tom Playford, while spending plenty on expanding South Australia's industrial base, was notoriously stingy when it came to education. Ugly asbestos prefabs mushroomed onto school playing areas, and extra teachers had to be found from somewhere. Belinda Bradshaw was promoted to deputy headmistress. Despite her extra duties she continued to work tirelessly for Dr Duguid and the Aboriginal cause. The original inhabitants were invisible. They did not enter hotels, swimming pools, clubs, or hairdressing salons, nor did they buy houses or apply for bank loans. The occupants of Duguid's house at Magill quietly observed the 'Day of Mourning' or Aboriginal Sunday, on the first Sunday after Australia Day, which they had been doing every year to mark the invasion of white man in 1788.

During 1955 Sveta had no less than ten different teachers. Some were dredged up from the collapsing Empire – like the sadist from India who loved breaking rulers over the back of Sveta's hands; or from inbreeding pockets of the dry north, like the weaselly pervert who, with hairs sprouting from the top of his nose, always had a gaggle of little girls sitting on his lap. Sveta had had enough of the darker side of Australian men, and knew to keep well away. There were lovely teachers too. Mothers like Mrs Heath, who with any snippet of education to their name were roped in; the delicate music teacher Miss Bell who drove an iron-grey Mayflower car, which she proudly told the class had come all the way from England by boat. Sveta had a deep crush on Miss Bell and longed to sit on her lap. Her own mother was not coping well with the new baby, and only that morning she was forced to run past all the factory workers in her dressing gown to fetch Mrs Taplow, while Tatiana screamed louder than the baby. Sveta became obsessed with Miss Bell and fantasised she was her daughter. But then Miss Bell, like many teachers, said she was leaving. Sveta was heartbroken, and risked a beating for being home late, by waiting by the school gate to get a last glimpse at the shiny iron-grey Mayflower.

Ivan was fed up with fusing pieces of metal together on the never-ending assembly line, which was spewing out thousands of Holdens for a car-hungry Australian market. He wanted out, and with the help of a loan from Mrs Fricker the wealthy widow Tatiana worked for, paid a deposit for a delicatessen that was being built in Woodville Gardens. This was in a new Housing Trust suburb on the edge of a giant sewage farm. The South Australian Housing Trust was building thousands of semi-detached houses out of asbestos cement, to cope with the acute housing shortage.

At last, with a sigh of relief, Ivan left the Holden factory assembly line, and cycled off instead to his new deli. Tatiana saw even less of him. Setting up the shop and learning the business with his limited English took up all of Ivan's time. He sold a huge range of goods, from cold meats, vegetables, cakes, and pies, to milkshakes, lollies, cigarettes and drinks.

People from the Trust houses, mostly poor working-class Australians, flocked to the shop, the only one around that stayed open until ten at night and on weekends. The Rosella Parrot shops always closed at 5.30pm on the dot each day, with half day closing on Wednesdays and an hour off between 1pm and 2pm. Ivan's business was a resounding success. Within three months Mrs Fricker got her loan back, with interest. Bill Portman sighed in resignation when he saw Ivan's FJ Holden car parked around the back of the now empty chicken yard. All the children in the street came around to admire it. These were the days when they could still count the number of cars that went up and down Pudney Street. Tatiana was temporarily happier, and even started helping Ivan in the shop, leaving Sveta and Sonia with the Taplows.

Mrs Taplow mumbled darkly to Mr Taplow. Her mouth set into a bitter down-turned bow, and a dull pain gnawed deep within her abdomen.

CHAPTER 8

Cockatoo Man

Midlato was saddened by the demise of Walter Bromley. For all his faults at least he had lived among them, not like the new Ngaityerli, William Wyatt who, like most white men, hardly took any notice of her people, even though he was supposed to be caring about them. Midlato and Kartanya were ushered reluctantly into one of the newly built brick huts at Piltawardli. It felt unnatural to live in such a stiff, ungiving structure. So different to a *wardli* constructed with leaves and branches, from which she could thrill at the moon scudding across the sky or be reassured by the fire, crackling at the opening. In the heat of the day the *wardli* was cool, and any breeze that fluttered by caressed her naked skin. This white-man prison stifled the air and trapped the insects and fleas. In a *wardli* she could just shake out the branches, and even relocate if necessary. What advantage did the white-skin abode offer? Only in the cold season the stiff sides gave shelter from freezing winds. But she would have infinitely preferred to be in the hills, protected by the great ancestor Ngano, as she snuggled under her cosy kangaroo pelt.

It was now the second winter, as the whites called it, that she had spent on the plains. It felt so alien, and it was so long since she had spotted a wallaby or kangaroo drinking at the river. The pelts to keep warm were becoming scarcer.

Midlato still kept her bone needle with which she used to sew the skins together in a special little bag she had woven. Every now and then she took the needle out and caressed it fondly.

At least there was food supplied during the cold season. Cronk, who was always asking for cockatoos, had moved into the compound as interpreter. He doled out biscuits twice a day, and sometimes sugar. It was nearing *wiltutti* again; time to gather emu eggs and wattle gum. Sadly, it wasn't the same as when her people would pack up and move down to the plains from the foothills. And it was harder to find emu and parrot eggs, with white-skins and their animals tramping everywhere. She was afraid of the 'bullocky', which were always escaping and lumbering where they shouldn't. The continual firing of cannons and quarry blasts which still frightened her people also scared away wild fowl and animals from the reed beds and the Karrawirraparri.

Midlato was in awe of the buildings that were made out of the limestone blasted from her land. The Holy Trinity Church, where she had watched Hindmarsh lay the foundation stone, now had a steeple and a clock, reminding the white inhabitants of home. Midlato, Kartanya and Milte-widlo would stare at the clock for hours, watching the arrows move and clapping in delight at a bell, which chimed when one arrow pointed to the top.

But word was out. A new big white governor was coming to the Tandanya plain.

Vitriol against Hindmarsh, that 'Colonial autocrat, John the First', as his garrulous opponents dubbed him, had boiled over to such proportions that violence had again broken out in the new 'Utopia of the South'. Mann, as well as losing his position as Advocate General, was suspended from court duties for 'conducting himself in a violent and indecorous manner'. Fisher was reprimanded by the green spectacled Judge Jickling, and bound over to keep the peace for quarrelling in public. All this news was brought first-hand by Robert Gouger to the colonial office in England. Hindmarsh was promptly recalled, and left Adelaide in July 1838. Hindmarsh's son-in-law, George Milner Stephen, stepped in as Acting Governor. It was felt that the squabbles between Hindmarsh and Fisher had retarded the development of the colony, so the dual offices of governor and resident commissioner would be merged to the sole authority of Hindmarsh's successor, George Gawler, who was to arrive in October 1838.

Midlato and Kartanya, oblivious to the petty shenanigans of their white masters, were mesmerised by the antics of the Acting Governor's pet monkey which was chained to railings outside his offices, on what the whites called North Terrace. They had also heard that the new Governor would be bringing with him new teachers for the schoolhouse being built at Piltawardli. They were pleased, as they wanted to go on learning English and teaching their language.

Midlato jumped at the sounds of the explosions; she counted twenty-one of them. She didn't think she could ever get used to this white man's thunder. They heralded the arrival of Gawler, and ignited much hustle and bustle among the whites. All the Adelaide Aborigines had been invited to a feast at Government House, which was actually a large hut made out of wattle and daub. Strange ladies had brought Midlato some clothes, insisting she must wear them to the feast. These garments felt stiff and prickly against her skin, as she assembled with a few hundred of her clans-people on the lawns. She vainly looked around for

Looty, whom she hadn't seen in a long time. Her feet had been squeezed into a pair of abominable contraptions; feet which ran happily through scrub, mud, and sand were now jammed into hard prisons. How could she feel the earth with the soles of her feet? These feet, these sensors that fed her information about the terrain she traversed. How could ghost-skins read the land when swathed in so much cover?

She stood miserably as ladies draped in masses of billowing flowery stuff looked down at her: as with most white people, eyes and mouths not matching. The mouths showed yellow-teethed smiles, but the eyes looked suspicious, hostile even. The flat tones of the language that slipped from their mouths were alien and dry. A lady bore down upon her. This one had a particularly prominent nose, like a bandicoot. She seemed to have made her deathly pallor worse by putting something like powdered chalk on it.

'White bandicoots' – she nearly giggled as she remembered Milte-widlo's description of ghost-skins.

'Hello, aren't you sweet?'

She squirmed uncomfortably.

'What's your name?'

A pocket of musty breath swept Midlato's nostrils. She was fascinated by the ringlets that sprang from the wattle yellow bonnet, wriggling each time the woman spoke.

'Good for keeping flies off,' Midlato whispered to Kartanya who was nearby, feeling equally ill at ease in her stiff clothes. Midlato felt herself encased not only in a physical prison of uncomfortable clothes, but in an indefinable mental prison which she didn't understand, and in which she had little room to breathe. The woman's eyes bore down on her as if she wanted to capture her, stuff her, and send her off to England as a curiosity, just like the thousands of cockatoos that were taking pride of place in Victorian glass cabinets. She was saved by a pair of laughing friendly eyes.

'Hello Midlato, how lovely to see you.' It was Looty, her parasol shading her pale face from the blistering sun. Midlato flashed her a beautiful smile, her squashed feet temporarily forgotten.

Murlawirrapurka was feeling confident. It was a festive occasion. He, King John of the Natives, had been specially summoned to be presented to the new big white Governor. And with him, all the Kaurna invited to partake in a massive feast held in their honour. This was more like it. This is what he had been waiting for, some recognition that this was their *yarta* that white man was commandeering. The Governor was going to address them, and Ngaityerli Wyatt would be translating. He had already spotted Governor Gawler riding on his handsome *pindi nanto*, and was impressed – especially by the feathers in his ceremonial hat. 'Cockatoo Man' they had dubbed him. His feathered headdress seemed more of an indication of common ancestry than the strange headwear worn by other whites.

Murlawirrapurka, Kadlitpina, Ityamai-itpina and a dozen other men were given blue soldier caps and brightly coloured sailor shirts and sashes. Oh, how festive they felt as they strutted towards the lawns east of the Government hut on a picturesque bend of the river. It seemed all of Adelaide's white population were assembled, resplendent in bonnets, parasols, and tall shiny black hats. From Governor Gawler's head burst forth a wonderful array of plumes.

The white multitude gave three hearty cheers as Murlawirrapurka and his band of followers strode in. The Kaurna men created quite a spectacle in their colourful garb, and wielding an impressive array of waddies and spears. They reciprocated joyously to the hurrahs with three more loud cheers.

Cockatoo Man nodded acknowledgement to Murlawirrapurka, glanced at his pocket watch and beckoned for the throng to hush. Murlawirrapurka was intrigued by the flash of gold, and wondered at these timepieces that *pindi-meyu* wore. Why did they need them? He could tell the time of day by the position of the sun in the sky, by the hue of the gums on the distant hills, by the feel of moisture in the air on his skin. His body was a tuning fork which vibrated with the energy of his land. He rested in it. He didn't have to decipher it through a mechanical contraption! Fingering the initiation scars on his chest, covered reluctantly beneath his hot shirt, he wondered what trials Cockatoo Man had had to endure. What did this white man see as he surveyed the world from under his feathers?

Gawler cleared his throat and started to speak, looking straight at Murlawirrapurka, 'Black men...' Murlawirrapurka, although having learnt quite a few English words, didn't fully understand what the Governor continued to say. Benevolent smiling and murmurs of assent issued from the white throng whenever he paused. But was he saying something about black men learning to imitate and love white men? Murlawirrapurka certainly was not happy about that. It was Wyatt's turn to translate:

'Black men – Great Englishman Governor now speaks to you. Englishmen very much love black men.'

So they should, thought Murlawirrapurka.

'Constantly, we will give plenty clothing, shirts, flesh, food.'

Absolutely! Just what he would expect – not that he wanted to make a habit of wearing this hot sticky shirt!

'Black men, white men are brothers, with one Father.'

Okay... but not too sure about the one father – is that Gawler? What about Tjilbruke, the Kaurna's esteemed ancestor?

'If English men quarrel with you, fight you, strike you, then quickly come to my house.'

Murlawirrapurka approved of this promise of protection, especially since settlers had shot and wounded his people near this very spot.

'Plenty by and by, you black men will speak English.'

That was okay. He, Kadlitpina, and Ityamai-itpina had many words already.

'If other black men come here; do not kill, do not fight them.'

Oy! Murlawirrapurka definitely did not like that – this was his *yarta* – if black men like the Moorundie and other enemy tribes came in, it was his duty to fight them, kill if necessary, and see them off! This was indisputable in Kaurna law!

Wyatt continued his translation,

'Black men must not steal great bullocks, sheep, or spear pigs. Not shoot or fight white men.'

Fair enough, this is what Murlawirrapurka was striving to teach his black brothers.

'You must watch white men make clothes, build houses, dig. By and by you build plenty houses and dig earth.'

Hey? Murlawirrapurka was not sure about this at all. It had been bad enough digging at the Piltawardli. He and Kadlitpina exchanged perplexed glances. Was Cockatoo Man really saying that they must become like good white men? How insulting. They stood in a state of shock and stared dumbly at Cockatoo Man, who smiled benevolently back.

The *Register* reported, 'Whether they understood what was said, we know not, but the vacant stare and senseless faces of many, evidently bespoke utter ignorance of the meaning.'

But any unsettled feeling was temporarily swept away when the Aborigines were invited to partake of a huge feast laid out on tables under the gums. They were all hungry, and enthusiastically tucked into roast beef, biscuits, rice, hot tea and delicious cool sweet drinks. Midlato really enjoyed the roast beef. So, this was the 'bif' that Milte-widlo had bragged about after visiting the *Buffalo?*

Mmmm, a bit like kangaroo, but with a different deeper tangy taste. And as for the coloured drink, it was delicious; a lot sweeter than the beverage her people made by swishing wattle flowers through water. She saw Looty again and waved.

After the feast, the Kaurna adults were given blankets. Murlawirrapurka's uneasy feeling was assuaged by the softness and warmth of these amazing pelts. He marvelled at them. Perhaps the white man would now take care of his people properly. He was distracted from his thoughts by Cronk, who informed him that the Governor insisted that he and his men display their spear throwing abilities. A couple of white men were putting up a large piece of board, painted with big circles, in the middle of the lawn. The spectators were moving back to make room, excited by the thrill of watching the big native chiefs throw their spears at the target.

'I refuse to be a performing cockatoo,' grumbled Ityamai-itpina darkly. Murlawirrapurka, who didn't usually go along with the impetuous Ityamai-itpina, agreed. How insulting to be asked to throw a spear at a piece of flimsy board! Murlawirrapurka was a warrior. A warrior who could run swiftly across the plain, and throw his spear with such lethal accuracy that it would fly great distances through the air and always hit its target. For thousands of years his ancestors had honed the fine art of spear throwing, and now this Cockatoo *pindi-meyu* wanted him to put on a silly performance. Had the feathered one not just insulted them in his speech, by proclaiming that black men must become like white men?

Murlawirrapurka, a master of theatrical performance, muttered to the others, 'Let's act dumb.'

He then made an elaborate show of bringing the target closer, miming that it was much too far away. Then one by one he, Kadlitpina, Ityamai-itpina and the other warriors, threw their spears with mock awkwardness and missed badly.

'Ooh,' squealed the ladies as Ityamai-itpina's spear landed a tad too close to the bottoms of their voluminous skirts.

'Jolly poor show, what?' murmured one top-hatted worthy to another.

Derisive laughter spread throughout the crowd. Murlawirrapurka could see the rotting yellow teeth of a spectator, as he guffawed like a European donkey.

These white men want me to be like them. Never!

The garish blue, red and violet sailor's shirt stuck to Murlawirrapurka's sweating back like a heavy oppressive mantle. His *wilyaru* scars, the honoured special markings of Tarnda, the totemic kangaroo, lay hidden by the trappings of an alien civilisation. He snapped.

He strode out into the middle of the gathered assembly. Ripped off his jacket, trousers and cap and threw them dramatically to the ground. Something he had enacted many a time in the *Ngunyawaietti*. His naked body glistened in the sun. Stunned shocked silence. He picked up two of his spears, strode back several paces and aimed for the target. With alarming accuracy, he drove the first spear through the bullseye and paused as he raised the second, looking magnificent as the Tandanya warrior he was. Everyone was mesmerised. Including Cockatoo Man. Gawler knew instinctively that with one flick of the black man's wrist, he could be dead. An electric stillness captured the air. Sweat was sucked out of many a bonnetted face, despite lavish ministrations of the powder puff. Perspiration puddled between Midlato's toes. Swish. The second spear lodged next to the first. Then, with great courage and dignity, Murlawirrapurka turned slowly towards the crowd, preparing to address them in English. He pointed at the spears still quivering in the centre of the target, and declared loudly, 'Varey goodey!'

He then pointed at the clothes lying in a tousled heap on the grass, and shaking his fist at them pronounced, 'No goodey!'

This was all described in the *Register*, emphasising how uncivilised he was. If he'd had more of the language, this is what he was trying to get across with his actions.

'I am a black man. I know how to throw a spear. That is how I live on this, my land. This is my true path. I do not want to be like a white man. And if wearing these ridiculous clothes makes me a good white man then I do not want them.'

The trouble was that his actions and simple words fell on deaf ears. The people he addressed did not want to hear his truth, or recognise the dignity he displayed. They preferred to tut tut at his shocking nakedness and make fun of how he pronounced English. This affirmed what they felt was their God given superiority over these 'savages'.

That night, Murlawirrapurka stomped out his rage in a *kuri*. The *kuri* was a dance of Kadlitpina's people, the Kaurna Wirra. Painted in white spots and stripes three dancers at a time, their knees swathed with green leaves, stomped their aggression into the earth, raising huge clouds of dust. They rustled, stamped and hollered until exhausted. Before them, swaying women shook bunches of leaves. With a deep intonation that emanated from the depths of their being, they harmonised with the rhythmic rustling that came from their men's knees.

Afterwards, the spent Murlawirrapurka sank his head into his hands in the warm glow of the campfire and mumbled despairingly to Midlato's *kammammi*,

'When will this nightmare end?'

'I'm afraid this nightmare is only just beginning,' she murmured, ever so softly.

The feast whetted the Kaurna appetite. Many took to basking 'mostly nude' under the windows of Government Hut and when asked to move, cried, 'wantum tucker'. Very quickly the Governor had a paling fence erected to keep them out. Within a week of the feast, several cattle and sheep were speared. It was almost like Gawler's injunction, not to hunt European animals, had the opposite effect. This 'pindi bullocky and theep tasted vary goodey.' And if these animals were eating all the black man's carefully prepared grass and driving away their game, then the black man had as much right to it as the white man. Moreover, if white men were not going to share their food with black men, and this levee was just a one off, then the black men were going to take it. Biscuits and rice were not enough. 'We are men, not parrots,' they grumbled. Three Aborigines were caught for spearing cattle and sheep, but escaped before being tried.

Two men who watched the whole scene at the Government feast with great interest were the new Piltawardli teachers, the Lutheran missionaries, Clamour Schurmann, and Christian Teichelmann. Schurmann was fascinated by the energetic *kuri* he witnessed that evening. He was struck by the passion with which Murlawirrapurka danced, and recorded it in his diary. Neither the missionaries nor Murlawirrapurka knew that their destinies were to be inextricably entwined with the future of the Kaurna race. These pious young men from Dresden had sailed out on the same ship as Governor Gawler, to undertake the task of teaching the Adelaide natives about Christianity. They had been helped in this endeavour by the patronage of George Angas of the South Australian Company who, with his Quaker sentiments, still wanted to do right by the Aborigines. On board the ship, discussions had already begun about how the natives were to be handled. Gawler preferred that the natives should be taught English as quickly as possible and assimilated into civilised habits, such as farming. Teichelmann and Schurmann, like Bromley before them, argued that it was important for them to learn the Kaurna language first and then, through it, convert the natives to Christianity. In this way, the hearts of the natives would be changed first, and then everything else would easily follow. Gawler, equally pious, was persuaded.

Schurmann was so enthusiastic about his new task that he was learning Kaurna words on the first day of his arrival. He was already accomplished in other languages, including Hebrew and Greek. Midlato conferred with her *kammammi*, who urged her to teach the two missionaries as she had

Bromley. Her *kammammi* also encouraged her and Kartanya to learn writing skills so they could record the Kaurna language. She said it would be very important one day.

Midlato found the Germans odd. She had just got used to English people and could understand their accents. The Germans' English words sounded very strange. But they were kind and, like Bromley, lived among them, moving into newly built huts at Piltawardli.

All the while, more ships spilled new immigrants on to either the sandbar at Holdfast Bay or the treacherous marshes of Port Misery, now renamed Port Adelaide. An uncertain future awaited them as the economy was on the point of collapse. Gawler's reaction to the absolute chaos he found was to deal swiftly with the plethora of incompetence, increase public spending, and splurge on a lavish building program. Action inspired capital investment. Work was started on a grand new government residence, and a steep £5000 was spent. This ushered in a cycle of overspending, but did give work to the thousands of labourers who, taking advantage of a free passage and promise of work, flooded in. Thomas Daniel, a basket weaver, and his wife Kitty arrived in Adelaide in July 1839 with their three children, accompanied by the Denham family with their eight children. The promise of a new life was not to be theirs. Within a year they would all be dead and, in a way, that would turn Murlawirrapurka's careful work on its head.

Establishments of trade and industry popped up all over the fledgling capital. Flett and Linklater opened their chain of drapery stores; Snooke and Co started manufacturing brooms; Mrs Watts made bonnets; Joseph Ind, the watermelon squatter, sold cart-loads of his watermelons, to the approval of the town's teetotallers, who thought them far better for quenching thirst than rum. Much to the disapproval of the same teetotallers, Emanuel Solomon built a 'sinful' theatre in Rundle Street in the middle of the new town. Midlato and Kartanya earned pennies by helping Mr Ind load his barrow, while Miltewidlo worked for Snooke and Co, gathering dried stalks for brooms. They all helped Job Malin build a flour mill on West Terrace, by fetching stringy bark and wood from red gums and peppermint trees. Midlato and Milte-widlo were mesmerised by the resultant windmills, which circled majestically above the former Tambawardli plain.

The extravagance of Governor Gawler's spending did not extend to his social life. He strongly disapproved of dancing and forbade it at Government soirees.

Even though 'John the First' had been dispatched, the colony was still bedevilled by intrigue and seethed with libel suits, which had escalated under the interim governorship of George Milner Stephen and his monkey. Gawler couldn't believe the gross ineptitude and irregularities he discovered in the supposedly model colony. Both Gilles the treasurer and Gilbert the storekeeper falsified reports, and failed dismally at keeping accounts. They were fired. Brown and Mann were sacked for 'gross insubordinacy'. George Stevenson lost the monopoly of the *Register* after a libel suit. The rival *Southern Australian* bellyached interminably that Gawler's appointment as joint governor and resident commissioner was contrary to the intentions of the colony's founders.

In the case of the luckless Light, Murlawirrapurka would say that whites could not distinguish between good white men and bad white men. He continued to be treated badly. Eking out a living from private surveys and selling sketches, he became overwhelmed by poor health as his tuberculosis progressed. Things were made worse when his house and belongings were burnt to the ground in early 1839. Light's friends showed him what kindness they could, but his remaining days were those of an invalid. He had some comfort in the fact that public and official opinion had at last moved in favour of his choice for the site of the city.

As the ships disgorged more immigrants, the Adelaide natives were squeezed out further. They were in a no-win situation. If they carried out their seasonal practises of burning to optimise the gathering of food, they were accused of threatening the property and livestock of settlers; if they demanded food they were accused of begging; if they just took the food, they were accused of stealing. Many waited at the ports and begged for 'baccy and bicketty'. New arrivals, charmed by their exoticness, gave it to them. Milte-widlo was impressed by how rich the sailors were and dreamed of becoming one. His command of English was such that he was now selling brooms for Snooke and Co to the many immigrants camping along the river. He and Itya also brought the campers branches and wood for fuel; or offered to cut wood in exchange for a piece of 'bullocky' or 'black money'. Itya found a new use for his weapons. He would spear settlers' potatoes and roast them over the fire.

Midlato went with Milte-widlo to earn a few extra coins. She was fed up with rice and biscuits. Occasionally, she was given garden produce by Bridget Hack. Peas were a firm favourite. But she really missed meat, so she was tempted to buy herself and her *kammammi* a little meat to eat. She helped Milte-widlo fetch water for a group of immigrants, and Milte-widlo supplied some gum tree branches and twigs to start fires. The settlers were delighted by the brilliant conflagration as the oil packed leaves flared up. Milte-widlo thought he would try his luck and dared to ask for white money. Midlato was scared – she had only ever received 'black boys'.

'White money – you want a sixpence? I tell you what!' said the settler, getting ready for a bit of fun. 'You say 'split sixpence' and I will give you white money.'

He was wise to the fact that the natives couldn't sound the letter 's'. Others moved in to watch the sport. Milte-widlo looked to Midlato – she was the scholar of the family. Poor Midlato. She had tried and tried to say 'Lucy' and 'Jesus' so many times, and had always failed. But oh, to buy a bit of bullocky for her *kammammi*, that would be good. Making a huge effort, she spluttered, 'P-p–pit tiktpent.'

The settlers roared with laughter and fell about clutching their sides. Midlato was mortified. What was so funny? She caught the coin as it was thrown at her. The bull neck of the dead king looked just like the bull neck of the guffawing settler. Crestfallen, she walked away.

'Never mind,' said Milte-widlo. 'I'll become a sailor and bring back lots of white money.'

'No, please don't!' She remembered her terror the first time he went on the ship. She was still afraid he might not come back.

Murlawirrapurka pondered the predicament of his people. They were being reduced to the state of beggars and white men's slaves, just for a bit of 'baccy' or food. One thing he knew was that white men, who outnumbered white women, ogled black women. White men had already been killed for interfering with them. Murlawirra had four young and pretty wives. White men were always commenting on them and indicated what a potent man he must be. He felt their respect. He fondly remembered the lithe bodies of his women as they sought his by the glowing embers of the fire, under a sky bouncing with stars. Many of the ghost-skins had no wives. And if they did, they were so encased in volumes of strange stuff he often wondered what lay underneath. Did their pale limbs ever quiver in ecstasy?

In his tradition, it was customary to offer the services of a wife to other men. He decided to do so with select white men. The first time he did, he was given a large silver coin. He deduced the settler must have been content. His wife was certainly smiling broadly, her own silver coin firmly encased in her hand. Soon, Murlawirrapurka had many silver coins and was able to buy plenty of 'bullocky' and 'theep' and share them with his people. Sharing was their law. Kaurna had no concept of hoarding – they lived in the moment – the idea of killing fifty kangaroos and hoarding them for the next month was totally alien. Their law was to fulfil present needs, not future desires. That was the white man's disease.

But the natives in outlying districts were becoming rebellious. The Wirra watched the encroachment of the white people northwards with increasing restlessness. With alarm, Wangutya, a kinsman of Kadlitpina, looked at the thousands of sheep and cattle trampling his sacred watering holes. His uncle, a prominent Wirra sorcerer, emboldened by what seemed like successful subterfuge, (storms, floods, earthquakes) continued his incantations. The Wirra found it impossible to do nothing when white men were just marching over their *yarta*, fouling their water with their smelly 'theep', and disregarding their ancestral burial grounds. White men were staking out land and putting up fences. The Wirra loathed these structures as much as they loathed white shepherds, who were moving in their cattle and sheep.

The Fowlers settled by the little Para River in what would become the town of Gawler. Mildred Fowler was afraid of the Wirra people, especially how menacing they looked during their all-night dances, or *kuris*. She was especially worried about James Thompson, her intended, who went out alone into Wirra territory as a shepherd. The area was lush and full of long green grass, which the Wirra had prepared from time immemorial to attract game, so that they could flush it out. Now white men were moving in their herds and driving out kangaroos, wallabies, bush turkey, emus, and countless other game that the Wirra depended on. Their discussions with Murlawirrapurka were very heated and he didn't know how long he could keep his hot-blooded northern brothers calm. He had a lot of help from the diplomatic Kadlitpina, whose own sacred waterhole was the Kadlitparri, the dingo river, in the midst of Wirra country.

Teichelmann and Schurmann plunged enthusiastically into learning all they could about the Kaurna people. Ityamai-itpina was one of Schurmann's first eager students when lessons began in the new schoolhouse at Piltawardli. Ityamai-itpina 'followed the letters so fast he was soon a help to me with teaching', wrote Schurmann. Midlato and Kartanya were delighted when Kudnartu came down from the north and joined them at school. Teichelmann and Schurmann were impressed by these girls and how quickly they were learning the new skill of writing. They loved writing in their own language and forming the letters on their slate boards with chalk. Midlato would take the slate to her *kammammi* and read the words out loud. Teichelmann especially liked Milte-widlo and took him under his wing. He thought this enterprising, bright young man a prime candidate for successful civilisation.

Schurmann was particularly impressed by the Kaurna's quick, intelligent assimilation of foreign materials and concepts. For example, the word for tent, 'turnkiwardli' was an algamation of two concepts, cloth and hut; 'parasol' was 'kurotura', a combination of 'kuro', crown of head, and 'tura', shade or shadow. 'Judge' was 'pepa meya', paper man. This was an insight into how the Kaurna saw British justice – just a pile of paper. The word 'yammaiamma', for teacher and doctor was an extension of the word *yamma*, which meant foolish, stupid or silly. In grasping the language, Teichelmann and Schurmann were gaining a little of the perspective on how the Kaurna saw white man and his ways, even if it was none too flattering.

The missionaries forged close relationships with Murlawirrapurka and Kadlitpina, again impressed by their brightness and innate 'grace and decency'. Kadlitpina formed a special bond with Schurmann, whom he addressed as Midlaitya, fifth-born son. Teichelmann was dubbed Kertamerru, like Kertamerru Murlawirrapurka, first-born son. Schurmann felt honoured by his Kaurna name and was assiduous in his task to get the nuances of the Kaurna grammar right. Kadlitpina was grateful for his care. Midlaitya Schurmann was intrigued by the creative art forms, such as the *palti, kuri,* and *Ngunyawaietti, which* the Kaurna employed to digest and absorb current, rapidly-changing events. Schurmann wrote down one of the songs Kadlitpina sang during a ceremony.

In this tense time when white man was driving out traditional Kaurna food, and not giving out meat in return,

Butterflies & Demons

Kadlitpina's *palti*, 'Birkibirki' (Peas) was very tongue in cheek.

Oh, my mouth waters for peas
Oh, plenty peas please
'Don't like cold bappy from Ngaityerli
Ah plenty peas please!
Bappy no good

The settlers were growing peas in abundance and, as Midlato had discovered, these were very tasty. But they were ridiculous in their smallness. Kadlitpina wanted to chew! He was sick of biscuits, rice, bread, and sugar. He wanted meat. He expressed this in his *palti*.

I want to chew. I want to chew. I want to chew.
I am thinking of roasted emu, game, possum, and kangaroo,
And not trickettty birkitti (biscuit) or peas
Please give me lots more, lots more than just peas! Please!

Wauwe Woman: It is amazing that this song has been preserved. So, writing down words does do some good.

Author: What is also amazing is that Teichelmann and Schurmann wrote down many of the conversations they had with Murlawirrapurka and the others. It is only recently that these diaries have been found and translated from the German, providing me with unique snapshots of these Kaurna ancestors which I have reproduced.

Midlato huddled miserably in her hut with her friends Kartanya and Kudnartu. They had few blankets and were cold. Another hot season had passed and it was the traditional time to go to the foothills, build their cosy *wardlis*, and put on their newly stretched possum pelts. Yet again they stayed on the plain. Life was getting more and more out of control. At least Cronk handed out food every day, even though it was more suited to parrots. If Midlato went down to the river to catch *kungurla* she was taunted by white children, who acted like they owned her beloved Karriwirraparri. She nibbled miserably on her biscuit and longed for the fires in the foothills, in which she and the women would roast the roots they had dug, and chew the delicious bones of the game their men had just caught.

Midlato also felt anxious because Milte-widlo had decided he would follow his dream of becoming a sailor. He'd had enough of selling brooms and firewood for measly brown money. The sailors at the ports seemed to roll in silver money and baccy. Having improved his English with Teichelmann's special tutelage, he thought he could go on to better things. Teichelmann was sad to see him go, but thought being a sailor and seeing the world an excellent next step in his protégé becoming civilised. It was with great foreboding that Midlato trudged through the marshes of Yartabulti to see him sail away in a merchant ship, to a place called Singapore. Because of its name she thought it might be a place where people sang. She just hoped Milte-widlo would return. She needed him to be with her, as life was becoming more and more unstable.

In late April 1839, the Adelaide Kaurna heard terrible news. A white shepherd had been murdered in the area to the north of Adelaide.

Oh no! thought Murlawirrapurka. *The Wirra have not heeded my counsel.* As Albert Taplow reluctantly gathered a posse together, news came of the murder of another shepherd, a James Thompson, Mildred Fowler's intended. Kadlitpina joined the posse and headed north.

Fear of black insurgence reached hysterical proportions as rumours flew thick and fast of wholesale murders of whites. As Governor Gawler was away surveying outlying districts, George Milner Stephen was temporarily in charge. He thought Gawler too soft and much too indulgent with the natives. Murders of shepherds! That was the proof of the pudding. A firm hand was needed. Many settlers agreed. Stephen did what any self-respecting, Acting Governor would do. He stopped the rations for the Adelaide Aborigines.

Midlato, Kudnartu and Kartanya ran and found Murlawirrapurka to tell him the bad news. He immediately confronted Cronk but was brushed off. 'Sorry – Acting Governor's orders.' Murlawirrapurka was furious. He felt the white man was not doing what he expected him to do, and what he had worked so hard to achieve – to distinguish between good black men and bad black men. It was obvious it must be Wirra men who had committed the deeds, but he and the Adelaide group were being punished. Unfair. The *South Australian* newspaper agreed.

'It is well known that the accused are not in the neighbourhood of Adelaide... the enactment therefore... condemns the whole group, men, women, and children to be starved.'

Murlawirrapurka had sacrificed much to play by the white man's rules. This was a travesty. Acting Governor Stephen's monkey was getting more food than his people. He marched with Cronk up to the newspaper office. The *Register* reported that the Aborigines' 'confidence in our friendship and even-handedness has been shaken by cutting off rations.' Murlawirrapurka insisted his statement be published.

'You white men have taken our land and you have driven away our kangaroo and emus. We have no food now but what you please to give us. We are few and weak; you are many and strong. You say that black men have killed white men. We say take and kill bad black men but do not kill and starve good black men, your friends, and their women and children.'

Many citizens of Adelaide were sympathetic to Murlawirrapurka's eloquent plea. They were outraged, and condemned Stephen for his action. Gawler soon returned and was horrified to discover rations had been stopped. He immediately restored them and, in so doing, restored Murlawirrapurka's faith in Cockatoo Man's sense of justice.

Taplow and the police party returned with six Wirra suspects who were put on trial. Flocks of their brethren flooded to Adelaide. It was a mockery to bring them to the unintelligible formality of a British trial. In fact, some right honourable men eloquently expressed the argument that as Aborigines had their own laws, they 'should be emancipated from the foreign albeit majestic vagaries of English law.' However, not all agreed with this sentiment. Other right honourable gentlemen wanted all six heads on a plate, immediately!

Out of the six suspects, two were sentenced to be hanged on May 31st 1839. The court clerk recorded the names as Yerricha and Wang Nucha. Yerricha should have been more correctly written as Yerraitya, which meant second-born, and Wang Nucha as Wangutya, the seventh-born male. The two men had no idea what was going on and had been convicted on flimsy circumstantial evidence. For example, Yerraitya had only one eye and his victim failed to stipulate such a salient fact in the evidence he gave before he died. Settlers were baying for blood. Yerraitya and Wangutya were the scapegoats.

Murlawirrapurka had his work cut out trying to quell a full-scale rebellion among the unfortunate men's numerous relatives and clans-people. He had also heard that the two white men killed had been on amicable terms with the natives. That saddened him. He tried to explain to the Wirra that the whites were here to stay, and because their weaponry was more lethal, they had to submit to white man's justice. He explained that because white man had so much abundance, he must be doing something right. Therefore, he was adamant that the Wirra must follow British law, saying that if they did, then things should work out for them as it had for the British. The Wirra were not convinced. Young Itya didn't help matters. He liked to mime the horrible way Michael Magee had met his end the year before, at the hands of so-called white man's justice.

During this bleak time for the Kaurna, another feast was organised at Government House. It was the new Queen's birthday. The Wirra children screamed in terror as on the 24th May 1839 all the ships in the harbour let off a cacophony of thunderous salutes to celebrate her 20 years. Midlato calmed them down by explaining that white men liked making a lot of thunder, but that they would all be tasting delicious 'bif' very soon. The *Register* wrote of the proceedings,

'His Excellency, in a speech which was interpreted by the Protector, assured the aborigines of the friendly disposition of the white man towards them, exhorting them to adopt the habits of civilised life, to work, to build huts, to wear clothes, to live like the white men and be their brothers.'

Hmmph, thought Murlawirrapurka, looking at the dark expressions on the faces of his Wirra brothers. However, all were hungry, and politics temporarily forgotten as they wolfed down the beef. Midlato and her two friends thought the plum pudding delicious and loved the new soft blankets they received. But their parents, their hunger assuaged, regarded this banquet for what it blatantly was: a sop. They looked at the pewter plates they were given, depicting the face of an alien Queen surrounded by the letters of an alien alphabet, and failed to regard them as a fair swap for the destruction of their way of life. Midlato, Kartanya and Kudnartu could read some of the letters and tried to explain to the uncomprehending adults who Queen Victoria was. But Midlato was also sorely disappointed. She fervently hoped that Cockatoo Man would pardon Yerraitya and Wangutya.

Mildred Fowler had made a special journey down to Adelaide from the Para River to watch the hanging. She was panting to see justice done for the murder of her shepherd lover. She shared the opinion of many colonists, that hanging only two of them was not good enough. In her opinion, all the 'abos' should be got rid of. They were 'savages' and a danger to themselves and others. She made her way down to the parklands of North Adelaide, and found herself a choice spot in front of the scaffold.

Schurmann experienced first-hand the misery and discontent of the Aborigines. He discussed the state of affairs with Kadlitpina in Kaurna and in English. Kadlitpina warned him that the Wirra were deeply disturbed and could possibly cause trouble. All the condemned men's relatives were camping around the Location, their usually happy demeanours clouded by the dread that hung over them. Many seemed frightened and withdrawn, staring in awe at the brutal changes the white settlers had brought to the previously virgin land.

Others stalked menacingly around the gaol, which was a flimsy two-roomed wooden building. This rickety affair was only secured by a wooden paling fence guarded by sentries, nervously wielding their Brown Bess muskets. Taplow, one of them, felt terrible, and berated himself that he was not living up to the Quaker Backhouse's exhortation to care for his disadvantaged black brothers. Things were going from bad to worse.

The last day of May dawned. The colonial authorities gathered up all the Aborigines and ushered them towards the gallows. They wanted as many as possible to witness the executions, as a deterrent to future incidents. Many whites, including Mildred, were afraid of the 'savages', and cringed away from them. As Yerraitya and Wangutya were brought to the scaffold, the relatives commenced a loud wailing. The two men were accompanied by Cronk. While Yerraitya shook with terror, Wangutya argued defiantly with Cronk right up to the last. He would not accept that an alien power had stormed his country and was forcing him to die by their law. This was unheard of. The Wirra had their own set of laws. The hangman and the sheriff, not wanting a repetition of the disastrous Magee hanging, made sure that the nooses were put in the right place on the black men's necks. Wangutya, proud seventh-born, knowing he had lost the battle, had a last look around; at Ngano, great ancestor lying in the east; at the glorious gums that he could so deftly climb to flush out possums; at the dear faces of his weeping relatives; then he was arrested by Mildred's face right in front of the gallows, and the triumphant grimace of her smile. He was shocked by the look of profound hatred in her eyes and searched deeply into them trying to fathom it. Mildred felt exceedingly uncomfortable, her smile fading quickly. She felt this black man was challenging the very core of her being. Aeons passed. She was extremely relieved when the hangman pulled the hood over those eyes, those eyes which would haunt her forever.

The carts were moved more efficiently this time and, to Sheriff Smart's relief, Yerraitya and Wangutya immediately jerked to their deaths. The Wirra looked on in shocked disbelief. After a stunned silence, a loud wailing pierced the air.

Schurmann wrote, 'All the natives, particularly the relatives and tribal friends of the condemned ones, were deeply touched and cried very much. On many mornings and evenings, I heard their touching laments and condolences.'

After the grief, the anger returned. When Wangutya and Yerraitya were buried in the gaol, this caused total fury. Kaurna cherished burial practises were not being respected. Who were these white usurpers? Night after night the Wirra challenged Murlawirrapurka and Kadlitpina, saying their conciliatory approach was selling all the Kaurna down the river. They thought the hangings unjust and wanted their own justice. They warned that other Aboriginal groups, especially those along the Murray, were fed up with white incursion and were determined to kill whites from now on. Kadlitpina reminded them that whites had superior weapons, and now numbered several thousand. The Wirra threatened more sorcery. Kadlitpina was so concerned he had to warn Teichelmann and Schurmann of the threats.

'Obviously excited he told us that the relatives of the two recently hanged tribesmen, full of wrath against the whites, would come in the morning and cast their witchcraft upon them, and that in consequence many white people would die. To console us he also said that they would speak up for the missionaries, so that they may be saved from death.'

Wangutya's uncle was determined to cast a spell on the Karrawirraparri to make its waters poisonous. Murlawirra and Kadlitpina exhorted him not to use sorcery.

'Why shouldn't we?' he said. 'The whites have used it on our people. The Ngarrindjeri told us that when they fought to protect their women, white sealers had shouted, 'A pox on ya!' and then hundreds of our people died of smallpox!'

They argued on, well into the night.

'And besides, they have killed our clansmen unlawfully – in our law we should kill them. They are about to kill us all anyway, eventually. This is our only chance to get our land back!'

Ityamaitpinna loved the fierceness of the Wirra. He looked beseechingly at his *burka*.

Murlawirrapurka stayed firm. Kadlitpina told Schurmann Murlawirrapurka's response to the Wirra.

'No charm. It is now enough. The white man has and distributes food. Enough that these two men have been hanged. We are other men.'

Schurmann, assuming that Kadlitpina had talked them out of proceeding with their witchcraft asked him why they had changed their minds. Kadlitpina interrupted him saying, 'Please don't ask. I am afraid that they might still do it.'

Matthew Moorhouse, the new Aboriginal Protector who replaced Wyatt at this fraught time, reported that everything was under control and that the Adelaide natives 'were in a perfect state of quietude – not injuring or spearing, or in any way destroying the property of the settlers; and had great confidence and attachment to the Europeans.' And the Wirra 'were labouring under a degree of fear and dread of the white population, on account of the two executions.'

Mildred had terrible pains in her stomach as she swayed north in a bullock's dray after the hangings. The doctor told her that as well as being pregnant to her dead lover she had dysentery, probably from drinking river water. The latter half of 1839 saw many deaths as the young, weak, and older citizens succumbed to diseases that raged through the young colony, and left many a family mourning more than one death. Hard hit was Thomas Daniel, the basket weaver. His three children, healthy on arrival, all perished within a few months. The Denham family lost three of their eight children. The upshot was that the Daniels and the Denhams resolved to get away from this place of death and seek a new life elsewhere. They decided on Van Diemen's Land and awaited a ship to take them. Little did they know what further horror was ahead.

Wauwe Woman: You're not suggesting that the Wirra did poison the waters are you?

Author: Well why not. It is so politically incorrect to write about Aborigines and sorcery? Wirra Woman seems happy about it. I, for one, think if they did use sorcery, good on them. That was their only weapon. Why not use it? They didn't just lie back and die without a good poke.

Wauwe Woman: Don't be so stupid. People died of dysentery because of the highly unsanitary conditions. By 1839 there were 17,000 new immigrants swarming into Adelaide. Sheep were killed on riverbanks, their stinking offal devoured by blowflies. And where do you think human waste went? The river of course!

We don't want to be associated with sorcery, because whites then dismiss everything about us. And anyway, the Kaurna blamed smallpox on sorcery – even though 22,000 people died of it in England in 1839, and we know that it was brought here by the whites. Many of our people just didn't seem to get that diseases can also be transmitted. Is that sorcery?

Author: Well, I think you are denying something that is essentially part of your heritage.

Wirra Woman: I am on the author's side. We Wirra are to be reckoned with!

Wauwe Woman: You're not trying to say that sorcery is real, are you?

Author: It depends on the world you live in. Even the Christians allude to sorcery in the Bible.

Wauwe Woman: Oh, stop it – let's continue with the story.

Author: Well, we're going to fast-forward to the 1950s and you, my *kammammi* chorus, will become part of the story and have a chance to influence the action.

CHAPTER 9

Port Misery

The Taplows lived in a cream coloured, square house with a red tiled roof.

'A roof with tiles,' Mildred Taplow emphasised over and over again. If her intention was to demean Sveta because the Pleznowskis only had a tin roof, she was successful. Sveta constantly felt demeaned. It didn't matter what Mrs Taplow said, her intention to make the Taplow family superior always worked. But the continual put downs also had an unexpected consequence which Mrs Taplow hadn't foreseen and would come to resent, bitterly. They drove Sveta to succeed. She got better and better at school.

At the end of the year she achieved an amazing 100% in her exams. As her parents were working in the shop, Sveta went to Mrs Taplow's house and proudly showed the glowing report card. She was unprepared for the response. Mrs Taplow went white, clutched her stomach and ran to the bathroom. Lynette Taplow was visiting. She was miserable, as Barry Guthrie was having a dalliance with a pretty Ukrainian woman. She did look at Sveta's report card but quickly looked away when Mildred returned. Mildred then totally ignored Sveta and the report card and continued.commiserating with her sister-in-law about the dreadful behaviour of Guthrie.

On the next Sunday visit to the Fowlers, Trevor's family effusively congratulated him on getting 95%. Mildred studiously ignored Sveta's shiny face. Sveta couldn't hold back any more and eventually piped up,

'I got 100%.' She was met with stony cold silence. After an excruciating lull which would have frozen a dog on heat, the conversation returned to how well Trevor was doing at school. Sveta was hurt and puzzled. In fact, she felt a bit crazy – like she didn't exist – like her efforts were useless – she was reminded again that she was an alien in an alien world. She always felt she didn't know the rules of this strange Adelaide society and was always falling foul of the unspoken ones.

The truth was that Sveta and her family were too much for Mrs Taplow. The woman felt that her utopian intentions to assimilate Sveta's family had backfired terribly. Her 'do gooder' assimilation tactics had produced a monster; the little flower Svitochka had flowered a bit too much from inside those peasant lace-up boots. With her bright little face and impossibly stupid plaits, how dare she get 100%! Mildred could not stomach the fact that Sveta had outshone her beloved Trevor, that the Pleznowskis had a Hills Hoist, that they owned a car, that they'd bought a delicatessen which earned them a fortune. She could not stomach the realisation that her neat, orderly, Anglo-Saxon, British Empire worldview was crumbling around her. Just like the Britannia statue, it was in pieces. The demon of envy and hatred grew and growled in her belly. Like her mother and grandmother before her, a virulent cancer that would soon kill her was growing within her entrails

Wirra Woman: Serves her right – after what her ancestor did to my beloved Yerraitya. Doesn't feel good does it, love?

Wauwe Woman: That's very unkind and sounds a bit vengeful

Wirra Woman: Well some of us are howling for revenge. We're not all saints like you! And anyway, demons are vivid portrayals of what lies unresolved in the substrata of human unconsciousness.

Wauwe Woman: But poor Mildred Taplow – she can't carry the can.

Wirra Woman: Of course not. Every Adelaidean carries the can to some extent. You can't just wipe out a whole people, steal their land, take advantage of their generosity, and get away with it. It won't just come out in the wash. Or you can just blame Wirra sorcery!

Wauwe Woman: The former Prime Minister Howard and his ilk would think that was hogwash. They believe whites were kind people, did their best within the constraints of their times, and have nothing to be sorry about.

Wirra Woman: Well I think *that* is hogwash.

Tatiana became obsessed by the Russian ships which occasionally docked at Port Adelaide. It did not work for her to suppress her past, as was the way of her New Australian friends.

As Katherina said, 'Just forget the past Tatiana. You have a new life now.'

Or the doctor who supplied her with sleeping pills, 'You are so fortunate. Count your blessings.'

Or Ivan, 'Hard work will fix everything.'

But she missed her family and Russia terribly, and just basking in the cyrillic letters on the side of the ships was a huge comfort to her. She pushed her pram endlessly around the docks of Port Adelaide, unaware of its turbulent history.

Collet Barker had been the first European to spot the inlet above Lefevre's Peninsula in 1831, just before his gruesome death. Even though Light had felt pressured by Governor Hindmarsh to put Adelaide nearer this port, he knew the place was wrong. It was marshy and dank, a mosquito infested swamp. The Aborigines didn't like it. For thousands of years they called it *yartabulti*, place of sleep or death. In fact, nobody except Hindmarsh liked it. It was such a miserable, unwelcoming place, especially for people who arrived there after having sailed half way around the world. It was quickly dubbed Port Misery.

The history of the port was infused with tragedy and misfortune. The first ships which arrived were bedevilled by capricious tides. Exhausted passengers and crew had to carry equipment and luggage through mangrove swamps, while being attacked by an array of ghastly insects. Large amounts of stores and baggage were lost. For years it remained a long, dangerous, and muddy walk, a daunting start in the new colony. In March 1838, Captain Burns of the *Giraffe* was attacked and speared. In July 1840, Daniel Gatway and his party were lost and spent a terrifying night in the swamp.

In that same year, John McLaren, manager of the South Australian Company, began to build a road across the swamp to a section of land situated much lower down the creek, and on which the present port now stands. The two-mile road cost the company a steep £12,000. The docks on which Tatiana now walked were built on huge piles that had taken engineering ingenuity to fix into place. Ships could then anchor more safely, and a small town sprang up, including a Methodist church. But this was not an end to the misery. The place was prone to sudden floods. People walking to church often had to be rowed home through floating sewage. Many drowned over the years, including two unfortunate employees of a Mrs Sinclair, Jane Jamieson, and Janet Samuel, in 1866.

Yet the most devastating disasters at Port Misery were caused by industrial fires. One, in 1857, nearly destroyed the fledgling port. On the aptly named 'Tragedy Dock', the *City of Singapore* exploded in 1924. The ship was loaded with cars, tractors, kerosene, and petrol. The deafening explosion echoed off the Adelaide Hills, and fire crews from all over Adelaide could not contain the fire for several days. A memorial was erected in the Cheltenham Cemetery to the several firemen who died. Two years later there was an equally horrendous Sugar Refinery fire.

Tatiana's Port Adelaide of the 1950s was still a depressing place but now had numerous wharves where ships from all over the world, including the Soviet Union, would dock. Tatiana heard that one of these ships was allowing visitors on board. Was this signalling a thaw in Khrushchev's relations with the West? With great excitement Tatiana took Sveta to visit the ship. As they joined the queue for entry up the ramp, Sveta was intrigued by the cyrillic letters on the side. But a shock awaited them. They were barred. Only Australians were allowed on board. When Tatiana remonstrated, the official said, 'You should have thought of that before leaving your motherland.' When she answered she had been forcibly taken away by the Nazis, the official just shrugged with an implacable, 'Nyet.' Tatiana felt deeply rejected.

In Adelaide, she felt shunned; it seemed impossible to understand the rules of these strange new people. And now on this ship, symbol of her home country, she also felt ostracised. She couldn't bear it. She walked up and down the dock, strains of accordion music on board tugging at her heart-strings. She just cried and cried. Sveta gripped her hand, helplessly. Tatiana and the little girl walked towards the water. For a long time, Tatiana looked into the inky depths. The dark swirling blackness beckoned her. She discerned fiery red shapes that seemed to call her. She saw figures, girls' faces – two of the many who had drowned here. 'Come join us. Come join us!' Sveta felt afraid as her mother swayed forward. Suddenly she heard shouts from behind. Two men came running up. 'Lady, don't jump. Lady, don't jump.' Burly arms pulled mother and daughter away from the water's edge. Sveta felt comforted by the kind voices, as they gently guided them to safety.

A few months later, Tatiana heard that another Soviet ship was docked at Outer Harbour, the original place ships had landed in the 1830s. She begged Ivan to take her in their new Holden. Sveta sat in the back with little Sonia as they drove through a flat, featureless landscape. When they reached Outer Harbour, there were no ships. Just a broad expanse of mud flats, mangrove swamps, and vast lonely emptiness. The Kaurna descriptions, 'a salt swamp where nothing grows', and 'a place of death', were fitting. Tatiana ran to the edge of the mudflat and screamed at Ivan.

'What hellhole at the end of the earth, have you brought me to? What will become of me?' Sveta rocked Sonia back and forth miserably, as her mother unleashed a demented howling and threw herself to the ground.

Ivan stood helplessly as Tatiana screamed and writhed. He couldn't understand it. He was trying to do everything for his wife. Nothing he did made her happy. He worked so hard, put food on the table, bought her a house and beautiful clothes, but all to no avail. There she was writhing in torment. He looked out over the vast flat expanse – the water to the west and the chimneys of Port Adelaide dominating the skyline inland. He saw flames leaping – not the flames of the terrible fire that claimed many lives in 1924, nor in 1926, but the flames of a warehouse in his native Odessa into which thousands of Jewish women and children were herded and burnt alive in 1941. He couldn't distinguish who was screaming. He shut his eyes and clenched his jaw.

As Tatiana howled into the earth, something deep within it stirred. The spirits that dwelled there heard the anguished cries. They reverberated with the howls of despair. They felt the sadness in the young man's chest. They discerned the fluttery rhythms of the little girl's heart as her world crashed in around her and her breathing reduced to an absolute minimum, staving off the terror that threatened to engulf her.

The spirits of that place gathered together around the family. A new suffering was manifest on their land, and in the tradition of the ancestors they wanted to face it, to understand it, to muster up ancient healing qualities to absorb it, to wander with it. They could see that Tatiana was tormented by many demons which appeared to be encircling her brain, rendering her impervious to influences of good. All they could do was to bear silent witness. Eventually, Tatiana began to calm down, and her sobbing gradually subsided. Ivan gently led her to his shiny FJ Holden, a car that was supposed to bring happiness to his desperately unhappy wife.

In bed that night, Sveta prayed fervently to God. 'Please stop Mama from screaming all the time.'

The burden of Tatiana and her craziness lay heavy on her thin shoulders, and she felt very alone.

That night, a council was held on top of Yurebilla, one of many such councils that had been held over the last 120 years, ever since the white-skinned ghosts had first appeared from the sea. The Tandanya spirits had watched over this land since time immemorial. They had seen their own people wiped out, and the few remaining ones dragged off to different territories where they died bereft. They waited patiently, and still wait patiently, knowing that one day their people would return to their land. They also had the task of keeping their own demons, who howled for revenge, at bay. They howled for countless deaths from horrible diseases; at the wholesale occupation of the land; at the desecration of the sacred sites; at the invasion by the ghost-skins who assumed such blatant superiority, disguised in fancy language. It took all their thousands of years of knowledge to try and understand these strange ghost-skins, many of whom rarely laughed and rarely sang; and then only in strange oblong buildings every seven days. The Tandanya spirits found it hard that these ghost-skins looked upon the keepers of this land with such loathing, and banished them from the beloved *yarta* they had tended so respectfully for over forty thousand years.

'It's not fair!' the vengeful ones howled. 'Our ancestors must be avenged.'

But the wiser spirits kept most of the mutinies down and let the ancient wisdom of love and respect overcome.

In the last few years a new influx of ghost-skins had come to the Adelaide plain. Very odd – a very different breed – many Tatianas and Ivans, looking awkward, lost, and disempowered. The old ghost-skins didn't seem to like them at all. They herded them into unattractive treeless parts of the city and sent them to work in giant noisy tin buildings that belched fire and smoke into the azure sky.

Wauwe Woman: So, what is going on here? We understand the nature of the suffering of our people who lost their land and of the usurpers like Jeffcott and Mildred. But we don't understand this new suffering, as shown to us by this Tatiana woman.

Wirra Woman: There is someone wanting to enter our circle who says she can explain.

Wauwe Woman: Let her in.

They gasp as they see Baba Yaga.

Wirra Woman: But you have been described as an evil witch. All Russian people are terrified of you.

Baba Yaga: – *warming her long thin hands over the fire* – Aha! This old hag image of mine is just a guise. Just like yours, you great grandmothers of the south. *She wags her bony finger at them.* I am very like you Red Kangaroo grandmothers, outside time, all knowing, all seeing, all pervasive. But sometimes it is necessary to be harsh, in order to remove dead wood. Like you, I am also a guardian spirit to the pure of heart. What has brought me to this god-forsaken end of the earth is Svitochka. I am here to watch over her. Nice view you have here. *Baba Yaga looks over the twinkling lights from the Tandanya perch on Mount Lofty*

Wauwe Woman: So, Baba Yaga, welcome. We like to think that this Kaurna circle can become multicultural. Tell us what the hell is going on with Tatiana?

Baba Yaga: Tatiana came from a very grim part of the world where Joseph Stalin was dictator for twenty-five years.

Wauwe Woman: Oh, a bit like Thomas Playford?

Baba Yaga: No, no. *She chuckles* You have a very different problem here. Playford is a benevolent dictator. The words 'benevolent' and 'Stalin' will never occupy the same sentence. He was a terrifying madman. Not called 'cockroach eyes' for nothing, you know. He murdered millions of people. He starved the Ukraine deliberately in the 1930s; several million people died and Tatiana's family suffered terribly. Her brother starved to death and her other brother died in a prison for stealing food for him. You think you've had it bad here.

Wirra Woman: Oy, you watch your Slavic tongue! We've been virtually wiped off the face of the earth! That's pretty bad.

Baba Yaga: Well, Tatiana and Ivan escaped the catastrophe of World War Two, in which sixty million died and sixty million were made homeless. They had to escape two giant demons, Stalin and Hitler.

Wauwe Woman: Oh, we have had our own problems with our own devils, the Moorundie and the Permangk. Our giant ancestor Ngano, on whom we now sit, was slain, saving us from the Permangk. But from what you say, it sounds like the white-skins of the north have had it really bad.

Baba Yaga: Yes, but poor Tatiana could not leave the Holocaust behind. She has unfortunately brought all her demons with her. She is haunted by them. Doctors in Adelaide don't know how to treat her. They just give her pills to dull her senses.

Wauwe Woman: Oh, Adelaide doctors are so stupid. It is not by accident that the Kaurna word for doctor is 'yammaiamma', stupid one. Do you know there was a Dr Wright who killed people with his supposed cures? We Kaurna wouldn't go anywhere near him! But can't Tatiana be helped by being married to Ivan? He is so dependable.

Baba Yaga: Sure, but there is the whole Jewish thing there. Tatiana comes from a very anti-Semitic background, so feels very guilty about marrying a Jew.

Wauwe Woman: Yes, we witnessed anti-Jewish feeling here. Solomon, who started up a theatre in early Adelaide, was shunned as the archetypal, miserly Jew.

Baba Yaga: Even though Ivan is steady and loves Sveta very much, I am worried about her. She is a happy, resilient little thing but she carries a heavy burden. *Baba Yaga's wrinkles sag with anguish.* I believe that Sveta has Tatiana as her mother for a reason, but it is very terrible to watch.

Wauwe Woman: Don't worry. You have us to help you now. We can see how the demons have ravaged Tatiana's brain and how Sveta is at their mercy. We know we cannot protect her from Tatiana. However, we can send her some helpers along the way.

Myrtle O'Donnell was rather nervous as she knocked on the door of 17 Pudney Street. She had seen an advert in a shop window on the Port Road.

'Wanted – woman to look after two young girls – live-in. Good wages.'

Although Myrtle was over seventy she loved little children, having sadly lost two of her own in infancy. And besides, she was sick of living with her irascible Irish sister-in-law. This was a chance to get away. The front wire screen door opened, and a skinny blonde child with plaits said 'Please come in.' Mrs O'Donnell followed the girl down the long dark hallway to the kitchen near the back of the house. Here she saw a nervous looking woman with a baby.

'I've come about the job. My name is Mrs O'Donnell.' When Sveta had opened the door, she saw a woman with a halo of soft white hair and the sweetest of smiles; Mrs O'Donnell in turn, saw an angel with blue eyes, who she fell for immediately. Mrs O'Donnell was shocked to discover that the household was a New Australian one, but once she had seen Sveta she was smitten. Tatiana, on the other hand, was worried by the fact that Mrs O'Donnell looked so old, but was desperate for help.

Within a week the woman with the halo of white curls had moved in to the front room. She didn't even know what caused her to look at the 'Wanted' notice in the shop window in the first place. She didn't really need the money. She was well looked after by Legacy, an organisation devoted to looking after widows and children of ex-servicemen. Her husband Paddy had been killed in World War One. Oh, that sad day over forty years ago, when she went to Port Adelaide docks to see him off. There had been so much jubilation and fanfare, as all the fine strong young men had heeded the call to Empire, and were kissing their loved ones farewell. Her hot-headed, vibrant Irishman. She had loved him so. How they had grieved the loss of twin girls from scarlet fever the previous year. Paddy was one of five and a half thousand South Australian men who did not come back. This was a huge slice of young vibrant manhood from a tiny population. Myrtle never remarried. There were few men left. And many of those who did come back, like Paddy's brother, just sat in a dark room, shaking, and not being able to bear the slightest noise.

Paddy O'Donnell. His name was up in cold brass letters on the War Memorial down near the port, but that did little to fill the aching empty years. But now she had Sveta and how she adored her. Sveta was overjoyed as well. Tatiana went to the shop every day with Ivan, and they came home late at night. Number 17 sang with sweetness. Myrtle had a big trunk full of treasures she enjoyed showing Sveta; a lace wedding veil; little knitted bootees; a beautiful book with a shiny red cover of Queen Elizabeth's visit. Myrtle O'Donnell not only was heaven sent, but also a great baker. Sveta loved the scones and heart-shaped biscuits this angel seemed to churn out so effortlessly from the gas oven.

Tatiana loved the beach. It seemed to calm her down. On a hot day Ivan would drive her there, knowing that she was always better afterwards. When she swam, she felt soothed. She didn't know that the sea around Adelaide was full of benign sea spirits of fishes, whales, and dolphins. Even though most had been wiped out by rapacious sealers and whalers, their beautiful energies laced the green waters of St Vincent's Gulf. Also, the white sands contained spirits of wonderful flowers which did not bloom any more – again stamped out by ignorant white-skins. But their spirits waited patiently for a time in the future, when white-skins who had taken over so bombastically would appreciate the land that they had raped, and nurture them again. Also, Tatiana felt soothed as she lay in the sun watching the Italians, gold St Christopher medallions glinting on their chests, as they jubilantly threw balls at each other. This was the time when the sun was still benign and white-skins hadn't yet polluted the atmosphere with harmful chemicals which destroyed the ozone layer.

But of course, the sun was still too hot for the white-skins, and every summer Sveta had to put cold tomatoes on her reddened skin. She didn't know that countless other children who had played in these sands before her had the perfect skin for this sun. In fact they, the Midlatos, the Yerraityas, the Kartanyas, had everything that was perfect for this land. They had the wherewithal to live in it, and knew where to find water, how to survive drought, where to find succulent vegetables and medicinal herbs to heal their bodies when they were sick; they knew how to tap into the wisdom of the ages.

The Tandanya *kammammi* women watched and waited, their ranks strengthened by Baba Yaga, an amazing wise being from a different hemisphere. As well as trying to understand this strange new influx represented by Tatiana, Ivan, and Sveta, a bigger menace threatened from the north. The Red Kangaroo grandmothers were aware of the terrible explosions of fire and black energy that devastated the land near Woomera and Maralinga, and had harmed the indigenous peoples who resided there. With mounting concern, the grandmothers also noticed a strange invisible poison that descended over the Adelaide plain, brought by winds from the north. They saw this poison infiltrate the bones of the white-skins as they went about their daily business. They were puzzled that the populace seemed blithely unaware of the poisons that seeped south from the sinister mushroom clouds that belched over the northern part of the state. This was an extremely strange new phenomenon, and they scoured the old songs, stories, and dreaming to discover any possible indication of this new scourge on the land.

Wauwe Woman: Well Baba Yaga – advise us, you all-knowing and all-seeing wise being. Do you know anything about these black mists from the north? Why do the Adelaide white-skins seem so unaware of it?

Baba Yaga: Well, it is a long dreadful story. It has its roots in the hemisphere from which I hail. The last great world ruler, the British Empire, which grew fat on people like you, is now declining, and the American Empire is emerging. However, there are other contenders. Stalin, the big northern demon, wanted to rule the world, and after he defeated the demon Hitler, he set out to conquer his new rival, America. What you have been witnessing is the atomic bomb; the latest weapon of power on this our planet. Stalin stomped through Czechoslovakia, where Sveta was born, to raid its uranium – the food of this horrifying weapon – and started to develop his own atomic bomb. America had already dropped this terrible weapon on another northern country of yellow-skins, and killed hundreds of thousands of them. Most just melted in the blast, and those who survived died dreadful lingering deaths from radiation sickness, or gave birth to deformed children.

Wauwe Woman: Oh Yurebilla. This is what our northern neighbouring clans have been reporting in the last few years. Invisible mists. Deaths. Eye diseases. Malformed children. Why are white-skins destroying our land like this? And why were the yellow-skins punished so catastrophically?

Baba Yaga: Hold your kangaroos! Too many questions! One at a time. American white-skins claimed that dropping bombs on Hiroshima and Nagasaki was the quickest way to end the war. But in reality, they liked their new powerful atomic toy. To make things worse, the Americans snubbed the British, who helped them develop the first atomic bomb. The British did not like this one bit. They don't like the fact that their Big Empire, the one that snuffed out you guys, is crumbling, and they are not bowing out gracefully. Nobody gives up power voluntarily. So now they are furiously trying to catch up with the Americans and the Russians. There is what is called a 'cold war' between communism and the free world. After being put unceremoniously on a back boiler by the new American Empire, the British decided to test their own atomic bombs, to claw back a bit of power.

Wirra Woman: Uh oh, so that's where we come in. Oh Yurebilla!

Baba Yaga: Yes, you guessed it. Where better than the outback of South Australia? Prime Minister Menzies, with the big puppy dog eyes, dishes it up on a plate. It is empty. Perfect. So, the British set up atomic stations at Emu Fields, Maralinga and Woomera.

Wauwe Woman: But our land is not empty. It is full of our people – the ones still living and all their ancestors.

Baba Yaga: Yes, but like in all parts of the world – indigenous people are dispensible.

Wauwe Woman: Let's hear what one of the Tjarutja people near Maralinga has to say.

'*Only a few moons ago we see black mist drop on Adelaide. Whites love making big racket in the Bush – A huge explosion and the wind changed. We saw the plume drift and settle on Adelaide. We saw the sickness soak into the white people's bones. And they didn't know. Our people knew. Old Jimmy – he said a black mist rolled over and chilled them to the core – he is blind to this day.*'

Wirra Woman: But why are ordinary white-skins not told about it? Why are Adelaide doctors smuggling out the bones of dead babies, without the knowledge of their parents?

Baba Yaga: Oh, that is to secretly test the effect of radiation on the Adelaide population. You think that is bad. You should hear what my countrymen do to unsuspecting Russians. They are laboratory mice for radiation experiments. Just recently a big town was deliberately exposed to radiation from a bomb, twice as powerful as the one dropped on Hiroshima. Thousands are believed to have died in the immediate aftermath and in the years following. The experiment was designed to test the performance of military hardware and soldiers in the event of a nuclear war. Oh yoy, yoy, yoy! *Tears roll down Baba Yaga's face.* Who cared about the children who had just returned to school after a lovely hot summer? Who cared about the little seven-year-old girls who were taken to school by their devoted babushki for the first time? Who cared that their babushki had lovingly braided their hair with big ribbons, which had melted so easily in the blast.

The grandmothers sit in stunned silence. At last Wirra woman speaks.

Wirra Woman: So, puppy dog Menzies is playing with the big boys. In our backyard! We know they dig up uranium in Myponga and Radium Hill. Should leave it in the ground, I say. Much safer there. We are having trouble with all our own ancestors. They don't understand. They want to know why white-skins come and play bad games on our soil, playing with forces they shouldn't be playing with. And white-skins dare tell us that our sorcery is bad! They call us Stone Age! Yeah, we didn't blow up our stones or mess with uranium. We so-called Stone Age have our own laws. Whites think them primitive. We think whites in their Nuclear Age are SO primitive – they killed us off, and now are killing their own people.

A wizened Kammammi stokes the fire. The lights of Adelaide twinkle below. The group sits silently and ponders this strange world they are witnessing.

Sveta learnt about Woomera Rocket Range reading the newspaper. She read how proud the Aussies were to be involved in the Space Race. She looked at maps of the world, which were satisfyingly British pink all over. The sun never sets on the British Empire. She read how brave pioneers came to Australia and settled the virgin land and hoisted the British flag. She remembered the pretty queen in green feathers. She remembered her first history lesson about

Matthew Flinders circumnavigating Australia in the Tom Thumb, accompanied by an 'aborigine'. She puzzled about these 'aborigines' and wondered where they had gone (Aborigine certainly was not capitalised in those days). She even looked up 'Aborigine' in her Arthur Mee Encyclopaedia but there was nothing about them there.

On the 12th October 1956 she was juggling a pair of balls on a Stobie electric light pole outside her home in Pudney Street. She, like all the Adelaide population, was totally oblivious to the fact that an invisible deadly mist was falling all around her. Over South Australia, the wind had changed and sent a cigar shaped cloud of radioactive debris from the latest atomic explosion at Maralinga over Adelaide. The radiation, more than 14,000 times the strength of background radiation, seeped imperceptibly into her bones.

The Nuclear Safety Committee went to great lengths to avoid acknowledgement of the contamination of Adelaide following the 1956 test; this included falsifying information in an article published in the Australian Journal of Science. Anyone worried about the tests was assured by the minister, Howard Beale, that radioactive fallout from the tests was not an issue, except for 'communists and a few fellow travellers'.

Ngarrindjeri people who lived around the south of the Murray were puzzled when they noticed masses of dead fish floating belly up in the river.

Later in October 1956, Sveta observed how Tatiana and Ivan were agitated about news on the radio. It was the Hungarian Revolution. Brave people in the streets of Budapest were standing up for freedom in the face of Soviet tanks. They vainly waited for help from the free world. None came. They were brutally crushed. Tatiana sobbed helplessly.

A few months later Zoltan, a Hungarian boy, came to her school. He had escaped to the land of the free.

Miss Bradshaw welcomed him, as she had Sveta. Miss Bradshaw thought Sveta was amazing. She was forever telling the other children what a wonderful example she was, of an immigrant who had come over not speaking the language, but was now better than the kids who were born speaking it. Sveta received so many merit cards that year. Mrs O'Donnell was delighted, and every time Sveta got a good report she gave her a small treasure out of her trunk.

But the love affair between Myrtle and Sveta was about to come to a tearful end. Myrtle was doing a great job looking after the girls but saw that Tatiana was becoming more and more unstable. She would scream at Myrtle over the slightest issue. Myrtle could see the woman was crazed and tried to be kind. But one day, for no apparent reason, Tatiana kicked Myrtle out. Both Myrtle and Sveta were devastated. Mrs O'Donnell gave Sveta the shiny red book of the Queen's visit and promised to come and see her often.

Sveta and Sonia were farmed out to some other neighbours, the Butlers, in a nearby street. Sveta became good friends with their son, John. She and John roamed far and wide, having all sorts of imaginary adventures. These were the days before the Beaumont children grabbed the headlines when they disappeared from Glenelg beach, the original Holdfast Bay where the first settlers had landed.

Tatiana spent more time helping in the shop, which gave Sveta unexpected freedom. John loved drawing maps and they would set out looking for treasure. This took them into what was one of the last unspoiled regions of Adelaide, the Grange Reserve. Here, they were seeing the land as Midlato and her friends had seen it over 120 years earlier. John was a budding naturalist, and delighted in running among the sand dunes and discovering unusual and rare species of trees and shrubs: drooping sheaoaks; silver banksias; black tea tree; quandong; golden wattle; umbrella bush; and kangaroo thorn. Every now and then they would stumble across a thicket of paperbark teatrees.

In Midlato's time, the area was thick with them and, interspersed with a variety of saltbush, they protected the flora and fauna from the westerly winds. John showed Sveta a rare bluebell, a chocolate lily, and muntries; a type of edible fruit which Midlato once gathered. John was also a budding birdwatcher and excitedly pointed out white-browed babblers and yellow-rumped thornbills. Within twenty years these would disappear altogether as they depended on a dense understorey of shrubs, which was diminishing rapidly.

Wauwe Woman: Ah, Adelaide has lost so much. Not only have they lost us and our happy ways but also the unusually enchanting sounds of these shrub birds, the babblers and yellow-rumped thornbills are just the beginning; so many of our birds have gone. Babblers, with their distinctive white brows, had the most amusing calls. They grizzled, miaowed, and gurgled to each other as large flocks of them foraged together in the dense shrubland.

Author: And the yellow-rumped thornbills?

Wauwe Woman: They were not as communal as the babblers, more solitary. Often seen in pairs or small flocks. I so miss their twinkling twitter on a beautiful *wiltutti* morning. Ah, what it was to walk these dunes with the sea glittering in the distance; so thick with scents, flowers, birds, and butterflies. Whites have no idea of the paradise they have destroyed.

Tatiana inevitably fell out with John's parents, and Sveta was sent back to the Taplows. Mrs Taplow didn't approve of Tatiana's tantrums but she desperately needed the money, so reluctantly took on the 'New Australian brats' again. Sveta didn't tell Mrs Taplow about the stack of merit cards she was receiving, and that she was not only the top of her class but in a unique category of her own. She also now knew that she was loved by other people, who did not continuously denigrate her. Mrs O'Donnell had shown her that.

Then the world was hit by Hong Kong flu. Sveta was only one in her class who escaped.

Baba Yaga: It's all that garlic that Tatiana fed her. Gave her great immunity.

On October 4th 1957, Sveta was riding her bike on the back road, looking up at a strange light that was travelling across the sky, when she ran into a man who was also looking up at the sky. What they were both transfixed by was Sputnik, which the Soviet Union launched onto an unsuspecting world. At school, she was told that this was all part of the space race and what Woomera Rocket Range was all about. But Baba Yaga knew better. Sputnik was a feather in the cap of the Soviets, whose message to the Americans was, 'We are winning the Cold War.'

Within a month, Laika the dog was sent up in the second Sputnik. Of course, she never came back. She was dispensible, like the Kaurna.

In South Australia, Thomas Playford was knighted.

Belinda Bradshaw had been busy with the Ephraim Trip case. Trip, an Aboriginal man, had been stopped on his way home from work with his non-Aboriginal workmate and neighbour. The police constable asked the two men if they realised they were breaking the law by being together. Though the constable did not pursue the matter, Trip was so incensed that he brought the incident to the notice of Charles Duguid. Belinda and the Advancement League began a campaign to get the consorting provisions removed from the Police Offences Act. Don Dunstan, MP for Norwood, drew up the petition, which more than 7,000 people signed, and by October 1958 the consorting clause was repealed.

Belinda Bradshaw was also part of a historic meeting in Adelaide in 1958 of Aboriginal Advancement Leagues from all over Australia, who decided that a united Federal Front would advance the cause of Aboriginal people, who were still regarded as non-citizens. Charles Duguid became the first President.

As Labour member for Norwood, Don Dunstan was a vociferous opponent of Sir Tom Playford's long regime, and exploited the cracks as they appeared and multiplied. On a federal level, he opposed the White Australia Policy. He faced staunch opposition. It would take much longer to crack that old chestnut.

Tatiana became more volatile and spent a week in a private mental hospital, where Sveta saw her drink loads of black coffee and swallow different coloured tablets which were doled out like sweets.

CHAPTER 10

Cuckoo Notions

'Y'travel over land and sea to make one convert... an'
when ya finished with 'im, why, that feller's twice as fit for
hell as you are y'self.'   – Robert Merritt

Midlato was excited. Not only was she learning to write
in Kaurna and English, she was proud that Teichelmann
and Schurmann were consulting her, her friends Kartanya
and Kudnartu, and their elders on a book they were
writing about their language. Schurmann, a gifted linguist,
zealously recorded the depth and intricacies of the Kaurna
language and grammar. While many of Midlato's people
were suspicious and shook their heads in disapproval, her
kammammi kept nodding happily, tears streaming down her
cheeks.

Midlato, Kudnartu, and Kartanya were the missionaries'
star pupils. They felt a sense of great importance in helping
them with the book they were writing. But the girls found
them strange, especially their insistence that they should
love a *meyunna* called Jehovah who would apparently save
them from eternal damnation. These concepts were so
alien to Midlato. And who was this Yova? Was he related to
Yeetut? She took comfort in her own ancestors. They made
much more sense.

Murlawirrapurka, Ityamai-itpina and Kadlitpina were happy that Teichelmann and Schurmann took such an interest in them and their customs, and all enjoyed long animated discussions. They also tried hard to hear the Germans' fervent message – that people were commanded to love and care for each other and follow Jehovah and Jesus, or be damned. This was puzzling to a people for whom values such as caring and sharing were assumed. The Tandanya people lived by their own laws, which if transgressed brought dire consequences, as graphically shown in their ancestor Tjilbruke's classic story of greed and murder. They didn't need foreign Yeetuts and Yovas to tell them to do what they had been doing for aeons. Tjilbruke seemed much more wise and compassionate than Yova. Tjilbruke's tears were imbued in the land – everywhere informing them, nourishing them, teaching them, and whispering to them in the rustle of eucalypt leaves.

Murlawirrapurka did not see whites showing a lot of love or sharing; it had just been one long bickering mayhem. Food was stored under lock and key and had to be worked for, begged or stolen. Many parts of Adelaide were now crowded with hovels in which poorer whites were packed together in the heat and dust, with pigs, goats, hens, and screaming infants. The genteel, starched into their collars, stiff petticoats, and shiny hats, didn't seem to share with their poor brothers at all. They preferred intoning about Yeetut in the Holy Trinity Church, under the big clock. If Yeetut was such an important ancestor whose main message was 'to love one another', why weren't they taking heed? Murlawirrapurka had had many a conversation with Cronk, who assured him it was no picnic for the poor back in England. The hovels and overcrowding there beat any squalor he might be seeing in Adelaide. 'Why do you think they're all coming here?'

Teichelmann and Shurmann found aspects of Kaurna culture unfathomable. For example, when Murlawirrapurka's brother died in August 1839, the Kaurna blamed Permangk sorcery. A battle was planned. Schurmann viewed this as superstitious nonsense and warned that if the fight went ahead and they committed murder, Jehovah would burn them in hell.

Wirra Woman: For all his good intentions, Schurmann had no idea of the world we Kaurna inhabited.

Wauwe Woman: And none of you whites still even have an inkling! You see our death rituals as superstitious Stone Age nonsense.

Author: Well, let me have a go at explaining!

In the Kaurna world, especially before the white man came, all was in balance. Over thousands of years they had evolved ways in which their life worked, and how phenomena like bushfires and long periods of drought were to be managed. There was enough food, little disease, and the other groups, including the enemies, respected the boundaries. The land and its people radiated the purity of the law. If there was disease or anyone died before their time, it was almost always a result of some disharmony caused by their own infractions, or by the sorcery or jealousy of others. The death rituals were designed to winkle out anything untoward, disorderly or chaotic. And Permangk sorcery had been implicated during the death rituals of Murlawirrapurka's brother.

Wauwe Woman: Not bad. It certainly requires a dramatic shift in worldview.

Ityamai-itpina scoffed at Schurmann's objections and threat of Hell, whatever that was? – It sounded not much worse than a bushfire! He insisted on the Kaurna people's right to abide by their own laws of revenge. He still grieved terribly for Yerraitya and Wangutya and was beset by vivid flashes of the botched hanging of the Vandemonian Magee. Ityamai-itpina felt his people's way of dealing with transgression was far superior.

Despite dire warnings from the Lutherans, preparations were made for battle. These battles were elaborate affairs. Scouts were sent out and the field prepared. Permangk and Kaurna painted themselves to look as ferocious as possible, and assembled their finest spears and sturdiest shields. The fundamental rule was that the group which experienced the first serious injury or death must accept defeat and retreat.

Wauwe Woman: Now I call that much more civilised. Much less likely to provoke the ire of Jehovah than the thousands slaughtered at Waterloo and Trafalgar!

On reaching the battleground, each side formed a long line facing the other, across a distance of about twenty kangaroo hops. Fierce yells, accusations, and abuse were hurled across the lines. At a certain point, when passions were suitably inflamed, a signal was given whereupon each side launched a volley of spears at the other. What followed was an intense, acrobatic, almost balletic display, as shields caught spears and men swerved and spun deftly, avoiding the lethal trajectories raining down upon them, before leaping forwards for further attack. It was here that the extensive knee shaking exhibited in the *kuris* and *paltis* paid dividends; a fabulous preparation for being able to weave and circle from flexible knees. Ityamai-itpina loved it. This is what his whole life as a warrior had prepared him for. He felt he could give vent to his passionate nature and exercise his extraordinary skills, which as a white man's lackey were denied. At this particular battle, two Permangk men were badly wounded and they retreated to their eastern camp in defeat.

Schurmann admonished Ityamai-itpina. 'War is bad and you quarrelsome people will go to hell.'

'Yes,' he replied, tongue-in-cheek, 'we are wicked. We shall be thrown into the firepit.' But he was serious when he warned Schurmann that he and other whites must not intervene. He had noticed the presence of police on horseback hovering around the edges of these intertribal fights and really resented it. He also resented the fact that Protector Moorhouse was exhorting him to dig and to build more fences at Piltawardli. He and Murlawirrapurka only did so if fresh meat was promised in return. They refused to become 'good white men.' However, Murlawirrapurka's charm and friendliness made him very popular in the growing town, and in addition to receiving money for the favours of his wives, he was given a great deal of food and other bounty, which of course he promptly shared.

Light died early in the morning of October 6th 1839 at Thebarton after having written, 'On the whole, I have made rather a sorry adventure to South Australia. Add to this my health entirely broken – I have now no strength and wasting fast.'

Guns were fired every minute as the hearse moved to Trinity Church. Four thousand colonists, including those bitterly opposed to Light's choice of site, followed it to his burial in the square that bears his name. Flags hung at half-mast. History vindicated his choice of Adelaide's site. He is now hailed as the 'man in the right place at the right time.'

However, there was another 'man in the right place at the right time.' But that man has not yet been vindicated by history, at all. Only the ancestors of the Kangaroo Dreaming recognised Kua Kertamerru Murlawirrapurka as that 'right black man', as he sat near the Tandanya Rock and watched the hearse move past, barely flinching at the repetitive retort of guns. He himself did not know it, and neither did the white people of Adelaide, then or now. The rock formation in the shape of a giant red kangaroo loomed up, red and luminous, behind him. He drew so much comfort from its presence, and dismissed an unsettling dream he'd had in which it had gone, just disappeared.

He wondered again for the thousandth time, was he doing the right thing with his softly, softly approach? Shouldn't he listen to the Wirra, join with them, and start an insurrection? At least that way the Kaurna would go down fighting, in dignity. Not this slow agonising death.

He puzzled endlessly about these curious white men. They never seemed at peace. They did not seem to listen to each other, nor share their innermost thoughts or emotions. In their plays, dancing, and song, the Tandanya people displayed the whole gamut of emotions: sadness; gladness; fury; joy; and all the subtle shades in between. Whites seemed so monotonous – their faces always twisted in suppressed condescension – so humourless. No wonder Adelaide overflowed with taverns – it seemed to take the grog loosener to get their faces to relax. And even then, their humour had an unpleasant edge to it, like with the King John sobriquet. It was as if the ghost-skins were poking fun at him every time they asked, 'so how's King John today?' How dare they! He loved the humour of his own people and wished he could share it with these dour condescending bandicoots; a humour which captured the endearing qualities of others, and included them in the great human family they were all part of. He felt an enormous gulf between him and the whites, as wide as the Wongayerlo. How could he describe to them how Aboriginal humour vibrated with the tapestry of life, enriching it with subtle colours and hues; or explain the jokes which his people shared when resting in the heat of the midday sun, bringing delighted smiles to faces, down which the sweat freely ran?

His culture's lifeblood depended on communication, humour, and sharing stories. These whites read tales in books. That seemed so lifeless to him. Why write down or read a story when there were so many other living beings to communicate with? It seemed so alien to bend over thick dry books, like these missionaries did in the flickering candlelight, straining their eyes till all hours. How could that be good? And this Schurmann kept pointing at his thick books as if he, Murlawirrapurka, was somehow the poorer because he could not decipher the arid symbols. He would rather look up at the heavens and decipher the subtleties in the ever-shifting passage of the stars. There was always a new inflection on a time-honoured story up there; always something to dance to and learn from. The night sky provided a perfectly illustrated book of Kaurna morality and culture.

He coughed. He did not know that the same disease that had killed Light was now taking root in his lungs.

Murlawirrapurka was feeling another great dilemma. While he had been happy to go along with the settlement of Adelaide, he always had his own Ngaltingga to escape to. But now Cockatoo Man was busily forging a road right through the middle of his beloved *yarta*, towards Encounter Bay in the south. Surveyors, lumbering cattle, dray carts, and dynamite were shattering its age-old silence. He found this extremely painful, and felt more sympathy for Ityamai-itpina, whose ancestral waterhole was one of the first to be desecrated as the embryo city of Adelaide spread its placenta over the land, transforming it forever. What was even more painful was that he himself had guided these white men with their instruments, had shown them the old native tracks, the lagoons and ravines and the sacred spots where his ancestor Tjilbruke had wept and brought forth clear crystal springs. Murlawirrapurka had done all this out of the goodness of his heart. He did not feel the reciprocation. He just saw greed in white-skins' eyes as they staked out his beloved land. That night, in a gathering in front of the Rock, he smothered himself in red ochre – drawing strength from its redness, which reminded him of his murdered uncle's blood, and danced and sang a *palti* that expressed his pain. Schurmann was moved by the despair shown, and it is thanks to him that snippets of Murlawirrapurka's *palti* were recorded.

> *One lonely blue-gum stands in the grass*
> *High above the little scrub of Murlawirra.*
> *Behind me, bald hill hides the lovely valley, Maitpangga:*
> *I'm sitting in my country*

Down in the gully Murlawirrangga water lies
And in the wirra far below me, the mallee box and kaiyera sigh

All these dear places, Kurtandilla, Wangkandilla
Rikarnungga well, the springs of Tiranangko
Ngaltingga where we find red ochre, all going
Over near Tarangga, the wilta stumps are drying out;
And at the river, wheat is planted, and fences; dray-ruts
    as deep as my knee
Ah Ngangkiparringa, where I used to be.

Albert Taplow was having a hard time policing the problems between whites and blacks. He had a new boss, Constable Sweetapple, who strongly disapproved of 'the disgusting primitive rabbles staged by these painted savages'. He ordered Taplow to monitor the battles between the Permangk and the Kaurna, on horseback. He could feel Ityamaitpinna's eyes on him as he skulked around the edges. He felt he was tarnishing something very old and pure by his presence, and was relieved when someone got injured and the battle was brought to a close. He had hated the hangings of Yerraitya and Wangutya, and knew in his bones that these men were innocent. The Quaker preacher Backhouse's warning of a curse burned in his brain; a curse white man would surely incur if he didn't take care of his black brothers.

In February 1840, Taplow persuaded his superiors to invite Murlawirrapurka, Ityamai-itpina, and Kadlitpina to be part of the mounted police force. He felt that their presence on horseback in future wrangles between natives and settlers might increase their stature in the eyes of whites, who regarded the Aborigines as little more than annoying dingoes. Gone were the days when the Chief

Judge made a big spectacle of showing how fair whites were to them. Gone were the days when rhetoric abounded that black man was a British citizen with equal rights. Gone were the days when the Protector was appointed to uphold the rights of the Aborigines. Now he was there to protect the white man *against* the Aborigine. Every time an Aborigine was murdered, the white involved easily got off, arguing the case for self-defence. Taplow had witnessed countless numbers of these incidents and felt desperate; he couldn't turn the tide. It seemed that white supremacy, enshrined in the eugenics of the time, was winning. The Kaurna were even being driven from their own river; they, who since time immemorial had revered the Karrawirraparri, drunk from it, eaten its fish, bathed in it, and danced around it, were now seen as a nuisance.

Midlato heard wonderful news. Milte-widlo was returning. She was overjoyed to meet him at the Port. 'How was Singapore?' she asked. He looked at her shiny eyes and did not have the heart to tell her that the black people that lived there were virtual slaves. 'Oh okay,' he said. 'But there is no nicer place in the world than the Tandanya plain.' His pockets jingled as he swaggered along the dock. He gave his sister a shiny silver coin. She examined it in wonder; the king with the fat neck had been replaced by a young woman with a slim neck.

Kudnartu clung to Midlato as she jumped to the sounds of the explosions. Twenty-one of them. She felt she could never get used to them. It was the beginning of the May 1840 Queen's 21st birthday celebrations. 4,000 colonists witnessed Midlato and her school friends sing hymns. Midlato was proud as Schurmann read out the Ten Commandments in

Kaurna. Then Gawler exhorted the natives to obey the commandments, not to fight or drink, and to live in houses as 'King John and Captain Jack are doing.' The coarse woollen pants Murlawirrapurka wore rubbed uncomfortably on his nether regions. Afterwards, 300 Kaurna, many of whom, like Kudnartu's family, had travelled far, pounced on 'huge tranches of roast beef, biscuits, rice and sugar', and wrapped themselves in the warm, finely woven blankets that were given out. The next day, Midlato took Kudnartu's young brothers to see the Holy Trinity church clock, a favourite pastime, especially when the bell struck the hour at noon. But something strange happened. Noon did not come. The sun inexorably did its thing and reached the middle of the sky, but no bells marked its arrival. The clock had stopped. For the next couple of years, it stayed stuck at 11.25. Midlato was intrigued by this, as she knew clocks and watches meant so much to white people. She felt she had everything in the sun, stars, and moon that she could wish for.

Wauwe Woman: Just another example of how whites were blinded by what they thought was a brilliant clockwork mechanical universe, which explained everything. It fed their illusion of being in control. They have been in a trance ever since.

Within a month of the celebrations, the Daniels and Denhams, who had lost six children between them, boarded the *Maria*, a ship that was to leave Adelaide for Van Diemen's land, where they hoped to start a new and healthier life. Little did they know what lay in store on that ill-fated voyage.

Teichelmann and Schurmann, after many long discussions with Murlawirrapurka and Kadlitpina, understood more of the Kaurna relationship to their land. But their mindsets didn't allow them to fathom the deepest meanings – that it was not the Kaurna who owned the land, it was the land that owned the Kaurna. The Kaurna were the humble servants to its law, suffused for tens of thousands of years with its ancestral wisdom, ritual, ceremony, and stories. However, the Germans understood enough to persuade Protector Moorhouse to take up the long overdue issue of their land rights. Moorhouse in turn persuaded Gawler that the Kaurna did have 'distinct, defined, and absolute rights of proprietary and hereditary possession'. Of course, this led to loud squawking among the gentlemen settlers. Gawler robustly defended the Aborigines' preliminary rights, and to his credit, acted. He granted sections of newly surveyed land near Encounter Bay to Tammuruwe Nankanere, a Ramindjeri man. Gawler was barraged by storms of protests. Landowners insisted categorically that they themselves had 'absolute right' of first selection of land, not the Aborigines.

For the next few months, arguments raged back and forth. An 'old settler' wrote in the *Register*, 'It would be difficult to define what conceivable proprietary rights were ever enjoyed by the miserable savages of South Australia, who never cultivated an inch of the soil, and whose ideas of the value of its direct produce never extended beyond obtaining pieces of white chalk and red ochre, wherewith to bedaub their bodies for their filthy corrobories.' This upright 'old settler' went on to accuse Moorhouse and the Lutheran missionaries of instilling 'Cuckoo notions' among the Aborigines.

Wirra Woman: 'Cuckoo notions!' How dare he? The whites were the big fat cuckoos who had flown in on their white birds, parked their bulky weight on pristine land, defecated their rot all over it, and strangled us dry! What planet was this 'old' settler on? *She is spitting with rage.*

Wauwe Woman: Yeah, but Moorhouse gave a pretty good reply – in the measured response of those times! And you've got to hand it to Gawler and Moorhouse. They really tried.

'With regard to the insinuation that the claims of the natives to proprietorship in the land are 'cuckoo notions' which the Protector and Missionaries "have instilled", I beg to say, that it is as incorrect as it is illiberal. We are quite ready to prove the antiquity of their territorial rights and ideas concerning these, whenever properly called upon to do so.'

The upshot of all this debate was that some lands were put aside for the benefit of the natives. Of course, these were far too small for a hunter-gatherer lifestyle. It was hoped that the Kaurna would become like white men and farm their land.

As Kudnartu gazed up at the now defunct clock, she was not to know that she would be one of the first Kaurna women to acquire some land. And she wasn't to know that it would bring about her early death.

The ancient law of the land, embossed in its every crag and crevice, was overridden by White Law written on its 'pepa'. Whites failed to understand that Kaurna law, which had evolved for tens of thousands of years, was inscribed in every rock, in every water-course, in every hue of the blue of the sky.

Wauwe Woman: And today – still no-one understands it. Even the black people educated in White Law at Universities. Look at the hoo-hah around native title.

Wirra Woman: Well, that is the only way some of us have to fight. We must use the structures of the white ways. We must learn their laws and use them to our advantage.

Wauwe Woman: See. Useless! Whites would have been a lot better off if they had their own version of a good old 'filthy corroboree' to settle their differences, rather than all this succinctly phrased high-minded twaddle. So what if South Australians had the distinction of being the first to recognise Aboriginal ownership of land? That nobility didn't stop them from stealing it. And as, no doubt, the story will show, our dear Kudnartu's descendants still have not got the land that is rightfully theirs.

Gentleman capitalists continued unhindered to buy up huge tracts of land. Gunpowder was used to dislodge large gums to widen the dray tracks for the new road south. Blasts struck terror into countless feathered and furry creatures as they fled from their sanctuaries, sacred no longer.

Murlawirrapurka gazed at his ancestral land and mournfully sang, Schurmann recording and translating.

> *Over the bald hills, a track winds on my right,*
> *Where I led them to the water,*
> *On our way to Maitpangga and Wirramu.*
> *…. I was dreaming…*
> *Like a child I foresaw nothing!*
> *Now I see, that the axes, the fences and the police house*
> *Are at Willangga, and the track comes nearer this way;*
> *   tomorrow Murlawirra,*
> *Then Maitpangga – (place of high cliffs)*
> *All go, all my country, all!*

Willanga, 'the place of green trees' was being blasted open, and while its quarries began spewing forth slate for the rooves and floors of Adelaide, the first game of cricket was played at Thebarton. Itya and Midlato earned a penny or two by hunting out lost cricket balls in the long grass.

The Kaurna had deep notions of reciprocity and expected a fair swap for the loss of their *yarta*. The white maggots had infested their ancestral tree and they were stuck without game, without pelts. They also refused to go along with the European hard work ethic. Frankly, they thought white life grim and boring. They were happy to don a few silly clothes to placate the white man's strange notions of modesty, desultorily knock up a fence post or two at the Location, listen to a boring sermon on the ire of Jehovah, but all the while they were itching to throw off these shackles, daub their bodies with paint, encircle their knees with rustling leaves and ecstatically dance as the moon shimmered on the water. Or, in *wiltutti*, leave the miserable concrete flea-ridden huts, take the children out of school, and set out for the bush where white man had not made too many incursions, and resume as much of the old life as they could.

This practice frustrated Teichelmann and Schurmann who felt that any progress they were making with the children was dashed every time they disappeared for weeks on end. Even though Midlato was one of their best students and could write and recite the Ten Commandments in Kaurna and English, it meant very little to her. Especially 'Thou shalt not kill.' She shuddered as she remembered the wailing of Yerraitya's family as his neck was broken and he hung lifeless from the gibbet. She just went along with the game. If she stayed at school for at least three months, she was promised another blanket for her *kammammi*.

Teichelmann and Schurmann observed that the Kaurna expected the white men to 'give them provisions and be completely their servants', but rather than see this as an expectation of reciprocity, interpreted it as an attitude of laziness. But despite their grumbles, the missionaries were prepared to try and understand the worldview of the Kaurna, as far as their evangelical paradigm could allow them. Kadlitpina appreciated this and shared more of his beliefs with Midlaitya, the Lutheran fifth-born. He told him the Kaurna dreaming story of a young boy, Tarnda, who brought joy to the life of his aged parents and went on to become a great hunter. In old age, he was transformed into an old man kangaroo and was a great and respected teacher of all the Kaurna men, and was named Monana. When his life was finished he threw many spears up into the sky to form a ladder, which he climbed. Kadlitpina pointed to the evidence of them shining brightly in the southern sky. He even suggested that Schurmann should undergo a scarification ritual so he could then be privy to men's secret knowledge.

After a lot of hard work, Teichelmann and Schurmann published their Kaurna Grammar book in August 1840. This included over 2,000 words of the Kaurna language.

The Southern Australian wrote, 'The German missionaries laboriously devoted themselves to the acquisition of the language of the Aborigines, and have, perhaps, carried their linguistic attainments in this department to as high a pitch of acquisition as has ever been done by any other persons under equally disadvantageous circumstances.'

Midlato's *kammammi* traced her gnarled hands over the book, gave a deep sigh of relief and murmured, 'these

Kaurna words on white pepa is what will save our people's language.' Even though cataracts were dimming her eyes, she could just make out the edges of the book. She knew that her eyesight was deteriorating rapidly because she didn't want to see what was happening to her people: the wholesale destruction of their culture and its oral wisdom. She didn't have a lot of faith in white man's books but she knew that this book, with its detailed vocabulary and grammar, would serve as a code that would be preserved until a time when future occupants of the Adelaide plain would be able to decipher it. She looked up at the shining faces of Midlato, Kartanya, and Kudnartu and saw how pretty they were, especially Kudnartu. This worried her deeply. She knew that the old customs of protecting such pretty girls on their path to motherhood were now gone. The future she could see, especially for Kartanya and Kudnartu, was grim.

Even with a grasp of the language, Teichelmann and Schurmann were unable to convert the Kaurna to Christianity. It was hopeless. The Kaurna were very happy with their spiritual beliefs, thank you very much. For all of Teichelmann's Jehovah blindness, he could recognise that the Kaurna were 'naturally proud and wise in their own estimation and express themselves perfectly satisfied with the tradition of their forefathers.' It had worked for thousands of years, and the Kaurna had not seen anything in the white way of life which interested them greatly. Sure, they liked the iron tools and axes but what else was there? Milte-widlo had earnestly tried to take up white ways, odd jobs man, broom salesman, sailor. In Singapore, he was shocked to witness the virtual slavery of black people. He confided to Teichelmann.

'Would not I be a fool to take on a life like that! These people are half-starved and at the end of the week they get half a crown, while I live here in comfort and can eat meat whenever I like. And what have I earned after all that? Nothing!'

Teichelmann had had high hopes for Milte-widlo, who in his estimation had become fully civilised, but was sorely disappointed when on his return from Singapore, he promptly 'divided the wealth he had gained among his countrymen, went around completely naked on the third day, and was worse than before.'

Milte-widlo did not want to sell his soul for a tiny wage. He would rather go into the bush and do what he loved best: sleeping under rustling gums; singing, dancing and hunting; and running with his ancestors. The sky and the land were his succour. Not pennies, baccy or cheap grog.

The Dresden men had many spirited discussions about religion with their black friends. To Teichelmann's assertion that all non-believers would be punished by Jehovah, Ityamai-itpina grabbed his spear and proclaimed, 'I am very strong, if Jehovah punish me I shall spear him.' When Teichelmann persisted that it was only Jehovah who had all the power, and not Tarnda the totemic Red Kangaroo, Murlawirrapurka objected.

'Why do you charge us with a lie and reject our opinion; we don't charge you with lies; what you believe and speak of Jehovah is good, and what we believe is good.'

Teichelmann replied, 'the truth can only be on one side and it is on our side.'

'Very well,' Murlawirrapurka answered, 'then I am a liar and you speak truth. I shall not speak another word, you may now speak.'

Author: I am so happy that the Lutherans recorded these exchanges. They really show us the calibre of Murlawirrapurka.

Wauwe Woman: Yeah, what a wise man!

Wirra Woman: What a patient man – if Teichelmann had said that to me I would have hit him with his Bible.

But Murlawirrapurka was saddened. White man wanted nothing from him. All the questions the missionaries asked about Kaurna practices were only to find a way to discredit them or convert him to follow their Yova *meyunna*. After a while even Kadlitpina stopped telling his 'secrets' to Midlaitya Schurmann. He would have heartily loved him to take scarification rites and have him as a bleached brother, but he knew that Schurmann had no room for him or the precious knowledge of the Kaurna ancestors in his strange northern heart. The gulf between them seemed too wide. When Murlawirrapurka's youngest wife killed an infant at birth, Schurmann was up in arms. Kadlitpina explained that it was an old Kaurna custom to kill newborns who were small and weak.

'But Jehovah sees this as villainy and will send such murderers to hell,' insisted Schurmann.

'Well,' replied Kadlitpina, 'I don't think this is villainy at all. And besides, Jehovah is quite welcome to fry me in hell.'

Murlawirrapurka became angry when the missionaries persisted and began pestering him about the baby.

'Am I the wife? Have I borne the child? Why do you scold me?'

Wirra Woman: What a modern man!

Wauwe Woman: Oh dear, the infanticide issue. Do you know how many abortions there are in the Western "Holier than thou" world?' 200,000 per year in the UK alone. Murlawirrapurka's wife decides to kill a weak infant and we all throw our hands up in horror!

Wirra Woman: Much more likely the baby had a pale skin and she didn't know how to handle this problem. Wasn't Murlawirrapurka selling her?

At least it shows that Kaurna women were in charge of their own procreation!

Just as Midlato, Kartanya, and Kudnartu were getting used to their Lutheran teachers, things changed dramatically. The Dresden society decided to send Schurmann to Port Lincoln and Teichelmann to Happy Valley in the south of Adelaide. Midlato and her friends were sad to see them go. Samuel Klose sailed from Dresden to replace them.

Protector Moorhouse observed that 'civilising the adult natives and making them good white men', was useless. The gardens they began reluctantly cultivating were neglected, and the huts were only used as storehouses for spears. Moorhouse began to concentrate on the children. He was disparaging of the Lutherans' insistence on teaching them in Kaurna and wanted them to be taught in English. Official policy towards the Kaurna was hardening. Moorhouse believed free rations made Aborigines 'idle and unsettled'. He wanted rations used as a reward for labour and as a means of 'training the Aborigines to habits of useful industry'. A more sinister policy was evolving – to keep children away from what was seen as the bad influence of their parents.

But before these new plans came to fruition, South Australia was beset by serious violence between blacks and whites. To Murlawirrapurka, who had worked so hard for peace, this was a cruel body blow. He was distraught when he heard that a large number of whites were found murdered in Coorong in Ngarrindjeri country. A boatload of people had left Port Adelaide on the *Maria* in June 1840 for Van Diemen's Land. Among them were the Daniels, the Denhams, and their surviving five children. The *Maria* was wrecked near Encounter Bay. The twenty-six survivors had been led peacefully across barren terrain by one Ngarrindjeri clan and then passed to another, the Milmenrura. But something went badly wrong and they were massacred.

'But the Milmenrura are the same people who looked after the survivors of the *Fanny*, two years earlier, and guided them to safety,' puzzled Murlawirrapurka.

Author: Hey you *kammammi*. I'm going to play devil's advocate here. Did you know that the *Maria* massacre was the biggest slaughter of whites by blacks in the whole of settler history?

Wauwe Woman: Yeah, but there were lots of mitigating circumstances; the sailors interfered with the black women and...

Author: You know I'm sick of all this stuff about mitigating circumstances – I know that white supremacists went the other way in the 19th century, talking about ruthless savages and so on, but the fact of the matter is, not just the sailors were killed – small children were killed: Fanny Denham, aged 8; Walter Denham, aged 6; Anna Denham, aged 4; just to name three of six butchered children. But no, we're not supposed to talk about them. In the black armband view of history there's always the genocide of thousands of blacks who were killed; that is what's talked about.

Wirra Woman: Hey hey hey! You watch it. You are beginning to sound like that right-wing historian, Windshuttle, and his crony Howard. We original inhabitants of Australia were destroyed – it *was* genocide. The Ngarrindjeri had their own reasons – they were protecting their land.

Author: No they weren't. These people were survivors of a shipwreck. They weren't attacking the Ngarrindjeri...

Wauwe Woman: Yes, the sailors were – they were flouting sexual mores; punishable by death in Ngarrindjeri law. And besides, it is still no excuse for the lynchings that took place afterwards. Now that was a kangaroo court if there ever was one. The Milmenrura didn't have a chance and were strung up like rabbits by so-called civilised white men. Gawler, supposed representative of British justice, gave the nod.

Wirra Woman: And besides, the authorities in England didn't support Gawler, the lyncher. They recalled him, and rightly so. Even George Stevenson wrote in the *Register* that Gawler was wrong to condone the lynching party.

Wauwe Woman: Even many South Australian colonists thought the tragedy was the result of cross-cultural misunderstanding and sexual abuse of native women. It wasn't just the innate actions of 'blood-thirsty savages'.

Author: Murdered children were stuffed into wombat holes. Sounds pretty savage to me.

Wauwe Woman: You can have the last word for the moment, Miss Smartypants, because you are the author. But we demand to return to this issue later.

Author: Okay, we will.

As well as being censured for mismanaging the *Maria* massacre, Gawler was accused of spending too much money and plunging the fledgling Adelaide into economic crisis. This was hardly fair, as crop failures and a severe depression in the eastern states contributed, as did the frenzied land jobbing of the first few years. The new expensive gaol quickly filled up with debtors. Even the enterprising Hack was on his knees. The stores in Hindley Street stood empty. Joseph Ind, the squatter, received notice to quit without compensation. On his abandoned watermelon garden there sprang a rash of Scottish thistles, planted, some suggested, in spite.

Meanwhile, more settlers were pouring in and couldn't find work. Samuel Klose, the new Lutheran missionary, survived on potatoes that had been planted by Schurmann. Midlato warmed to Klose immediately, gathered berries for him, and showed him how to roast buttercup roots.

The economic depression had other dire consequences, which would cause more heartache for Murlawirrapurka. Plunging world wool prices lead to surplus stocks of sheep and cattle in New South Wales. Squatters decided to sell them to Adelaide, and so began the great sheep walk. Flocks of up to 6,000 sheep were transported by armed ex-convicts. The Aborigines around Rufus River, in northern South Australia, became fed up. In August 1841 they attacked, killing two overlanders and dispersing 5,000 sheep. Major Halloran, who had so proudly led the lynching party to

Coorong, was dispatched with a posse. Halfway, he was called back to Adelaide. Chomping on the bit, he was annoyed that he couldn't go and teach this bunch of natives a lesson, like he had in the Coorong. When he returned, he found that Gawler had been recalled and that new instructions were to be followed for dealing with the Rufus River incident. The British did not want a repeat of the Coorong lynchings. Not good press for the image of a law-abiding civilised British Empire. The new Governor Grey was uncompromising in his stance. Moorhouse and Taplow were sent with the next posse. Despite trying to reason with the shepherds and the Aborigines, violence still erupted, and not even Moorhouse could prevent a massacre. Dozens of Aborigines were killed. 'Lynching' was substituted with the standard chestnut, 'self defence'. Albert Taplow was in torment. Teichelmann observed the reason for the Rufus outrages was the same as in the Coorong; white men demanding black women, and failing to reciprocate.

Wauwe Woman: So it all boils down to sex. The abduction of Kirrila was just the beginning of one long fight over women. Even the great *pepa meya*, Jeffcott, killed a man over a woman and then drowned in his hasty dispatch to make sure his fiancée wasn't getting off with another.

Murlawirrapurka was saddened by the massacres of the Rufus River Aborigines. This was an example of Aborigines banding together to protect their way of life. It had failed terribly, as had other armed incursions in the eastern states. White fire-power was just too great.

When Governor Grey replaced Cockatoo Man, tough economic measures were introduced. The natives felt the pinch. Handouts became more meagre. The Kaurna watched as the colony struggled. To Ityamai-itpina's way of thinking this was inevitable. He had been appalled by white man's extravagance, like when Cockatoo Man had planted a huge expanse of grass all round the new Government House and had fenced it off. Gone were the days when he could take a leisurely stroll wherever he wanted to. Now he watched the enormous amounts of water that were dredged up from the river to keep this expanse of grass green, so that ladies in their white parasols could sit on it and drink tea. Whites were so obviously destroying the land, and flouting all the ancient laws. Like Cronk, they shot hundreds of birds, just to stuff them. This seemed so disrespectful. Whites had no idea whatsoever of the rhythm and balance of his sacred country.

As the colony floundered, Ityamai-itpina watched and waited. Perhaps whites would now take their *pindi nanto*, get back in their boats, and go back to where they came from. And then, at last, the Kaurna could reclaim their land and livelihood.

But the whites were saved. The disgraced former colonial treasurer, Osmond Gilles, discovered silver, lead, and copper in his own backyard. This, and further discoveries, bolstered the colony until adequate quantities of wheat and wool were produced for export. Whites survived by the skin of Gilles' yellow teeth. Ityamai-itpina, sorely disappointed, wandered further away with his spears. He was tired of seeing his land eroded, plundered, misused, and spoiled. He could see the ancestral spirits pining for the former gratitude that the black man always graced them with. Exploitation had supplanted gratitude.

Murlawirrapurka, who had been popular with Gawler, found Grey well disposed towards him and continued to enjoy his privileged position in the colony. Often wearing a panama hat, he made new friends readily. One of these was a teacher and artist, William Cawthorne, who took great interest in him and Kaurna customs, and regularly invited him to his house, which was a stone's throw from the river. When Adelaide life got too tedious Murlawirrapurka went off to the bush and began spending more time in his native *yarta*. He was coughing more and more, and his chest felt easier when out on his land. He could run free in the wind and nostalgically remember a time when there were no white people.

However, a growing menace from the east diverted his attention back to Adelaide, to reestablish his position as *burka* of the Tandanya clans, and deal once and for all with a terrible evil that was befalling his people. The one thing his ancestors could not abide, much worse even than the white invasion of their land, was encapsulated in one word; Moorundie. The abhorred traditional enemy of the Kaurna were straying into Kaurna territory. These people, worse than the Permangk, were filtering into Adelaide, attracted by the supply of food and blankets. The Kaurna believed much of the evil that befell them, since time immemorial, was caused by the sorcerers of this ancient river enemy. Thus, any incursion by Moorundie onto the Adelaide plains was always repulsed quick smart.

Moorundie had sporadically raided Kaurna territory for women and red ochre. But basically, they were content with their own *yarta*, the Murray River. This mighty waterway amply fulfilled their needs. They fashioned canoes out of the numerous trees that lined her banks and caught huge river fish that kept them all healthy and fat. During night-fishing sprees, the river danced prettily with the small sandalwood fires that flickered from their canoes. But with the advent of the city of Adelaide, envy grew as they watched the Kaurna rake in the advantages of white civilisation: delicious bullocky; baccy; grog; biscuits; and blankets. They wanted some of the action and began to appear on the mud streets of the town. Murlawirrapurka conducted ceremonies to see them off, and regaled them with ancestral warnings. 'Stay on your own *yarta* – listen to Tjilbruke's stories of greed and trespass – only bad will come of this!' Battles ensued, with deaths and injuries on both sides.

But the Kaurna, weakened by disease, and disruption of the old ways, couldn't keep the numbers back. Moorundie began to drift into the Piltawardli Location. Midlato froze each time she saw a Moorundie child, and refused to sit in the same classroom. Moorhouse, to his credit, saw that this was a problem and tried to devise ways to keep the Moorundie out. Klose witnessed several interclan fights, which resulted in what he described as a 'bunch of bloody heads!' The battles regularly occurred around the Queen's Birthday celebrations, when the Moorundie would come hoping for a handout. Albert Taplow was ordered to monitor any battles from atop his horse. In April 1842 such a battle incurred a fatality among the Ngarrindjeri, who had sent men to help the Kaurna. In 1843, another battle was narrowly averted.

Taplow, sitting on his gray horse, which stood sixteen hands high, was impressed by how the aggression remained contained. However, Sweetapple, his superior, thought that this 'rollicking noisy stuff' should be abolished, and the sooner it was stopped the better. Sweetapple was critical of Moorhouse and the way he tried to protect the natives. If it were up to him, he'd banish them all from Adelaide. He was instrumental in removing their 'disgusting wurlies' from the banks of the river by burning them. He had been in the party that killed several Aborigines at Rufus River, and believed interference from the Crown was uncalled for.

'What do men prancing about in their fancy carriages in London,' he would rant at Taplow, 'know about the tough life of the pioneers who are continually being harassed by these savage heathens, always trying to steal and never doing an honest day's work in their life?'

Taplow remembered Backhouse's sermon back in 1838 about his duty as a Christian towards his black brethren, and secretly thrilled at the magnificence of the natives painted in red and white ochre who wielded their spears and shields with such dexterity and courage.

Moorhouse failed to keep the Moorundie out of Adelaide, and even opened a second school for them in 1844. Murlawirrapurka was furious. Moorundie were being sanctioned in Kaurna territory 'to which they had no hereditary right.' The Queen's Birthday celebrations of 1844 were looming. Aborigines started arriving from all over the countryside wanting 'lanty bullocky and lanty blanket'. They were hoping that the recent reversal of fortunes in the colony might mean that 'no good Gubnor Gay that bloody rogue' would stop giving out 'piccaninny tuckout'. The constabulary had been warned that the aggression between Moorundie and Kaurna was reaching fever pitch.

Murlawirrapurka was determined to rid the Tandanya plain of the Moorundie, once and for all. He enlisted the help of the Ngarrindjeri and Ramindjeri clans, and Adelaide began to fill up with several hundred Aborigines. Taplow was nervous about the impending showdown. Matthew Cawthorne, Murlawirrapurka's artist friend, had witnessed many of these battles, and wrote and drew wonderful descriptions. He appreciated the grace and artistry, as well as the relatively small amount of bloodshed.

He observed that 'the Encounter Bay natives have arrived and are making shields for this interesting occasion. All are in high expectancy, parading up and down the streets in small parties with their spears and cuttas (fighting sticks), wirris (clubs) and shields.'

The Moorundie, with their allies the Permangk, were camped in the eastern Park Lands preparing their weaponry. The great fight was scheduled for 22nd April 1844 in the western Park Lands. Murlawirrapurka, looking magnificent in red and white ochre, his shield, wirra, and spear at the ready, and flanked by Kaurna and Ngarrindjeri warriors, waited expectantly. He was determined to banish the Moorundie once and for all. Cawthorne, from a rise near Adelaide, could see a massive 'moving body of blacks' converging on the designated battlefield from the direction of the sea. He described them as all 'in high glee – tattooed, oiled, ready.' This is what they had always been primed for – from their initiation rites, their secret ceremonies, and their ancestral tales of courage. They could forget for a while that an alien white race had appropriated their lands; that emus and kangaroos had retreated; that their children were being taught Arithmetic; and that strange animals were flooding their plains. They were charged with the energy of glorious battle – where they could pit their strength and skill against enemy tribes, and rest assured that the strongest would win.

Only it wasn't to be. Three mounted police had been alerted to the fact that hundreds of blacks were about to do battle. Taplow, wearing a brand-new policeman's uniform, was one of them. As they left the barracks, Constable Sweetapple thrust a musket at him.

'Looks like we're going to have trouble with the natives today.' Sweetapple cursed and swore as he headed the men and horses towards the western Park Lands. 'Bloody savages, messing up the parks, hollering and shouting – I'm going to put a stop to this once and for all!'

Taplow nervously followed.

The battle lines were drawn. Murlawirrapurka, Kadlitpina, Ityamai-itpina all stood tall, magnificent, ready. The signal to begin the spear throwing was just about to be made. The air was still. Albert Taplow dared not to even blink. *'Please let them have the dignity of one last battle,'* his heart implored the heavens. But it wasn't to be.

Constable Sweetapple thrust his steed between the two armies and fired his gun in the air.

The shot rang out, stark and alien. The Moorundie froze in terror. Murlawirrapurka was shocked. The police, though sniffing around the edges of battles in the past, had never so unceremoniously intervened before. The cannonball of reality shattered the magnificence of the occasion. White man's rules descended like a shroud over Murlawirrapurka's heart. All became slow motion as he watched the constable order the blacks to place their spears and weapons in a pile on the ground. Like some grotesque shadow play, they all meekly complied. Magnificent tall warriors visibly shrank in stature as they divested their weapons and laid them down. It was as if three mounted police had cast a spell on several hundred blacks. Taplow, the supposed white victor, propped up on his big steed with his big gun, felt terrible. Then it got worse. Sweetapple ordered him to trample over the pile of shields and spears with his horse. He froze. He saw the anguished face of Murlawirrapurka, the pathetic looks of the Moorundie, the disbelieving eyes of the Ngarrindjeri.

He couldn't move. He looked beseechingly at Sweetapple. The implacable face of white supremacy that belied the benevolent meaning of his name, looked back at him stonily. The look insisted, '*that is an order – obey!*'

Shooting pains shot through Taplow's eyes. He remained rooted to the spot. Sweetapple, with a gesture of disgust at Taplow's inertia, impatiently prodded his own steed forward. The horse's hooves trampled over the battle regalia. Carefully carved shields caved in; glass pointed spears securely bound to well honed shafts of wood snapped; painstakingly crafted *wirras* cracked. Taplow let out an involuntary groan. Something magnificent was being destroyed forever. Murlawirrapurka stared at the pile of broken weapons disbelievingly. He had held on and on – to the slender thread of hope that he and the white man could be friends. He knew then and there it was over. He had failed his ancestors, his uncle, and future Kaurna generations. His people were finished. He could not defend his land; not from the Moorundie; not from the Permangk; and not from the British Empire. Aeons of the rhythm and song of his people was ended – in this pile of broken spears. He had done all he could. He had stripped himself bare to accommodate the white man.

Kua Kertmerru Murlawirrapurka – Kaurna warrior – was broken hearted. Taplow, sitting limply on his horse looked into the anguished eyes of the defeated warrior. A blindness flashed through Taplow's brain. It blotted out what he didn't want to face.

CHAPTER 11

Demons

Sveta felt sorry for Mr Taplow. Every Saturday he lay in a darkened room with a debilitating migraine. She and Trevor were not to make a sound. She felt for Mr Taplow as she herself was often gripped by bad headaches. They had started soon after her mother had burnt her comics and refused to take her to the John Martin's Christmas Pageant.

Little did anyone know of the mammoth struggle in which Mr Taplow was engaged. For a start, he didn't mind when the first waves started to hit on a Saturday morning. He was relieved to get away from Mildred and the look of self-sacrifice glued to her face. Safely tucked away in his room, the wicked assault of the debilitating pain was preferable. Dr Peters had given him tablets for when the first symptoms hit. But they seemed to do no good at all. And he did not dare tell Dr Peters what these symptoms were. The first was usually at breakfast, when Mildred thudded about the kitchen, dutifully frying eggs and bacon, hoping her husband would be well enough to water the trees in the orchard, and attend to the countless chores which were piling up.

'The almond trees are very dry you know. I have so much mending and sewing to do. And then there's those New Australian brats coming over today. Their crazy mother can't look after them properly. I don't know. And I'm paid a pittance. But I have to do it... on your wage... and then there's some loose tiles on the roof, and then...'

It was about at this point that Albert didn't see Mildred anymore. His consciousness was swamped by a horrifying black shape that seemed to emanate from her large stomach. It had bulging eyes and seemed to be staring at him accusingly. Clutching his tablets, he staggered off mumbling, 'Migraine, migraine,' and escaped to the darkened room. Here he could get away from Mildred and the terrifying demon that seemed to live in her stomach. Sweating profusely, he swallowed the tablets and lay down on the bed, trying to dismiss the ghastly image. The migraine always followed a particular course. A bright light hovered to the left of his eyes and began to bore into his skull just above his left ear and explode into his brain. Different coloured sparks would form a ring that kept forever exploding outwards, larger and larger. The sparks would then turn into long multicoloured spears. They showered down upon him, piercing the soft tissues of his brain, before disintegrating into a series of agonising explosions. He saw huge faces of black men. They frightened him. They were not like the Aborigines he had occasionally seen hanging around outside pubs up in Port Adelaide, lolling about in a drunken stupor. These men were startlingly naked, daubed in red and white, and grimaced at him with impossibly white teeth. They beckoned him to look at a white man with whiskers and cravat, who, from a pulpit, boomed down at Taplow, 'You did not heed my warning and now a curse is upon you!' Taplow's mouth twisted in terror. Everything went black. He slipped into a state of shadowy limbo and fitful sleep, only aware of the pain that would randomly shoot through the left side of his head. It was always late afternoon before it subsided. Feeling weak and thirsty he would stumble unsteadily back to the land of the living. He was always relieved when he saw Mildred looking normal again, her striped apron swathing her large abdomen. The demon was gone, at least for another week.

While Albert Taplow struggled with his own demons, Tatiana was being subsumed by hers. There had been a temporary lull when Ivan had built a luxurious house close to the shop. Tatiana spent a lot of time and money choosing furnishings and carpets. Ivan, still as parsimonious as Sir Thomas Playford, clenched his jaw tightly as Tatiana bought lush curtains, kidney-shaped dressing tables, and expensive tulip light fittings. He had been alarmed by how much it had cost when she was admitted to the private mental hospital, and hoped that letting her buy what she wanted might do her more good. Tatiana also enjoyed working in the shop. The customers loved her pretty face and the fact that she always put a few extra slices of Fritz or corned beef into their packages. Ivan clenched his jaw even more tightly every time Tatiana went visiting. She would raid the shop's cabinets and take a side of ham or a luxury cream gateau as a present. Vlada and Kirov, who had graduated to a dilapidated asbestos dwelling among the tomato houses of Henley Beach, welcomed her joyfully. In return, they would rustle up a banquet and stay up all night talking and drinking, Tatiana enjoying the convivial camaraderie. One time, Tatiana arrived in a terrible state, pushing a pram, holding baby Sonia in one arm and with Sveta in tow. Looking nervously about her, she pushed the pram into Vlada's back porch. There, she lifted the covers. To Vlada's shock, it was full of money – £5 and £10 notes. She had never seen so much cash and was afraid.

'Vlada, I've left Ivan and I must hide this money!' The breakaway did not last. A grim-faced Ivan came in the car and collected the money, his wife, and their children. Another spell in hospital followed, and more pretty coloured pills. The doctor looked at Tatiana and said, 'I can't understand this – you have a good husband, two lovely children, and all the money that you should want. Why aren't you happy?' Tatiana just looked at him, through lithium stunned eyes. There was just no way she could even begin to explain. She also felt the doctor didn't really want to know the answer.

The brand new house with its bright shiny linoleum did not make Tatiana happy. The luminous pink tulip shaped lights did not make her happy. The latest state-of-the-art air conditioner did not make her happy. In fact, she felt riddled with guilt. She had begun to correspond again with her family in the Soviet Union, courtesy of a recent thaw in the Cold War. She did not tell them she was married to a Jew. Anti-Semitism had run rife in the village she had come from. She did not tell them she'd had an illegitimate child. An aunt who had become pregnant out of wedlock had been excommunicated. She did not tell them she was rich. From what she could read between pieces blacked out by censors, her family were poor. She sent them lavish parcels containing velvets and materials. She missed them terribly and longed to return. But as she was regarded as a hostile westerner who had betrayed her country, that was impossible. And as her demons told her, it was only a matter of time before the KGB would come for her. In fact, she became convinced that the KGB were looking for her. She imagined they were shining lights in the windows at night to try and find her. Tatiana moved her bed into the hallway away from all the windows. Sveta fervently wanted to believe her mother. Perhaps the KGB *were* persecuting her and would claim her. She too had seen the pictures of the terrified Mrs Petrov. One evening Sveta placed a neat mosaic of stones around the windows. She showed them to Tatiana next day.

'See Mama – totally undisturbed. Nobody has come.' But the demons in Tatiana's mind were telling her something different. The KGB were just very clever. Look at the elaborate plans they made to hunt down and annihilate Trotsky. She insisted that Sveta accompany her to the central police station in Victoria Square. She wanted to ask for the same police protection that kind Prime Minister Menzies had given the Petrovs.

Wauwe Woman: Oh look, there's Tatiana and Sveta coming out of the police station.

The Kaurna grandmothers were sitting among the marigolds in one of their favourite places – an original sacred Kaurna site, the Tandanyagga.

Baba Yaga: Yes, Tatiana thought she could get protection. She took poor Sveta along to translate.

Wauwe Woman: And are the police going to give it?

Baba Yaga: You must be joking. The woman detective was very rude and unkind. She ignored Tatiana, and whilst polishing her red nails, drawled to Sveta, 'This is wasting my time. Your mother needs a doctor.'

The grandmothers looked at Sveta's dejected face as she walked with her mother past the marigolds glaring in the hot sun.

Wirra Woman: Can the doctors help Tatiana?

Baba Yaga: They just give her pills which suppress the demons deeper into her subconscious. The pills cause her to have dreamless sleep. The demons just go underground and have nowhere to play. At least in dreams, the demons can act out a bit – expend some energy.

Wauwe Woman: We don't really like talking about demons. We will be accused of witchcraft and sorcery. White man will say we are backward. But we see that Tatiana is encircled by them. In our tradition our wise women and men, known rather derogatorily as sorcerers, help people tormented by demons.

Wirra Woman: It was the same in the Christian tradition. In the Bible, it says you can cast out your demons if you go to church, and that the blood of Jesus will get rid of them.

Wauwe Woman: We would really like to try and help Tatiana

Baba Yaga: Go ahead. But she must seek it first.

The group sat quietly among the marigolds, the Kaurna women fondly remembering the huge joyful gatherings that had once taken place in this very square. Instead, an imperious stone queen surveyed her subjects. Then Baba Yaga spoke.

Baba Yaga: But I have a question for you, oh Kaurna grandmothers. I've been following the story of the terrible massacre where the Milmenrura killed the twenty-six shipwrecked survivors in Coorong, South Australia, in 1842. Why did they kill all those children?

Wauwe Woman: You're one to ask. How many poor children have you fattened up and killed?

Baba Yaga: Yeah, but I had good reason.

Wauwe Woman: Well, so did the Milmenrura. Come with us on a journey and see if we can find some answers.

Baba Yaga felt herself enter a vibrational field of swirling mosaic patterns as she was hurled back through time. Gradually the swirling subsided, and she saw a pristine silver sand beach. Black men were leading a band of dishevelled white people along it. The women draped shawls around their shoulders. Some carried small children. Baba Yaga didn't really know if she wanted to be here, to witness. But she knew, as in her own tradition, all history was recorded somewhere. Nothing was ever lost. She zoomed in on an altercation that was occurring between two sailors and two Milmenrura men. It was over women. The argument became very heated, and one of the sailors, with hardened leather face and squint, cursed and spat at one of the natives. Baba Yaga found herself looking through the eyes of this Milmenrura warrior.

She gasped at what she saw. Even she, hardened by the poisonings and gruesome murders of the Stalinist purges when her own people were gripped in the most evil webs imaginable, was shocked, as she witnessed what lived in that sailor's eyes. It was pure contempt, laced with something else that was so bad that not even hatred came close. It was a derisory disdain, a blind unfathomable superiority, a dark viscous prejudice – as if the receiver of the look did not deserve a place in the world of men – as if the receiver of the look was a slimy cockroach that must be eradicated – as if the receiver of the look, just because of the hue of his skin, was to be ground beneath a white man's boot.

This same Milmenrura warrior, Mongarawata, who was the subject of the poisonous look, had helped Pastor

Longbottom and his family in similar circumstances just two years earlier. Then, he had been gratified to see humility and gratitude in the Pastor's eyes – a certain graciousness. But not so with this shipwrecked sailor, who seemed of the same ilk as many of the whalers in the area. Milmenrura sorcerers had been warning for a while that these white men who were beginning to spread over their land were not black men risen from the dead – but white evil beings who had come to destroy them. The Milmenrura were the protectors of their sacred territory – like Murlawirrapurka, giving of their resources, of their services, of their hearts; as they had with the *Fanny* survivors – and they were determined to protect it from white evil.

That night by a roaring fire, Mongarawata immersed himself in a ceremony, to receive guidance as to how to handle the situation with the shipwrecked survivors. As he settled into the rhythm of the dance, he saw a glimpse of a future he found horrendous to behold. In the vision, he could see his beloved land, but could not see his people in it. The white man had spread his poison everywhere. Strange iron animals belched fire and filth into the air. Pollution swilled the mouth of the sacred river. Large mushroom clouds billowed their deadly mist from the north. He was shocked to see a bedraggled people, his future progeny (a grey whitish colour), who had been driven from their land and who skulked in filth, decadence, and disease. The whites had smothered the once beautiful land with vast iron tracks, hard wide paths, and huge ugly shelters.

Baba Yaga, as she looked through his eyes, saw what Mongarawata saw – his people's death as a race, their lands, children, and women annihilated from the face of the earth.

He couldn't absorb that – he couldn't bear the disrespect for his ancestors, the disrespect for his wives, the disrespect for his future progeny, the disrespect for the harsh terrain they were marching through, and the blatant disregard of the thousands of years of graft and knowledge it had taken to be able to live there. Next morning he awoke, the vision still strong. He rubbed his eyes vigorously, and despite the utter beauty of the dawn, could not dispel the reality of the vision. Later, another big argument developed about the women...

Baba Yaga: Stop, I don't want to see any more. I understand. Did Mongarawata hang?

Wauwe Woman: Lynched. Yes, he took the rap. But he was fierce right up to his end. Tolmer, a police officer present at the lynching, wrote of his 'countenance, the most ferocious and demon-like I ever beheld', and when the hanging was botched...

Baba Yaga: Oh no, not another botched hanging – I thought the British were efficient.

Wauwe Woman: No, they didn't get the nooses right, but Mongarawata did not struggle. He just hung there 'glaring upwards at the crossbeam' until finally the lynching party got their act together. But I want to know; does the author understand?

Author: Yes, I understand! I understand why the Milmenrura snapped – and why they annihilated the children who would just grow up in the tradition of these white barbarians. There was no reconciliation across that divide.

Wauwe Woman: Is there today?

In the kitchen of the brand new house with the swirly patterned carpets, Ivan was counting his money on the shiny silver and red formica table. It was hot outside; filthy, in fact. But the kitchen was cool. The air conditioner hummed in the corner, turned low, so as not to blow the notes off the table. Hundreds of them were laid out in neat piles. The delicatessen was raking in a huge turnover each week.

Ivan adored his shop, and loved getting up early and stacking the shelves with all manner of goodies – displaying lavishly boxed Old Gold chocolates, refilling the lolly containers with sweet delights, and carefully displaying luscious Balfour sponges in the cake cabinet. As soon as he topped up his Coca-Cola ice-box with glass bottles of coke, they were snapped up by thirsty customers. He scooped delicious melting dollops of Amscol ice cream into McNiven's cones for hot, perspiring customers. The working-class men who inhabited the acres of Housing Trust semis which surrounded the shop received their wage packets every Friday. Even though the money was hardly adequate to feed their large families, they didn't seem to balk at spending it on stacks of cigarettes for the grownups, and bursting paper bags of lollies for the kids. The notes from their wage packets ended up on the red formica table.

As the king counted out the money, the queen entered the kitchen. Ivan's heart sank. He thought she had gone to sleep. Tatiana, bright eyed, announced.

'I can't sleep.'

'Have you taken your sleeping pills?'

'No, I'm sick of taking them – they're not doing me any good. I've thrown the packet away.' She picked up a sheaf of £5 notes.

'Look at all this money. Enough for us to go away on a holiday – perhaps to Surfers' Paradise.' She looked hopefully at Ivan. She so badly wanted to have a holiday. In all the years of the delicatessen, Ivan had only ever taken half a day off at Christmas.

'You know I can't leave the shop. There is no-one to look after it while I'm gone.'

The usual refrain.

'Pay someone – you have enough here!'

The usual riposte.

Stalemate as always.

Ivan started collecting the money grimly and putting it into a box. The last thing he wanted was to go to Surfers' Paradise. What would he do on a beach all day anyway? He loved his shop. It was his haven.

Tatiana saw red. She started grabbing the money and throwing it at him.

'You're just a stingy Jew. I should never have married you. I wish the Nazis had killed you off too!'

Ivan grabbed the money from her and pushed her away. He ran out the front door with the box and jumped into the FJ Holden. He knew when Tatiana got like this; all hell would break loose. She would start screaming, the children would wake up, frightened, the kitchen would get smashed up again! He would just drive away and sleep in the car.

Tatiana ran after the car, shouting, 'you stingy Jew!' She staggered up the road out of breath. She looked at the dark street. The pale fibro houses glowed in the moonlight. Everything was hushed. She returned to her house and hurled herself on to the front lawn, crying in despair. She called out to the stars above.

'Somebody help me, somebody help me!' In her anguish, everything went black.

She opened her eyes and saw a group of shadowy mothering shapes sitting around a fire. *I must be dreaming,* she thought.

'*Ngai wangandi marni,*' said one of them in a strange language which she had never heard. She found it very soothing.

'Welcome, you are at home. Welcome.'

Then another shape spoke to her in her own language.

'Tatiana, dorogaya, we are so pleased you have called for us. We have been waiting.'

Tatiana was amazed to hear the familiar heartening tones of her own mother tongue. She looked at the speaker. The hook-nose and iron teeth glinted in the light of the fire.

'Baba Yaga, is that you?' This was a shock. Baba Yaga was smiling at her in such a gentle way. Her mother and grandmother had always warned her how evil Baba Yaga was.

'You are at home here,' said yet another shape. Tatiana was dazzled by this woman's teeth. They accentuated the blackness of her face, which she was now making out more clearly by the light of the fire.

All she could say, rather stupidly, was, 'You are so black!' The only black people she had ever seen were at Aden, on the way to Australia.

Other black faces all looked at her kindly – murmuring, 'Yes, you are home – welcome, welcome.'

Tatiana felt the demons swirling about within her, not knowing where to settle. They could always find something to attach themselves to: an unfriendly look; an unkind word; a horrifying memory; her brother dying of starvation in her mother's arms; the anguish of the last glimpse of her mother's face as she was shoved into the Nazi cattle truck; charred bodies of children in the firestorms of Magdeburg. But not here: the love in the circle held her firmly. It was keeping all the monsters at bay.

'Talk to us, sweet one. Tell us what is troubling you.'

Feeling comforted as Baba Yaga held her hand, she began to speak. She was surprised how easy it came. She never felt able to talk to the doctors who offered a formula of supposed care that could not camouflage the matching crispness of their clinical eyes and white coats. Tatiana started speaking in halting English, and then in her native tongue. It didn't matter. She felt understood by these people. She told them about Ivan and his 'work, work, work,' mentality – of how he preferred to count his money rather than spend it; her terrible loneliness; how she ached for her family and her home country; her guilt of punishing and beating her beloved daughter Sveta – she just didn't understand what would get into her – she loved Sveta deeply, yet beat her terribly. She broke into sobs. Her tale was interspersed by sympathetic clucks and murmurs as the grandmothers received her pain.

A brew bubbled over the fire as she talked. An old black woman murmured an incantation. The brew was passed around the circle, blessed by each member and then offered to Tatiana. She drank the healing bitterness of the herbs. A curl of dark energy left her and vanished into the light of the flames. To the soothing chants of the group, Tatiana sank into a deep sleep.

Next day, Sveta came into the kitchen for breakfast. Her favourite breakfast of all time, semolina swirling with black cherries, was on the table. Tatiana, the perfect mother, pinny on, smiled at her from the sink. Sveta was shocked to see her mother looking so happy. Tatiana looked brighter and clearer than she had in a long time.

'Sveta, dorogaya! I want to talk to you, but eat your breakfast first.' Sveta spooned the delicious kasha into her mouth and wondered what was going on. She hadn't heard the Russian word for 'darling', nor had her breakfast cooked, in such a long time. When she had finished Tatiana brought some tea and held Sveta's hands as she spoke to her.

'I know I have been difficult to live with, and I have been giving you and your sister a very hard time. I am especially sorry for the way I have treated you, how cruel I have been to you. I just don't know what came over me. I am very sorry for the way I have beaten you. I don't know if you can ever forgive me. I am so sorry.'

Sveta looked into her dear mother's heart shaped face and was so pleased to have her own sweet mama back. She forgave her instantly.

Tatiana continued. 'You are now twelve years old. You have just started High School. You are a young adult. I want you to go into Adelaide on your own next Saturday. You are now old enough.'

Sveta had never gone into town on her own before. It seemed very big and scary, and she wasn't sure she could find her way around. She couldn't believe her mother was saying all this. This mother who was always so anxious about every move she made – this mother who wanted her home from school on the dot of four o'clock – this mother who obsessed about her every movement. This mother, looking remarkably normal in her flowery apron, was now telling her to go into big Adelaide, all on her own!

'I want you to get yourself something very beautiful to honour your passage into young adulthood.'

With this she gave Sveta a sheaf of notes.

'Make sure you buy yourself something you really like when you go into Adelaide.'

The following Saturday, with great excitement, Sveta boarded the bus. She was wearing her brand new watch she had received for her birthday, and in her bag was the money Tatiana had given her to spend.

Later that day Tatiana walked into the shop. It was a lull after the lunch crowd had cleaned out the little glass side oven of pies, pasties, and sausage rolls. Just pastry flakes were left, which Ivan was clearing out.

'Ivan, I want to talk to you about Sveta.' Ivan continued cleaning out the oven trays.

'Sveta is twelve years old now, and we need to spend some money on her.'

Ivan's dander was up immediately.

'Whaddya mean we must spend money on her. We just spent a fortune on her High School uniform and all the new books.'

'Yes, I know all that,' said Tatiana. 'But she is a young woman now and I want her to have a sewing machine and sewing lessons.' Tatiana had always regretted that she had not been taught to sew. 'And I would like her to learn music. I want her to have a piano.'

'A piano! Whaddya think I am? Made of money? What she need to play piano for!'

He furiously started to polish the glass front of the display cabinet.

'But Ivan, what is all this money for?'

Ivan was close to bursting a blood vessel.

'I tell you what it is for. I built you a beautiful house, full of expensive furniture. Sveta, she needs an education. Sonia, she needs an education. You want clothes, holidays. Nah! I need Sveta to work in the shop. No fancy piano!'

Tatiana felt the tension rise in her stomach. She tried to stay reasonable but it seemed hopeless. She hated the intransigent meanness that flared from Ivan's nostrils. She felt the clarity she had enjoyed the last few days begin to cloud over. She looked at Ivan's pinched, miserly face and felt fury. The demon inside her head began to stir.

'Ivan please, listen. It is very important. We must discuss Sveta's future. She does very well at school, but needs to learn other things too.'

Ivan went on cleaning. 'There is nuttin' to discuss. Now I must finish this. Customers will be in soon. Where is Sveta? I need her to help.'

'I sent Sveta to Adelaide. I told her to buy something nice for herself.'

'You what? I slave away all day here and she prancing in Adelaide spending money!'

As his voice rose, Tatiana's demon rose. All the anti-Semitic feelings of her past stirred in her guts and fed the demon, hungry for tidbits of hatred, hopelessness, and blind prejudice. It grew frighteningly fast. Through its eyes she saw an ugly, mean Jew who stood in the way of her happiness and the happiness of her children. Calm and clarity slipped out of the back door, unnoticed. She went to the till, took a handful of coins and threw them at Ivan's face. Taken by surprise, he staggered backwards. Above the till were the next casualties – attractively arranged boxes of Milk Trays and Old Gold chocolates were unceremoniously swiped sideways. Next went all the cigarettes – neatly stacked they were – piles of Craven'As, Peter Stuyvesants, Camels, and Rothmans, bouncing effortlessly off the shiny surfaces of the mirrors. Tatiana, now in rampaging mode, could not stop. She picked up the jars of lollies and smashed them to the floor. Ivan, who prided himself on the neatness and spotlessness of his shop, scrabbled to pick up the scattered pink and yellow balls that rolled everywhere.

'Stop it you bitch! Stop it! You want to destroy everything I've worked for!'

But Tatiana's demon was wild. It wanted to destroy the shop, it wanted to destroy the Jew, it wanted to destroy this offering to Mammon. Down came all the silver milkshake containers with a clatter. The demon liked that! It engorged itself with the hatred and vengeance of aeons. Ivan tried to stop the raging Tatiana, but with superhuman strength she pushed him away. She lunged at the cash register, wrenched out the tray and threw it all over the shop. Customers who were just about to enter scurried back outside in alarm. Coins hit the walls and rolled all over the floor. Ivan could see his shop, his empire, his hard-earned palace, being ripped apart by this mad woman, his wife. He went berserk. The jaw that held fast when Jewish neighbours swung from gibbets after the Odessa siege, the jaw that held fast when Jewish women and children were herded into large sheds and burnt alive, the jaw that held fast when his beloved parents were marched to their deaths, snapped.

'You fucking bitch. You fucking ruin my life!'

He bashed Tatiana repeatedly across her face and arms. While she reeled, with blood dripping from her mouth, he pushed her roughly through the back door of the shop and into the corrugated shed outside, where he kept crates of drinks and extra supplies. He slammed the door shut and drew the bolt. Ignoring Tatiana's demonic shrieking and frenzied banging, he rang Dr James. Trembling with fury, he rasped down the mouthpiece.

'Tatiana has gone mad. She has stopped taking her pills. Come quick.'

Sveta walked down Rundle Street, in central Adelaide, going into all the shops. She loved the freedom. She was a young adult who could decide where to go and what to spend. She felt a little small and a bit frightened of the crowds, but relished being part of them. She went into the Myer basement where all the bargains were. Even though Tatiana had said she could buy what she liked, Ivan had instilled in her a fear of spending too much money. She thought if she bought something as a bargain then she could put any money left over into her piggy bank. Save it for a rainy day. 'You never know when you might need it,' Ivan would warn, remembering bitterly that money could have saved his parents from the Nazis. Among the sale items in the basement she found a red, white, and blue jumper. These were her favourite colours – the colours of the Union Jack. The jumper was reduced from £4 to £2 pounds and fifteen shillings; a good save! She bought it. She decided then to go down Hindley Street to a delicious German cake shop. Tatiana often took her there and giggled, 'Don't tell Ivan.' She bought a chocolate cake and a creamy coffee. If this was being an adult, she loved it. She walked past Government House to her bus stop. It was now well and truly sealed off from the general public. No longer could anyone, whatever the hue of their skin or sound of their language, innocently invade those hallowed grounds for a picnic. She enjoyed the bus ride home, exhilarated by her adventure. As the bus reached her stop, she noticed a crowd of people around the shop, and an ambulance. The exuberance of her outing turned into fingers of ice that clutched her heart. Something was wrong. She rushed around to the back of the shop, only to see her mother being put on a stretcher. She seemed to be asleep. Dr James was putting away a syringe. Ivan, pale and tight-lipped, told her to go home and look after Sonia.

On May 6 1960, Trotsky's killer Mercader was released from Lecumberri prison and flown to Moscow. He was decorated a 'Hero of the Soviet Union'.

In the west of South Australia, near Maralinga, a two-headed lamb was born.

In Hendon, Mrs Taplow was diagnosed with terminal stomach cancer. It had grown to the size of a cabbage.

CHAPTER 12

Comets

'When beggars die, there are no comets seen; the heavens themselves blaze forth the death of princes.'
— William Shakespeare

A profoundly dejected Albert Taplow led his horse from the scene of Murlawirrapurka's aborted last stand on the Tandanya plain. William Cawthorne, who had witnessed the carnage of the weapons, wrote, 'The astonishment that this act produced was truly remarkable – some looked quite aghast, others were confounded, and many doubted their senses, whether such a collection of beautiful windas (fighting spears) and shields, kylahs (hunting spears) midlars (woomeras), were absolutely to be destroyed... Poor fellows they were very much cut up. I pitied their hard case. Oh! It was cruel of the police.'

Murlawirrapurka broke out of his trance and angrily confronted Cawthorne, who wrote down the exchange.

'What for policeman do this? When white men fight in Adelaide, black fellow say nothing. When blackfellow fight, policeman come and break spears, break shields, break all; no good. What for, you no stop in England!'

Murlawirrapurka had come to the end of his tether. He was sick of having to endure humiliation after humiliation.

His good humour had run out. Why hadn't the white man just stayed in England?

'But what for you fight?' asked Cawthorne

'What for? Me tell you,' replied Murlawirrapurka, 'but no good tell you.' (When had white man listened to his counsel or asked him for advice – he was just a joke – King John in his silly panama hat – a curiosity for a settler to throw a shilling to. Or give his wife a cheap fuck!)

'You write in the paper,' he continued to Cawthorne, 'and tell white men what for we fight. Before white man come, Murray black fellow never come here. Now white man come, Murray black fellow come too. Encounter Bay and Adelaide black fellow no like him. Me want them to go away. Let them sit down in at the Murray, not here. This is not his country!'

What would Cawthorne know about cultural authority and the deep law of the land and its boundaries? Murlawirrapurka had spent long hours explaining it to Teichelmann and Schurmann in both Kaurna and English. He thought that they may have understood a bit. But an impenetrable shield circled white men's brains. They lived on another planet. Totally ignorant.

But the Moorundie – they had cultivated their deep affinity for their land for thousands of years – they had their own strict customs, taboos, and knowledge. They knew all too well the boundaries and the rules. It seemed white man was spreading the curse of greed; the Moorundie were seduced by white man's abundance, blinded by his bottomless waterhole of baccy, grog, and biscuits. Avarice and envy led them to stray from their boundaries and into the sacred place of the Kaurna. They should know better.

Murlawirrapurka had finally been stripped of everything; land, traditions, livelihood, and now of his Kaurna cultural authority, and it was due to the white invasion.

'Why for you not stop in England!'

The Kaurna grandmothers sit in silence, heads bowed as they hold Murlawirrapurka and his plaintive cry in their embrace, across the trajectory of time.

Wauwe Woman: It killed him, you know. He died within nine months. All of thirty-five he was. Not even grey headed yet. Usually we only accord grey heads with the title of *burka*, 'old wise man'. But he was a *burka* way before his time.

The Queen's Birthday celebrations that year were a subdued affair, with 800 natives, mostly Moorundie, attending. As Cawthorne wrote, 'Moorhouse announced that they were to file up to Government House to receive some bread and beef and some of them received blankets also, but I am sorry to say many were disappointed in both.'

The glory of the old days, when there was even a glimmer of hope that the white man would honour the black man, were long gone. For Murlawirrapurka the dance was over. Since the Wirra hangings, the Rufus River massacres, and now the Moorundie invasion, he felt overwhelmed by the trauma his people were facing. Events were happening too fast to be absorbed by the time honoured traditional methods of dance, song and storytelling.

He felt sad and defeated. Eight *wiltutti* had come and gone since white man had landed on the Tandanya plain. A few random tents had now expanded into a burgeoning town. The number of whites had rapidly increased to ten thousand. The number of Kaurna had rapidly decreased to a trickle. He himself had lost two wives and five children. He mourned each one terribly. Schurmann had recorded the death of the first son.

'The following incident …is evidence of the tender love of parents for their children. A small child of Murlawirra died, whereupon all who were present mourned so deeply and so loud that it was moving to see and to hear. The father held his child, wrapped in a kangaroo skin, on his lap, his head covered with a blanket. He poured out streams of tears, which were constantly renewed when the others, one after the other, threw themselves down beside him, lowered their faces over the child and brought him a rich offering of tears.'

Murlawirrapurka was coughing more and more, and feeling weaker. He spent his time quietly at Piltawardli. Another son died. He cradled the child in his arms and looked sadly up at the star-studded night. As he tried to find consolation in the great celestial river, the Wardliparri, he was arrested by the luminescent blue of the Ngakallomurro, or 'parakeet ashes', known to whites as the Magellanic Clouds; dwarf galaxies perched just outside the Milky Way. In Kaurna lore, it was here that flocks of beautiful birds were lured by trickery, and then killed and roasted. As he stroked his dead son's hair, he felt kinship with these birds. It seemed a giant cosmic trick had been played on his people; they were tricked, trapped and now being roasted alive. It had taken the wanton destruction of his weapons to face the blatant truth: his people were being destroyed. While he had his spears, he still had the illusion of power over his destiny. He had seen the warning signs when a spectacular comet appeared the previous year. He had ignored them.

The great comet of 1843 caused widespread panic all over the world, similar to that caused by the meteors of 1832, which had so frightened Midlato and augured her mother's death. Apprehending the approach of Judgement Day, crowds filled the churches of the Christian world. Movements like Methodism reaped a harvest of new souls. In New York, fifty thousand people donned white ascension robes, because their leader William Miller proclaimed the end of the world.

The comet, with bright silver nucleus, had emerged in the southwestern sky, its giant forked tail sweeping fire into the Wongayerlo, and terror into the hearts of local indigenous people. Schurmann noted the effect on the Port Lincoln clans, who told him that comets were 'harbingers of death'. It was even more portentous if the tail was forked. The Moorundie were convinced that the appearance of the twin-tailed comet was the result of powerful Wirra sorcery. It was retaliation for the imprisonment in the Adelaide jail of a principal of the Wirra clan for attacking a shepherd. The Moorundie were so worried about this that they went to the explorer Edward John Eyre, stationed on the Murray, and pleaded with him to go to Adelaide and secure this man's immediate release. Only this would avert the evil intended by the comet. Otherwise they told Eyre the comet would overthrow Adelaide, destroy all Europeans and their houses, and then sweep destruction up the Murray River. Murlawirrapurka had been so caught up in this plausible explanation that he ignored what he knew deep down, the real message of the ominous forked tail – the death of his people.

And now, Murlawirrapurka stroked the limbs of his precious little son, limbs that would never grow into those of a Tandanya warrior, and wept bitter tears. The end of his world had come. In his anguish, he drew sustenance from the image of Tjilbruke spilling tears as he carried his beloved dead nephew over his *yarta*.

Midlato wandered about distraught. Her *kammammi* was now totally blind, and she tried to comfort her as much as she could. At least she had warm blankets, which Midlato's attendance at school had ensured. The young girl felt deeply sad throughout that winter of 1844. It seemed the world was dying around her. She avoided the Moorundie children who skulked at the edge of her river. Summer came and with it, hordes of grasshoppers. All the gardens of Adelaide were destroyed, as a plague measuring three miles wide and seven miles long flew in 'as thick as snowflakes in Europe'. At the Piltawardli, everything was eaten down to the roots.

Just like us, thought Midlato as she covered her *kammammi* lovingly, and looked in on Murlawirrapurka who, coughing incessantly, was now confined to his *wardli* at the back of the Location. She felt that the plague was another omen. Kadlitpina was convinced it was the Wirra sorcerers. As grasshoppers chomped their way through Adelaide and obliterated Christmas, a dying Murlawirrapurka asked Midlato to help him walk to a rise behind Piltawardli, so he could watch the sunset. He leaned on Midlato's shoulder as their beloved Tindo sank into the Wongayerlo. As the sky turned orange, Murlawirrapurka glimpsed something hovering above the horizon. Another comet! This was unbelievable. Never had comets appeared so closely together. He felt his ravaged lungs tighten, as little breath remained in them to sustain him. He pointed the comet out to Midlato, thinking his eyes were playing tricks. Midlato saw it too and her stomach convulsed in dread. Yes. Unmistakable. This comet seemed to emanate from the rays of the setting sun. Its bright silvery head was similar to the previous comet but this one had a smaller tail, unmistakably forked; like the tongue of a serpent dripping fire. Murlawirrapurka didn't even dare to acknowledge to himself what this meant. His high level of initiation in the Tarnda clan had given him access to deeper secrets, which though bringing greater knowledge also brought the concomitant burden of responsibility. He sighed deeply and let Midlato lead him back to Piltawardli. They told the blind *kammammi* what they had seen. She didn't seem shocked. She just nodded knowingly. They all felt that the comet was auguring the end of the Kaurna as they knew it. Only the *kammammi* knew an even deeper significance. She just squeezed Murlawirrapurka's hand tightly.

Murlawirrapurka, his health failing fast, continued his vigil watching the comet as it brightened over the evening sky. It was as awesome as it was fearful. He had tried to ignore the truth when he had seen the forked tail of the previous comet. He had clung to the hope that he could just share his beloved plains with the whites and keep the Moorundie out. But now the ancient enemy was here. He looked towards the east where the giant ancestor Ngano lay, purplish and magnificent in the evening light; the giant had given his life, keeping eastern men out, and continued to lie there guarding the beautiful Tandanya plain. Murlawirrapurka felt he had let him down. Eastern men had seeped in. The ancestor had died in vain. The *burka* knew that the appearance of this new comet, so quick on the forked tail of the previous one, was portentous, and driving the message home. The Kaurna no longer controlled the Tandanya plain. It also augured his own death.

Murlawirrapurka died a few days later, on January 2nd 1845. Midlato felt the ancestors had come to take him home.

Cawthorne recorded, 'His bier is stuck around with spears and he is to be carried down to his own country, Mypunga. He is lamented by both blacks and whites.'

The *South Australian* honoured Murlawirrapurka with a lengthy obituary.

'King John was one of the first natives the settlers of the province ever saw, and, by constantly mixing with the whites, he had acquired a considerable knowledge of the English language and, by many, was looked upon as a great favourite... He was always decent and peaceable with respect to the Europeans, and would occasionally submit to labour, but nothing could alter his habits of vagrancy, or love of wandering in the bush, far away from the haunts of civilised man. His opportunities for hearing the Gospel spoken to him in his own tongue were numerous, and he would listen patiently to any statements on this subject, but his attachment to the superstitions in which he was brought up, were invincible.'

Wauwe Woman: And there you have it! A succinct description of the clash of worldviews.

Murlawirrapurka's remaining two wives carried his body all around his beloved *yarta*. Every evening they would stand, tears streaming down their faces, and watch the comet which grew brighter above the Wongayerlo. The funeral rites lasted several months, and he received all the honours accorded to a *burka* of the Kaurna people.

Wauwe Woman: We buried him properly – he was a great *burka* – we don't care how strange white men think our burials – curiosities in anthropological museums – superstitious gobbledy-gook – quaint. You know, when we traditionally moved Murlawirrapurka's dead body to all the corners of the white man's compass, white man had no clue of the subtle energies we invoked; the spirit of that great man was blended with the spirits of the land, the spirits of his ancestors. As a result, the great *burka's* energy is still with us.

Wirra Woman: So, you can understand how dreadful it was for us when the bodies of Yerraitya and Wangutya were not given to us. Or our body parts taken to museums.

Wauwe Woman: We can't even begin to explain the importance of our death rituals. White man is so one dimensional, and to make things worse he thinks himself superior. We see him with his gun as bolster, crudely walking through our territory – no rhythm – no sensitivity – absolutely no song! No real knowledge – just book knowledge calcified in his brain, setting in stone a fixed viewpoint he has on the world; Latin and Greek phrases, honed with a cane in expensive British boarding schools, giving him the illusion of refined intelligence. Hmmph!

Murlawirrapurka's dried body was put up in a tall gum tree high above his beloved home territory. The brilliant silver comet with the forked tail dissolved into the starry dome.

Back in Adelaide, Midlato walked to the Tandanya Rock. To her shock, it was gone. Blown apart by gunpowder and used to build Parliament House. Like all conquering nations who destroy ancient civilisations, the British were no exception. They had blown a hole in the Kangaroo Dreaming. Kaurna's main *Burka* was gone; and now the main religious centre was gone too.

Midlato stood desolate in the yawning emptiness. She noticed something scurrying among the gaping holes where the Rock had stood majestically for aeons. A surprise. A bush-tailed bettong. These gentle inquisitive creatures had been virtually eradicated by white man's cats and foxes.

Wauwe Woman: Yeah, also like the spotted-tailed quoll which had once preyed on wallabies and insects. As white man's dictionary describes, 'It was not abundant and its presence and subsequent disappearance went almost unnoticed.' Just like our people.

Midlato continued at school despite the fact her clans-people were urging her to marry, join them, and leave school. The handouts from the Protector were diminishing. Her people were no longer prepared to sit through exhortations of how Jehovah would punish them if they did not relinquish their beliefs, in order to get a biscuit.

Klose was having financial problems and could hardly subsist on the small stipend from the Dresden Society. His days were numbered, as Governor Grey agreed with Moorhouse and disapproved of him teaching in the Kaurna language. Midlato loved learning and writing in her language, and wanted to stay at school to continue to do so. She constantly consulted the Kaurna textbook Schurmann and Teichelmann had published. And she wanted to stay with Klose. She and he were fond of each other. Klose loved his students right from the beginning. As he wrote to Dresden, 'During the lessons, the children sit quietly and pay attention, so that it is a pleasure to be with them. I am just waiting for a time when I shall possess a sufficient command of the language to be able to tell them stories from the sacred history, for they are not lacking in intelligence, as is generally believed. Not at all! I find no difference if I am among European children or among these, other than they are black and not clothed. Often, as a matter of fact, their faces appear so familiar, as if I had seen them as whites in Europe.'

Klose set about translating more of his Bible into Kaurna and was pleased when Midlato and Kartanya's written work improved in leaps and bounds. Examples sent to Dresden impressed the society with their neatness and perfection. At the time of Governor Gawler's departure, the children wrote letters of farewell and thanks in the Kaurna language. Midlato was proud to have mastered the quill and ink, and proud to gracefully curve the precious Kaurna words over 'pepa'. She missed her friend Kudnartu, who had gone back up north to work on a sheep station.

Midlato and Kartanya were able to read and write in English, and understood the English number system. In learning how to tell the time on the big church clock, they had a glimpse into how white-skins thought and saw the world. Midlato became quite a seamstress, and had sewn a shirt for Klose and a dress for herself. She glowed with pride when Klose told her it was as good as shirts he had brought with him from Dresden. She marvelled at the fineness of the needle, but still kept her old bone needle with which she had once sewn possum pelts. Even though she hankered after that time, she was not prepared to go back to the old ways. They had lost their original enchantment, as the beautiful land was now owned by settlers. She was constantly hard pressed by Aboriginal men to leave the school and marry, but she desisted. Her friend Kartanya did succumb, and much to Klose's disappointment left to get married. Midlato felt bereft. Her two closest friends had now gone. She had heard that Kudnartu had attracted the attention of John Adams, a white shepherd.

Klose knew his time was running out, and anxious that the children would be indoctrinated as much as possible in the Dresden way, stepped up the teaching of the scriptures in Kaurna. He vainly battled to the bitter end to gain converts. But whatever he tried, the Kaurna would not give up their beliefs. When chastising a group of young men who were about to be tattooed, 'I told them that was not right since Jehovah had given them a good, healthy skin, why should they now pierce it. The response was: 'Yes we know all that; the whites do not do it, but that is what the blacks do.'

'If one proclaims the Word of God to them and draws attention to their sins, while referring to such truths as the fact that Jehovah will punish them in eternity, they burst out in loud laughter.'

Wauwe Woman: Sounds a pretty healthy response to me!

Moorhouse finally withdrew all support. He decided to close down the Piltawardli Location and combine the Moorundie and Kaurna children into one school, where only English would be taught. But worse was that he wanted to continue a practice already started at Piltawardli: the precursor of the 'Stolen Children' phenomenon. Native children were to be separated from their parents and compelled to sleep in dormitories.

The Dresden missionaries' long battle to teach the Kaurna in their native language was finally lost. Reluctantly, they admitted defeat. Ever since Teichelmann and Schurmann had sailed over with Governor Gawler, they'd had to fight for their belief that the best way to convert the natives was by learning their language. Gawler and most whites didn't think so. They were of the opinion that learning to write in Kaurna would only encourage the natives to stick to their ways and beliefs; 'by adhering to the native language, the children are more deeply confirmed in their original feelings and prejudices, and more thoroughly kept under the influence and direction of their own people.'

Ironically, Piltawardli school was to be moved to where the sappers and miners lived, near Government House. This had been the headquarters of those who exploded the banks of the Torrens for stone: the very men who had blasted the Tandanya Rock into oblivion.

The inevitable came abruptly. On the 3rd of July, in the winter of 1845, sappers barged into the Piltawardli Location and began ripping the rooves off the natives' huts. Rain fell on Midlato's blind *kammammi*. Klose confronted the sappers and said they should leave at least one roof up, to give the old woman and six other old people shelter. 'No, it is the Governor's order that no native shall remain any longer within the fence!' With that they tore down the last hut. Midlato led her trembling grandmother to shelter under a tree.

That evening, Klose and his wife gathered the remaining children, nine boys and nine girls, for a farewell tea. His wife baked a cake which she served with wild mint tea. Midlato was in floods of tears, and could not understand why Klose was not coming with them. Many children were crying, and Klose himself was sad, as this was the end of an era.

Midlato and the remaining children walked disconsolately to the building vacated by the destroyers of the Tandanya Rock. She was forced to share lessons with the enemy Moorundie. The white people did not seem to realise how awful that was for her. Fortunately, she could escape at night to the separate Kaurna dormitory. All the lessons were now in English. Midlato was sad. She used to love reading the hymns that were written in her own beloved tongue.

Her *kammammi*, because of her frailty and blindness, was eventually allowed to stay in a *wardli* at the Location. But no food was sent and the old woman came close to starving. Klose intervened and asked for provisions from Protector Moorhouse. Next day, a half a sack of flour and ten pounds of sugar arrived. Midlato begged an egg from Bridget Hack and made her grandmother a cake. But the woman was getting weaker. She summoned her granddaughter, and because she could no longer see, held her hand tightly. Tears fell from the sightless eyes.

'I must go soon, my precious *kamilya*, my daughter's daughter. I am sorry to leave you like this when our people are so wounded. You are young and must stay strong.'

She put her hands over Midlato's face. She remembered how pretty she was. And this worried her terribly. She had managed to use her influence to keep Midlato in school and not be married off to the many suitors who were waiting to nab her. She knew that now she could not stop them. She had been sad when Kartanya who, like Midlato, was so good at white man's learning had been whisked off, and when Kudnartu had gone north and was now betrothed to the white shepherd John Adams. She shuddered at what lay in store for these girls. Used as prostitutes in exchange for sheep. Her heart ached for the dismal future of her people. Their song was being trampled into the mud by greedy, dissolute white men, and their bullocky and theep. But she took consolation from the fact that the ancestors had whispered to her that the song would just go underground – the white man would stamp it down ferociously or blast it away, like with the Tandanya Rock, but would never be able to destroy it altogether. The rhythms of the songs would quiver in every eucalypt leaf, in every small yellow stamen of a wattle flower, in every teardrop of Tjilbruke's magic springs.

'Just remember, my sweet *kamilya*, that whatever happens I am with you always. Our old way of life is over, but our spirit is strong. White man does not know it yet – but we have deep wisdom – a wisdom garnered over aeons – a wisdom that glints in the eye of a spotted quoll or in the vibrant blue of a blue tongue lizard, in the red and yellow of a *pilyabilya's* wings. One day, white man will be able to hear it. This fact is written clearly in the stars. It will not happen in your lifetime but it will definitely happen. You take your white learning and live with whites, but you also teach what you know to anyone who is able to listen.'

Midlato nodded miserably as her *kammammi* continued.

'If you were to go and marry, I would be giving you a fire-stick to carry with you – but instead I place a fire-stick in your heart. Let it glow always with the heat of my love. And don't hanker for a golden past – life is a constant unfolding towards something new – hopefully always better.'

Large tears fell on to Midlato's hands. She rubbed the precious drops over her face, soaking in the salty wisdom of this wonderful woman, without whom she didn't know how she would cope. The next day she tramped along the river and hunted out some fat white grubs. Her *kammammi* savoured the creamy and nourishing goodness. It was her last taste of the old days before she silently joined her ancestors. Midlato lay sobbing on her frail chest, imbibing every bit of ebbing warmth.

Kadlitpina and Ityamai-itpina were lost without their *Burka*. The centre of their world, as symbolised by him and the Tandanya Rock, had been destroyed. They felt impotent as Moorundie begged for baccy on the streets of Adelaide. Further insult ensued as their *wardlis* were banned from the Adelaide centre and burned. Instead, strange destructive English habits were transplanted on to their sacred territory. As well as the ridiculous water-guzzling lawns that sprouted around lavish villas, the gentlemen therein engaged in a curious pastime upon their *pindi nanto*. It was called 'hunting with foxes.'

In Kaurna law, animals were never hunted and killed for fun. Imported foxes multiplied and devoured a host of defenceless marsupials. Ityamai-itpina couldn't bear it any more and abandoned his sacred country. He took his family further north. Kadlitpina moved away too. Many of the Kaurna who stayed in Adelaide soon fell foul of some British law or other and ended up in gaol. Klose visited many of them in prison, and managed to have at least one death sentence commuted. The prison experience was to become part and parcel of Aboriginal life: degradation, humiliation, and deference to the white man. In the next century, prison would become the new initiation rite for young blacks.

Wauwe Woman: Give me circumcision and tattooing any day
– a much more noble way.

Midlato endured school where Moorundie classmates off-
ended her sensibilities. It was made more bearable when her
friend Kudnartu came back and joined her. The white
shepherd Tom Adams wanted to marry her, and she
returned to school to learn sewing, cooking, and more
English. Midlato often wondered what it would be like to
be with a white man. She felt caught between two worlds.
In limbo.

One evening in the dormitory, she was surprised by a
visit from her old friend Lucy Bradshaw. Lucy's brother, a
doctor in North Adelaide, was looking for live-in help for
his three children. Midlato jumped at the opportunity. She
was delighted to be near her beloved river, and to have
the opportunity to see Lucy. While she still saw a lot of
Kudnartu, she embarked on her new life with relish. She
enjoyed taking the Bradshaw children down to the river
where she taught them the Kaurna way to catch *kungurla*.
She also taught them string games.

However, she had to make sure she was always accompanied
by the children whenever she was out. Danger stalked her
from men, both black and white. Black men pestered her
to come back to what was left of the old way of life. She was
tempted. She would have loved to go hunting and fishing
and beating rhythms for the *palti*. But she knew that life
was over. She would inevitably just become entertainment
for white men. It broke her heart that Kartanya, who had
married a black man, was continually being sold to white
men for food.

But Midlato also had to be on her guard from white men. The colony was still seriously short of women, and she was continually being cajoled. She was lucky. An Aboriginal servant girl had been badly beaten by a settler in October 1846, after he attempted to rape her in full view of five soldiers of the 11ᵗʰ Regiment. Midlato remained protected within the harbourage of Dr Bradshaw. He was kind and decent, not like Dr Wright, whom she had often seen rolling home drunkenly from some tavern or other.

Wauwe Woman: Ah yes, Dr Wright, our drunk disorderly *yammaiamma*. What happened to him?

Author: Well, he stood for trial for manslaughter in March 1845, after a patient in his care died. Negligence, drunkenness, and overuse of opium and morphine were alleged. He was acquitted on a technicality, but the judge held him morally responsible because he was drunk. In defence, he claimed to have 'taken only the quantity becoming a gentleman after dinner'. He eventually sloped off to the goldrushes in the eastern states.

One of Dr Bradshaw's regular patients was Albert Taplow, who suffered debilitating headaches. Besides giving him opium, there was little Bradshaw could do. Taplow was of a nervous disposition and always jumped if he saw Midlato. One afternoon, he surprised her in the doctor's hallway by mumbling, 'I'm so sorry. I'm so sorry.' His headaches became so bad that he was unable to fully execute his duties as a policeman. He was given a desk job and settled quietly with his wife and children in Norwood, where he set up a Quaker meeting house.

The time for Kudnartu's marriage drew nearer. Midlato helped Kudnartu make her wedding dress for the civil ceremony. It was the first official union in Adelaide between an Aborigine and a white. Bishop Short refused to sanction this marriage in a church.

Kudnartu was getting a mixed reaction from her relatives. Many thought she was selling out. Midlato was one of the very few who understood. Both she and Kudnartu had walked into the white man's world too far to go back. They could speak good English. They could sew with white man's materials and cook English food. They had glimpsed white man's universe. Klose had given them geography lessons with maps and objective measurements. They had learnt the monetary difference between a penny and a sovereign. They could see that white man had usurped the black man and there was no going back. They lived in a curious half-way world.

With the help of Mrs Klose and some of the Methodist ladies who had taught them to sew, the young girls had fun assembling the wedding dress, blue muslin with lace on the bodice and full sleeves. To get the dress to billow out more stiffly, they fashioned a horsehair underskirt to fit beneath the petticoats. Midlato and Kudnartu giggled at the preposterous nature of English dress, but also could not help marvelling at the finery of the materials. Midlato helped coiffure Kudnartu's long thick hair into ringlets. But to try and stuff it into a poke bonnet looked ridiculous, so they let it hang over her shoulders. To complete the outfit, Kudnartu wore dainty heeled white lace-up boots boots with a delicate blue leather trim.

The wedding on January 27th 1848 created quite a stir. The bride attracted favourable comments about her looks and clothing. A reporter noted in the *Register* that Kudnartu, 'Is, for one of her race, remarkably good looking, and has a pleasing expression of countenance... and speaks good English.'

As Midlato continued with her domestic duties, she watched the development of Kudnartu's marriage with great interest. She was able to catch up with her when she and her husband came to Adelaide for a trial two years later. Kudnartu had found the body of a murdered neighbour and was called to testify. It was wonderful for them to see each other. But if Midlato had any illusions of what it was like to marry a white man, they were blown by what Kudnartu told her.

After her marriage to Adams, Kudnartu had been awarded with some land, previously put aside by the Protector for Aboriginal occupation, Block 346 at Skillogolee Creek. Moorhouse believed John Adams to be an opportunist who had only married Kudnartu to gain land. As a poor shepherd, he was not in a position to acquire land himself. However, whatever his intentions had been, taking possession of this land proved difficult in practice. The newlyweds couldn't even afford to put up fencing. Being a carpenter, Adams built a modest house, but the money ran out. And he spent much on drink. One of the biggest problems was that their land was on a sheep and bullock track, and several drays stopped each day at the watering hole near their house. This meant that animals stomped all over their property and their droppings attracted legions of blowflies. But far worse, drivers, drunk on rum from a nearby tavern, turned their lascivious attentions on Kudnartu. Attempts by Adams to get help from Kudnartu's supposed Protector to alleviate this state of affairs were fruitless. Moorhouse did not trust

Adams and was suspicious of his motives. Unfortunately, the vulnerable Kudnartu did not receive the protection she needed.

Midlato went to court to support Kudnartu. The latter, 'neatly dressed in the costume of white women of her class, her hair hanging about her head in rich profusion', tried to appear like the Mary Ann Adams she had now become. When the court asked her if she was a Christian, she could only tell the truth, which was that she had learnt prayers at school, but hadn't continued with them. As she said this she caught Midlato's eye. They nearly giggled remembering the silent resistance they affected when warned of Jehovah's ire. Midlato felt insulted on Kudnartu's behalf when the court suggested she was not a reliable witness, because as she was not a practising Christian she couldn't be trusted to tell the truth. Who were these white men? Lucy Bradshaw, who accompanied Midlato, was outraged.

Kudnartu and her husband had spent a good deal of money to come to Adelaide for the trial, but their expenses were not paid. Lucy was angry at that too, and helped pay for their return journey.

Kudnartu gave birth to two sons, Tom and Tim, but the marriage floundered. Adams, fed-up with being called a 'lubra shepherd' and not getting any further help from Moorhouse, disappeared for long periods. Kudnartu had no one to protect her from the bullock drivers.

Midlato's other friend Kartanya gave birth to a little girl, and she and Midlato performed a secret ritual for the baby by the sea at full moon, invoking the blessings of Kartanya's *kammammi* Kirrila. They named the baby Medika, after the blossom that laced the air that *wiltutti*.

Midlato and Kartanya were shocked when they heard of Kudnartu's death in February 1855. She had been found by her husband, and was reported to have died of natural causes.

Wauwe Woman: Sounds very suspicious to me. Adams had left her, turned up after several months, and said he found her dead. There was no death certificate. The woman was in her twenties for God's sake, and healthy. Adams was always after her land and still kept trying after her death.

Wirra Woman: Oh, apparently it has been stated categorically that there were no suspicious circumstances.

Wauwe Woman: What, like all the numerous other 'accidental' deaths of Aborigines?

Wirra Woman: Well, there is a possibility she went out of her mind?

Wauwe Woman: What, are you suggesting she was mentally disturbed?

Wirra Woman: Perhaps. She may have just lost the will to live. Adams kept pissing off. That, in Kaurna terms, is really shameful. A Kaurna woman would feel that she had failed her husband. Even more shameful in that Kudnartu had stepped out of her culture and married a white man. It would be doubly degrading to her that he had left. She would feel she couldn't go back to her people.

Wauwe Woman: A bit like Tatiana – who had married a Jew and had a baby out of wedlock.

Wirra Woman: Yes, very like Tatiana – she too was thrown into an alien culture and was not happy. Like Tatiana, Kudnartu represents those people who slip between the cracks of society's rigidity and intolerance and are cast out. Like Tatiana, Kudnartu had her own version of being dehumanised, enslaved, and sacrificed. She would have been sick of the bullock drivers. They would have raped her continuously.

Wauwe Woman: Are you sure?

Wirra Woman: Look, she was a pretty woman – 'black velvet' they would have called her. She was a sitting duck: a few drinks; the lonely road of the bullock trail; no women. What do you think? Bullockies considered Aboriginal women fair game. I think she got sick of those dirty beasts lurching at her with the thick white maggot growing in their filthy trousers. I think she'd had enough. Also, there was the prejudice against her husband, the 'Lubra Shepherd'.

Wauwe Woman: Are you suggesting suicide?

Wirra Woman: No, I think she just pined, and lost her will to live. She was in between a rock and a hard place. Like an untouchable, stuck between two conflicting worldviews. The pain was immense. I think the ancestors just came and slipped her away.

Wauwe Woman: Well maybe so, but I like to think that us Kaurna women are made of sterner stuff. And besides, she had two little boys. I reckon it was a cover up. No one bothered to get a coroner's report. I think she was let down badly by Moorhouse, who was supposed to be her Protector. Her children were whisked off to a mission and never were able to claim the land that was rightfully theirs. I think it was a terrible disgrace!

Midlato, gripping Kartanya's hand, sobbed on Lucy's shoulder. Kudnartu had represented hope for her. Hope that an Aboriginal person could be assimilated to white ways. Kudnartu had become Mary Ann Adams. She had learnt arithmetic, reading, and writing – a lot better than her white husband. She had left the old ways behind, lived in a house on her own land, had given birth to two lovely little boys, but had not been able to survive.

Kudnartu's children were sent to Poonindie, the mission that had been established north of Port Lincoln in 1850, by the Anglican Archdeacon Mathew Hale. 'A Christian village of South Australian Natives, reclaimed from barbarism, trained to the duties of social Christian life and walking in the fear of God.'

This was a totally isolated place and inaccessible from Adelaide except by boat. The sinister policy of taking children away from their families had begun. Midlato remembered with pain, sleeping in the dormitories at the new Adelaide school. She just hated it. At least at Piltawardli there would always be a *wardli* with a friendly fire in front of it. She could sit with her people and search for reassurance in the starry dome above. She felt for the children who were taken up to Poonindie, away from their land, away from their families, away from their language. She felt for the mothers left behind. The worst was when Kartanya came running up to Midlato drenched in tears. Her little girl Medika had been forcibly taken away on a boat to Poonindie. Midlato held her tightly as she wailed in agony on the docks at Port Misery.

In Poonindie, the children, having lost their families, had to give up their own language, their own beliefs, their own customs. Did not the white people know they had hearts? It was believed that only thus would they learn white ways, banished from the influence of their families. Many suffered from illnesses, probably including stress at leaving their families, and living in what was to them a foreign land. Some survived, and their descendants became excellent farmers. Others, like Kartanya's little girl Medika, remained withdrawn and sad and always gazed longingly out to sea. Even as a fully-grown woman she would rock back and forth and wail inconsolably.

Quakers in Adelaide were appalled with what was happening to the Aborigines. One, a member of Taplow's Quaker meeting house in Norwood, wrote, 'Shame Upon Us! We take their land and drive away their food by what we call civilisation, and then deny them shelter from a storm... What comes of all the hypocrisy of our wishes to better their condition? The police drive them into the bush to murder shepherds, and then we cry out for more police... What can a maddened black think of our Christianity to deny him the sod on which he was born... You grow hundreds of bushels of corn on his land but deny him the crumbs that fall from the table... They kill a sheep, but you drive his kangaroo away. You now drive him away from his own, his native land – out upon it; how can God's all-seeing eye approve of this?'

Whether 'God's all-seeing eye' approved or not, the Kaurna disappeared from the streets of Adelaide, and by the late 1850s no indigenous people were recorded as living there continuously. A small band lived in camps at Port Adelaide. One of them was Kartanya who sat wistfully looking out at the Wongayerlo, aching for the beautiful little girl who had so cruelly been taken from her. She remembered her childhood, when she would sit at Ngaltingga and look out over the Wongayerlo waiting for Kirrila, her *kammammi*, to return. Sometimes Midlato would travel to the port and find Kartanya and they would sit quietly together looking out over the sea. Midlato felt privileged that she could stay safely on as a governess to the Bradshaw family.

Other children were siphoned off from their parents to various missions, including Poonindie and Point McLeay. The Kaurna language ceased to be spoken. Its last known speaker was Iparrityi who died in 1929. She was Ityamai-itpina's daughter, and spoke nostalgically of her family's sacred waterhole, which was now swallowed up by the Adelaide Botanic Gardens. She always relayed the story about how frightened she had been when her father returned from the *Buffalo*, dressed in the blue jacket with the metal buttons.

Many of the Kaurna texts disappeared, either to the Lutheran society in Dresden or with Governor Grey when he took up his next position in South Africa. Teichelmann and Schurman's Kaurna book disappeared.

Like the spotted-tailed quoll, the Kaurna were 'not abundant and their presence and subsequent disappearance went almost unnoticed.'

CHAPTER 13

Butterflies

At Poonindie near Port Lincoln, Medika never did stop gazing towards the sea. Somewhere on the other side of it was a mother whose face was indelibly etched into the core of her being and whose arms she ached for. She never could take an interest in the Bible lessons, and refused absolutely to answer to the name Martha. 'Medika,' she insisted, thumping her heart. Kartanya had named her Medika with great love. It meant 'flowers', and she was determined to keep it. The other children were also given biblical names and forbidden to speak in their own language.

Poonindie was described in 1873 by the Adelaide Observer as an Australian Arcadia, and it was noted that 'It is impossible for any thoughtful man to visit the Poonindie Institution without being deeply interested... It is an immense step in one generation – from the ignorant savage life to the order and discipline pervading this little self-supporting settlement.'

Medika eked out her days in this supposed Arcadia, rocking back and forth. The staff always thought she wasn't quite right in the head and perhaps should be in an asylum. In the first few years of the colony, South Australia's mentally ill were dumped in the Adelaide Gaol. The first asylum was built near Ityamai-itpina's sacred waterhole in the Botanic Gardens. In 1870 its inmates were transferred to the newly built Parkside Lunatic Asylum, a grand Victorian affair in the east of the city.

However, Medika was tolerated at Poonindie. She was kept quiet by a steady supply of 'baccy' for her pipe, her only consolation. Land hungry white settlers eventually coveted the farm at Poonindie, and it was closed down in 1894. Medika was put on a boat that went east. Had her dreams come true at last? When she arrived at her destination she ran about distractedly looking for something. After a few days, she stopped and resumed rocking back and forth. She and other Poonindie residents had been transferred to the Point Pearce mission on Yorke Peninsula, which was Narungga country, and yet another gulf away from Kaurna country. Medika was given bags to sew, but had them taken away when she took to stabbing herself with a needle. She just smoked her pipe and gazed sadly into the distance. The Great War came and went. Medika rocked back and forth. The Great Depression came and went. Medika rocked back and forth. She began ripping her clothes off. The staff didn't know what to do with her. She was put on a boat again. This time the boat took her to Adelaide. But the sadness was now too deeply embedded for her to register that she was back on her beloved *yarta*. Kartanya's face still lived deep within her consciousness but was overlaid by so many layers of grief that it became too painful to capture the image. Minda Home, a charitable institution set up for 'mentally retarded children' took her in, even though she was now in her eighties. She continued to rock and sometimes bang her head on the wall and cry for no apparent reason. She took refuge in 'baccy' and made such a terrible fuss if she wasn't allowed to smoke that her pipe was tolerated. Then Gayle came into her life; a severely disabled little Down syndrome child. It was love at first sight, and they became deeply attached to each other. They spent all the time they were allowed to be together entwined in each other's arms.

The Second World War came. Minda Home was overcrowded. It was decided to unload the 'ineducable' children to Parkside Mental Hospital. But Medika's demented howling as the 'ineducable' Gayle was put on the bus was so horrendous, that it was decided that Medika should be sent too. She had senile dementia after all, and was unbelievably ancient. Surely she was close to death.

Parkside Mental Hospital, as it was now called, sat grandly behind high stone walls; more like a prison than a hospital. On closer inspection the buildings were decrepit, the furniture older than the Ark, and the food disgusting. Dr Hugh Birch, the medical superintendent who rivalled Premier Playford in parsimony, had ruled the place with a rod of iron for over thirty years. At the age of fifteen he broke his neck performing daredevil stunts on his bicycle at Semaphore Beach. Through sheer will he survived, but always walked with a shuffling gait. He indulged his cruelly aborted penchant for speed by racing cars around the empty streets of Adelaide. His large blue Jaguar made an exotic splash in the Parkside grounds. He was of the opinion that money should not be wasted on the mentally retarded or the psychotic, and advocated frugal use of electricity unless it was for the 'shock machines', the first of which Birch himself had built.

Gayle and Medika were thrown together into a dark 'retard' dormitory into which they were locked every evening at six o'clock. A kerosene lamp was occasionally shone through a slit in the door to check on the inmates. Medika and Gayle were always ensconced together on an ancient horsehair mattress. Every morning Medika took Gayle's soiled sheets and sluiced them in a big tub outside.

It was nearing the end of Birch and Playford's long reigns in their respective dominions. The dire conditions in the mental institutions of Adelaide were coming to the attention of the public. As with schools, Playford spent little on the hospitals. Well meaning people walked around Parkside and tut-tutted in disbelief at the Dickensian conditions. The stench! Fifty people sardined in a ward with only two toilets. But even more appalling was that mentally retarded children were lumped together with psychotic elderly patients. A wizened old Aboriginal woman, even. Outrageous. This time, Medika's demented howling was dealt with by a new wonder drug. Largactil. This concoction miraculously transformed management problems in mental hospitals. Lunatics could now be drugged into docility.

Ward C was an old stone building where geriatric women were stuffed. A giant outside staircase linked its three levels and was enmeshed in wire netting, in case inmates were tempted to end their miserable existence by jumping off. In front of the building were large bitumen courts surrounded by eight-foot high cyclone fences. Here, patients were 'aired', a necessary procedure as the inside rooms and corridors they were herded into stank. Medika joined a squadron of ancient women who had been forgotten by the world. After several weeks of mournful moaning, Medika approached the matron, aggressively brandishing the pipe she still kept. She demanded 'baccy'. Matron was horrified. There was a strict rule at Parkside. Women were forbidden to smoke. But Medika was very insistent. Even huge dollops of Largactil did not dull the fierce glare that shot from her eyes. It caused Matron sleepless nights, until finally she felt obliged to bring the matter to the attention of Dr Birch. There seemed little hope. Birch was a hard man who stuck to his decisions and didn't mind being unpopular. But something about this black woman intrigued him and he decided to shuffle over to Ward C and tell her the rules himself. He met Medika in the airing court. She stood there defiantly brandishing her pipe. Though physically handicapped, Birch was a powerful presence. As Dr Cramond, who eventually took over from him, said, 'He never shirked anything I knew of and could be a very formidable and awkward customer.' However, in that airing court, as the sun beat down melting the bitumen, Birch met his match. Having been cruelly separated from Gayle, Medika was determined that she would find solace in her pipe. She had never bothered to learn more than rudimentary English but Birch got her message, loud and clear. The social worker Barbara Franck reported that the wizened old Aboriginal crone had brought out a rare side of Birch; a deeply buried liberalism. Medika became the first woman in Parkside who was allowed to smoke.

Wirra Woman: Yeah! Thank Monana! Have you made all that up, author? Or is it true?

Author: All true – all recorded. I told you my research abilities would come in handy.

Medika liked to take her pipe and 'baccy', handed out by the tight-lipped matron, and climb to the top of the staircase and look out. Here she had a bird's eye view of the hospital. The main building with its clock tower sat impressively in the centre of its large grounds. Ward Z, at the back, was a grim stone fortress which housed the criminally insane. A spiked wall plus a deep ha-ha made sure these wretches never had even a faint hope of escape. Inmates in other wards were penned within galvanised iron fences. The grounds of the hospital were surrounded by a forbidding twelve-foot high stone wall. All who entered were counted in and all who left were counted out. Medika was comforted to see the building in which Gayle was housed, and with her sharp eyes could even spot her if she was outside. At these times she would frantically wave, tears coursing her cheeks. From her perch, she could also see over the walls of the hospital and spot gum trees in the distance and the blue haze of the Adelaide Hills. When she first spotted her ancestor Ngano, stretched out in the east, something deep within her stirred. She felt him calling out to her. Snippets of unused words swelled in her heart. A welcome sense of peace flooded her being. She spat out her pills and sang to herself in a strange language.

As with Medika, Parkside was also to be Tatiana's last home. But first, Ivan, his kitchen table still heaving with pound notes, sent her to St Anthony's private hospital. Ivan told the doctors that Tatiana was violent and demented. Here, she underwent the speciality of the hospital, insulin coma therapy.

Wauwe Woman: Monana help me, what's that?

Baba Yaga: Well, it was started in my part of the world by Dr Sadek, a Polish guy. It was believed that inducing a coma was of benefit to psychotic patients.

Wauwe Woman: Monana save us from the Yammamai. A bit like Dr Wright, who killed his patient with ten times too much morphine.

Every morning Tatiana and fellow patients were injected with insulin. This induced sleepiness, sweating, drooling, and uncontrollable twitching, before they fell into a coma. A nurse was ready with a mouth-guard in case of seizures. After two hours glucose was administered via a rubber tube inserted through the nose into the stomach.

Wirra Woman: How on earth can anyone think that is good? And white people condemn our sorcerers!

Baba Yaga: Well, the doctors believed that a prolonged coma would induce different brain rhythms, which would hopefully stop psychotic thoughts. You must remember schizophrenia was, and still is, a bugger to treat.

Wirra Woman: But both Tatiana and Medika were right in thinking that people were out to do them in. It was appalling what happened to them. They just need a little kindness; to sit around our fires, unburden their traumas, cry their unexpressed grief and drink bitter herbs. Then they would be okay.

If Tatiana could have trusted anyone enough to unburden herself to them, and could speak English well enough for them to understand her, psychoanalysis could have been an option. But this would have cost Ivan several pram-loads of money. And besides, medical insurance at the time was such that he received a rebate if Tatiana had technical procedures, but not if she spent time talking. But the private hospital was extremely expensive. And Tatiana didn't seem to be getting better. In fact, a side effect of the coma treatment was that she developed twitching and excessive drooling. This made her look even more crazy.

Ivan looked at the hefty hospital bills, looked at his wife whose mouth twitched uncontrollably, and reluctantly sent her to Parkside. The woman who loved to party was shunted into a grim existence. The woman who looked like Marilyn Monroe was encased in Salvation Army clothes. The woman who escaped the gulags was now incarcerated somewhere worse. Behind high stone walls, she joined a legion of people whom society had discarded; war battered soldiers, unwed mothers, demented spinsters, those who just couldn't cope anymore, and a fair smattering of Slavs, Poles, and Italians. And one wizened Aboriginal woman. Tatiana was sent to Ward C with the geriatrics, while the hospital decided what to do with her. The first thing she did was to climb up the staircase to see if she could escape. At the top, she was surprised to find Medika, smoking her pipe. They just looked at each other and Medika beckoned her to sit down. They sat silently together and gazed out over the hills, Ngano, the ancient ancestor, glowed pinkish in the evening sunset. The deep agony of being ripped from mother and country bound them on a level where there were no words. Something about the old woman was very familiar to Tatiana. She tried to grab hold of a dream she fleetingly remembered: black faces; a flickering fire; murmuring voices; strange bitter herbs. She felt a strange peace.

A few days later Tatiana climbed to the top of the tower again. The old woman was not there. Only her pipe remained. They said that she was well over a hundred when she died.

Wauwe Woman: Ah Medika. Did she live to such an old age? Very unusual for us mob.

Author: Yes, the records at the hospital say she was about 105.

Wirra Woman: Yeah, òur life expectancy is usually a good twenty years less than a white person.

Wauwe Woman: They always say that Iparrityi, Ityamaitpinna's daughter, was the last of the original Kaurna race. No one knew about Medika. Good research!

Tatiana picked up the pipe and felt sad as she gazed over at the hills. The dream of being around a fire with Baba Yaga and kind Aboriginal women would drift in and out of her consciousness. She was sure they were beckoning her. She longed to be among them. One afternoon, the call of the hills was so strong she felt that she had to go. With energy and determination she slipped across the bitumen court, scaled the tall cyclone fence, and ran towards a gate in the high outside wall. Medical orderlies in green peaked caps, on which were stitched an insignia of the crown, ran after her and forced her arms into a canvas jacket. As she screamed and kicked they tied her into it and marched her back. She was put into the more secure Ward K.

Here, Tatiana became more encrusted in the dehumanised and depersonalised world of the institution. Her demons grew fat on Largactil, lithium, and a host of other drugs which were being used experimentally. The demons lurched clumsily inside her brain. Regularly they were shocked into a stupor by electroconvulsive therapy, which doctors now decided was more effective than insulin comas. As Tatiana thrashed about uncontrollably, at the mercy of fierce electric currents, the demons thrashed with her, but were not defeated. When everything calmed down and Tatiana was back in the ward, shaken, disoriented, and drained, they recovered fast. They began whispering messages to Tatiana,

'You'll never get out of here alive.'

'You are being punished for marrying a Jew.'

'The doctors are trying to poison and kill you.'

This, of course, reinforced the doctors' diagnosis. At the next case conference, in their starched white coats, they were satisfied to announce, 'This patient is suffering from paranoid schizophrenia. Step up the drugs. Step up the treatments.' Tatiana, in her shapeless dress, was sent back to hell.

Baba Yaga: Ah yay yay yay yay yay. *Wauwe woman caught her as she swayed in despair.*

Once a week, Sveta visited her mother at what everyone called 'the loonybin'. She steeled herself as she walked up the long driveway and turned left at the main building. She hurried past the cyclone fences, where demented white-haired women ran at her, and clawed at her with bony fingers. Past Ward C, where blobs of humanity would shuffle up and down aimlessly on the outside staircase. Taking a deep breath, she finally reached Ward K, where she trawled through several security checks. How would Tatiana be today? Would she hurl herself at her daughter and scream, 'Get me out of here – they are trying to kill me'? Would she just stare ahead with non-seeing eyes? Would she be pretending to smoke a dirty clay pipe that she always held in her hand? Would she be trembling and dribbling after ECT. No, today Tatiana peered at her and said, 'You not fool me. You not Sveta. You Debbie Reynolds. She is pretence to be you.'

It was at times like these Sveta wondered who the hell she was. Why was life so terrible? What had happened to her beautiful mother who loved to sing and dance, who loved telling stories, who loved making vareniki?

Baba Yaga: Ah yay yay yay yay yay. *The kammammi clucked sympathetically. It was terrible to witness such a hardened old crone sobbing uncontrollably.*

Fortunately, in some areas, Tatiana's will still prevailed. The *kammammi* circle had conferred a lasting benefit. For her fourteenth birthday, Ivan bought Sveta a beautiful piano. She learnt to play Mozart's Minuet in G. She had never heard classical music before. It soothed her to the core. Ivan also enrolled her into a sewing school. Every Saturday morning, she travelled into Adelaide for lessons and learnt to make pretty dresses and neat little suits that curved around her growing bosom and hips. After her lesson, she walked down to the Torrens River and watched the black swans float serenely by. As she strolled past the bandstand where the Salvation Army would play on a Sunday, she was surprised to see some Aboriginal boys sitting on the grass. Miss Bradshaw, whom she still regularly visited, had told her that there was a loosening of some regulations regarding Aborigines, and many were drifting back in to Adelaide. One of the boys turned to Sveta and said hello. She liked his friendly face and beautiful smile.

'Hello,' she replied and stopped. They started to have a friendly chat. Suddenly, from out of nowhere, a vanload of policemen swooped upon them. The Aboriginal boys were rounded up. Two burly policemen towered over Sveta and started interrogating her.

'What did those black buggers say to you?'

Sveta was really taken aback and very afraid.

'Oh, just "hello",' she stammered.

'Did they make any indecent proposals to you?'

Indecent proposals? Sveta didn't know what they were talking about.

'We were just chatting. They were really nice.' In the background, she could see the Aboriginal boys being pushed around. Shoved quite nastily. What was going on?

'What did they say to you exactly?' The policemen were not letting up.

'Just hello – they were just being friendly.'

'Aah friendly, eh? Just how friendly? How friendly were they being? Did they touch you? Come on, you can tell us.'

Sveta was now really confused. She was a fifteen-year old girl and had just been having a friendly chat with some dark-skinned boys. That was all. Was this a crime?

The police seemed annoyed with her answers. They took down her details, which made her really afraid. The Aboriginal boys were pushed into a police van and driven off.

The black swans grunted as Sveta walked towards her bus stop, confused and uneasy.

She went immediately to see Miss Bradshaw, who had now retired. Belinda continued being actively involved in Aboriginal Affairs. She supported Dr Duguid's tireless work in the Federal Council for the Advancement of Aborigines, and its national approach to indigenous affairs. But Aboriginal people continued to be treated abominably, and had the status of non-citizens. Belinda cried when Sveta told her about the Aboriginal boys at Elder Park and shook her head sadly. Sveta thought she looked very tired.

Dr Cramond took over from Hugh Birch as Superintendant of Parkside Hospital. He set about to winkle money out of Playford to give the hospital a long overdue makeover. He met Sir Thomas in the old treasury building in Victoria Square. From a large leather armchair, in front of a fire which burned mallee roots, Playford disarmed him with a lecture about how to plant an apple orchard. As an orchardist, Playford knew that reticulation of water was vital to grow good apples.

'Surely as an educated person you understand that?

'Yes...?' Cramond nodded, perplexed. What had this to do with the dreadful conditions in the hospital?

'Well, you run off and write a paper about the reticulation you are doing at Parkside.' Sir Thomas was showing him the door, 'Metaphorically of course. It is only then that I would even consider releasing any money.'

Cramond went away wondering how he could ever squeeze any money out of this smug Scrooge, who had now been in power for over thirty-five years. So he invited Playford's Health minister, Sir Lyell McEwin, to visit Parkside. Cramond demonstrated 'reticulation' in action to the pompous dignitary. He showed Sir Lyell the iron baths outside the 'retard' wards, where Medika had once sluiced Gayle's soiled sheets. Cramond explained how the faeces from the 'retard' patients were emptied into a creek that meandered through the hospital grounds and then over to the hallowed Victoria Park racecourse nearby. Sir Lyell's visit to the races the following Saturday was just not the same. Money suddenly became available.

The Parkside face-lift was dramatic. The walls came down. More staff members were appointed. Flowers were planted. Inmates were now called residents. Parkside was renamed Glenside. It was too late for Tatiana. She had developed a habit of attacking doctors and trying to escape. A straitjacket was often used to restrain her. ECT was stepped up.

It was not long before Sveta discovered that Belinda Bradshaw was suffering from leukaemia. There seemed to be a lot of people Sveta knew who suffered from cancer; a Ukrainian woman in the next street who used to sew for Tatiana died and left two daughters; a woman who regularly came into the shop had also died. Cancer seemed a strange, cruel, and mysterious disease.

Sveta visited Belinda Bradshaw at the Royal Adelaide hospital. She was shocked to see how thin she looked.

'Come sweet Sveta, come and sit by me.'

Belinda appraised the teenaged girl, remembering fondly the little Svitochka who hardly spoke English. The plaits had been supplanted by a ponytail, and Sveta wore a red, white, and blue jumper that was far too small for her burgeoning bosom.

'How is your mother?'

'No good really.' Sveta's eyes filled with tears.

Belinda Bradshaw didn't know that some of those tears were also for her. Sveta looked at the sparse wisps of hair that had once been swept into a bun. This kind sweet woman had been the closest to an aunt she'd ever had. She had all but lost her mother, Mrs O'Donnell had died, and now she couldn't bear losing Miss Bradshaw too.

Belinda had some string in her weak hands.

'Here Sveta, I want to show you something that a wonderful person showed me a long time ago. She was an Indigenous Australian and her name was Midlato. My great aunt, Lucy Bradshaw, came over on one of the first ships to South Australia. She befriended Midlato when they were both young girls. They had a special connection; Midlato insisted it was because they were both fifth-born. Midlato lived in our house when I was very small. She taught me many things, including these string games. String was so important to the Kaurna – each strand symbolised that we are all woven within the intricate web of life, that we all belong to the earth, that we are all part of the whole.'

Belinda wove the strings between her frail hands and then passed them over to Sveta.

'You know, Midlato played these games with me for hours and told me wondrous stories of her childhood, before white man came. And then sad stories of what happened to her people afterwards. But you know, despite her huge loss, she had the best laugh I have ever heard. She would delight in telling me the problems she had trying to say the 's' sound, and how that led to so much grief. For example, she couldn't pronounce my great Aunt's name. She could only say Looty. She certainly wouldn't have been able to say your name, Sveta.'

Belinda's eyes were alight when she spoke about Midlato, and smiles creased her wan face.

'She gave me so much that woman. Do you know she described to me how, as a girl, she found wild honey? She sat quietly at a waterhole until she heard the humming of a bee come to drink. She filled her mouth with water and squirted it on the bee, stunning it temporarily. Then she retrieved some cockatoo down feathers from her basket and, with a little wattle gum, attached them carefully under the bee's wings. She then placed the bee on a leaf to recover. When the bee flew off, she chased it, following the distinct white fluffy frill, jumping if necessary over shrubs and mounds, till it led her to the sticky sweet magic of its hive.'

Belinda stroked Sveta's hair. 'You know I always loved that story, as it showed me that the Kaurna were into tagging long before white scientists. Oh, those people were so clever and so respectful of their piece of God-given earth.'

Sveta looked at the shining eyes of her dear old teacher. She loved hearing these tales. It reminded her of Tatiana, who had regaled her with fascinating stories of gathering wild berries and mushrooms with a babushka Sveta never knew, as sun filtered through tall dark forests.

Belinda recollected one of the last times she and Midlato had gone out together; she a young girl and Midlato an old woman, white hair sprouting around her beautiful lined face. The Bradshaw family had gone to the Adelaide Town Hall in December 1909 – a Glee Club fund-raising concert. The Glee Club had been formed by the Point McLeay mission, near Encounter Bay, where Aboriginal people including Ngarrindjeri, Ramindjeri, and Kaurna had been incarcerated since the 1850s. The programme consisted of dancing, music, and impassioned speeches. A girl called Ruth sang 'Old Folks at Home', echoing the sadness of Negro slaves in America. The audience were very moved by her beautiful heartfelt rendition; it was easy to feel empathy for an enslaved race in another part of the world. However, they felt less comfortable when confronted by two speeches about the race they had enslaved in their own backyard. The first was by David Unaipon who had mastered white learning, and was skilful in many areas. His accomplishments were such that his face would become enshrined on a future $50 note. He knocked on the head any notion that Aborigines were 'ignorant savages'. The other speech was delivered by Philip Rigney, whom a reporter dubbed 'The Black Patriot'.

Belinda Bradshaw had been riveted by his heartfelt words.

'This is a beautiful country... one of the finest on earth. I do not know of any other, but I have read of them. And it cost you people nothing.'

Belinda remembered how he stopped and looked around at the audience who had paid just a silver coin to come to the concert. They fidgeted uncomfortably as he continued.

'It cost you nothing. Nothing in blood or treasure: nothing in purchase. It came to you as easily as it went from my people, and, if the Government only gave us a little of the best of it, we wouldn't be here tonight asking for your help. Instead of that, we have come to you to solicit your assistance towards the purchase of material roofing for our huts. The settlers have burned off or otherwise destroyed all the grass we used to employ in thatching our cabins.'

'You know Sveta, Midlato sobbed uncontrollably all the way home. She couldn't believe that her people, so articulate, so eloquent, and so learned, were reduced to begging for a roof over their heads, in their own beautiful country. And she told me how her frail *kammammi* had had the roof ripped off her own head so many years before.'

Sveta cried too when she heard the words of Philip Rigney, The Black Patriot. She felt a kinship with Midlato and greater compassion for Tatiana who had been so unbelievably bereft without her home country.

'Come closer.' Belinda said, seeing the tears on Sveta's cheeks.

'Yes Sveta, Midlato, like you, had lost everything; the language which moulded you both; your place in your own cultures; your mother countries; your mothers. But like Midlato, you will never lose your spirit. Let your tears flow – that is one thing Midlato's people always did. They let their tears flow freely. They followed the example of their ancestor Tjilbruke, who was not ashamed to let his tears fall in abundance. With every tear shed, hope and peace did spring. The Kaurna deeply grieved their loss as their precious song stopped being sung.'

Sveta let herself sob. She felt her heart would break. Her own Slavic song, nurtured in the hearts of generations of babushki and their little grandchildren as they gathered 'svitochki' in the spring, had been blown to smithereens. But with Belinda Bradshaw's support she surrendered to her grief. A grief she shared with Midlato, Kartanya, Medika, and Tatiana. Midlato's beloved country was living and breathing but unavailable to her. Sveta's beloved mother was living and breathing but also unavailable to her. After a while Sveta felt a little easier. The terrible burden had been lightened a little. Belinda dabbed the girl's tears with her delicate white handkerchief.

'I would like to tell you what Midlato told me just before she died.' Belinda sighed as she remembered that beautiful black face, kindness and depth etched into every line.

'She said that no matter how much adversity you suffer or how hard life is, you must stay strong and keep a vision of good.

'She said her people had been enclosed in invisible threads – like a suspended chrysalis encircled in an alien outer casing; inert and just hanging in limbo, waiting one day to re-emerge. Deep within the pupa was the Kaurna butterfly, black with sparks of gold, red and white. She told me that her first word to my great aunt Lucy had been *pilyabilya*. These gorgeous butterflies are now virtually extinct in the Adelaide area. Their habitat, like that of the Kaurna, has been destroyed.'

'*Pilyabilya,*' repeated Sveta. 'How beautiful.' The Russian word for butterfly came back to her: 'Babochka.'

'Babochka,' repeated Belinda. 'That is beautiful too.'

'You know it is a version of Baba or Babushka, which means grandmother. I never knew my grandmother. I wish I had.'

'Yes, Midlato had a wonderful grandmother. She spoke of her '*kammammi*' with great fondness.'

Belinda looked into Sveta's blue eyes.

'I believe, as did Midlato, that this new butterfly will be a combination of the old and the new. You know what, my dear Sveta, I am positive that you will be part of its wet unfolding wings.'

Belinda Bradshaw, like many South Australian citizens who had been subjected to the invisible seepage of radiation in their bodies, died of leukaemia. Of course, any link is always strenuously denied, and no proper epidemiological study has ever been carried out. Anyone who suggested such research was seen as unpatriotic and a communist sympathiser.

In the bowels of Parkside Mental Hospital, Tatiana was having her head shaved. She was being prepared for a lobotomy. This operation, which involved cutting the frontal lobe of the brain, was reserved for people for whom no other treatments were working. Tatiana had now undergone several different drug regimes and countless electro-shock treatments. It was finally decided that, other than the effects of severe disorientation, dribbling, and twitching, they did not seem to be doing Tatiana any good. Her delusions were getting worse. For example, she would insist on putting bowls of water under her bed at night. She explained to medical orderlies that this was the only way she could stop 'Them' from electrocuting her.

'God, how nutty can you get!' the orderlies smirked to each other.

Of course, nobody linked Tatiana's 'paranoid delusions' with the fact that she had, for years, been strapped to a bed and subjected to all manner of comas and violent electric currents which, not in her wildest dreams, would she have ever asked for voluntarily. Surely any sane person would do what they possibly could to avert such dreadful assaults to their bodies?

The medical orderlies finished their preparatory tasks, the gold crown insignias on their peaked caps glowing eerily in the light of the operating theatre. In Mexico, the KGB had hacked Trotsky's head open with an ice-pick. In Adelaide, doctors used a more refined instrument, a 'leucotome,' to slice through the nerve fibres which connected the frontal lobe with other parts of the brain. Moniz, who invented the operation, was shot by one of his patients. However, he was still able to collect an award for his invention, albeit in a wheelchair. The award was the Nobel prize for physiology in 1949.

Sveta went to see her mother after the operation. As she looked at Tatiana's shaved head, she fleetingly glimpsed something rather horrific. She dismissed the image quickly from her mind. What Sveta spotted was a mangled demon. It had met its match. Sliced into bits by a 'leucotome'.

The demon was dead, but so was Tatiana. She never spoke again. Her body lived on for another ten years.

In the Adelaide Hills near Yurebilla, a circle of grandmothers sat in silent communion. They held the spirit of the woman with the heart-shaped face, who had come to their land with such high hopes; the woman who, in their own way, they had tried to help. At the same time, they rained sweetness on Sveta, who found the loss of her mother to a strange half-world almost intolerable to bear.

Baba Yaga: Well, I must be off. I am going to leave you and return to my northern homeland.

Wauwe Woman: What, you can't leave! What about Sveta?

Baba Yaga: I am satisfied that she has survived intact. Because of you people and your quiet magic, Adelaide is one of the most benign places on earth. Sveta has you now and is imbued with the wonderful spirit you, Murlawirrapurka, and your other ancestors have weaved into the land. The British Empire failed to destroy that. I will leave her in your capable hands. I feel reassured that of all the places on earth that Sveta could have landed, Adelaide is okay.

Wauwe Woman: But what about Tatiana and the butchery that was done to her? We feel dreadful that that happened on our Kaurna soil.

Baba Yaga: To her, and countless helpless people all over the world. You should see what doctors did to people in so called mental hospitals in the Soviet Union. It was no picnic there either, I tell you. Man's inhumanity to man knows no bounds.

Wauwe Woman: But Sveta has to bear what happened to Tatiana.

Baba Yaga: Yes. One day she will have a vision in which she will face all the demons. She will see the demons that plagued Tatiana, Albert Taplow, and Mildred. Only when she is strong enough to do that will she be able to transform those demons into butterflies.

CHAPTER 14

Promise to Obey her Lords

'Without the interior journey, we remain alien to ourselves and to others. The latter doesn't require the experts, the leaders. It requires only the willingness of one! And that one is myself!'
– Lillian Holt: Rhetoric, Reality, Racism, 2003

Wauwe Woman: I'm annoyed that you have sent Baba Yaga back. We liked having her here: a good babushka to have on the *kammammi* team.

Author: Nothing to do with me. She wanted to go back. Besides, she had finished her job; to make sure that Sveta survived intact.

Wauwe Woman: Well did she?

Author: Well Sveta and I are the same person. So, judge for yourself

Wirra Woman: So you're the one who promised to obey her 'Lords' for all those years.

All the kammammi chortle with glee.

Author: Oy! I didn't make fun of you lot, not being able to say 'sixpence'.

Well, what do you think of my story?

Wauwe Woman: Not bad for a white-skin. But we're still not sure about white-skins telling our story. We want to tell our own stories

Author: Well I was telling *my* story – revised since I knew about you lot. When I was plonked in Adelaide, I always thought my story was mingled only with the British. But since knowing you mob, and having powerful visions and dreams, I have discovered that where I landed in Adelaide has a far richer story into which to slot and merge my own. Your story has also become my story. That is just the nature of it. Destiny has landed us in the same boat together. Just like it put my mother and Medika into Ward C together.

Wauwe Woman: And the story continues. As you have written, the time between the 1840s to the 1960s was bad for us. But things got better in the 1960s. Our people started waking up.

Wirra Woman: In fact, some of them got pretty stroppy. Charlie Perkins, an Arrente man from near Alice Springs, was separated from his family and brought to St Francis mission school in Adelaide, as a ten-year-old boy. The missionaries tried their hardest to assimilate him, but he was having none of it. He became a trailblazer for our people. He was outraged that RSL Halls did not allow black people to enter, and caused havoc outside an RSL Hall in New South Wales. The local Anglican vicar was so upset by Charlie's ungentlemanly antics that he had him hounded out of town. And then there's Vincent Lingiari, a Gurindji from the Northern Territory, who refused to obey the Queen's Lords.

The kammammi giggle again.

Wauwe Woman: We call it a 'cinder in snow' story, where a tiny spark of hope is kept alive for our people. Just like

Murlawirrapurka and his integrity. His kindness was his strength but also his undoing. Murlawirrapurka thought he could continue to be a custodian of his land and customs, while accommodating the white man. What he learnt too late was that the usurper always trashes his lackeys. Always. Vincent was a man who learnt that lesson. He was strong enough to stand up to the usurper.

One of your Lords, Lord Vestey – in fact, he is a polo playing chum of Prince Charles and Master of the Horse for the Queen – grew fat on the Gurindji. His forbears, the Vestey brothers, stole several thousand acres of Gurindji land in the Northern Territory to breed cattle. Any troublesome Gurindji warriors were shot like dingoes. Those who managed to survive worked as drovers for the Vesteys, and were lucky if a scrap of discarded offal was thrown their way. The good beef was frozen and sent in shiploads to Britain and Europe. The Vesteys became obscenely rich. William Vestey was skilful at evading tax, and bought his title for £25,000 in 1924. The Gurindji were ground into the dirt. Virtual slaves.

They were good stockmen; they knew the land and knew where to find straying stock, but as Billy Jampijinpa, a mate of Vincent's, described, 'We were treated just like dogs. We were lucky to get paid what we were due, and we lived in tin humpies you had to crawl in and out on your knees. There was no running water. The food was bad – just flour, tea, sugar and bits of discarded beef like the head or feet of a bullock. The Vesteys mob were hard men. They didn't care about blackfellas.'

It was 1966! And it was still illegal to pay an Aboriginal worker more than a specified amount in goods and money.

Wirra Woman: And you know when they requested a tap, the Station Manager said, 'You are blackfellas, you can carry your own water!'

Wauwe Woman: So in steps our hero, Vincent Lingiari. He was a Gurindji elder who'd had enough. He led 200 men out on strike at Wave Hill, traditionally sacred Daguragu country, on the Vestey estate, demanding equal wages and conditions.

The word on the street in Darwin was, 'Strike won't last a week. Those blackfellas haven't a chance in hell.'

But something was crystallising in Lingiari's mind. Wages, better humpies, grovelling for a tap, were not where it was at. As an elder, he was proud custodian of the Gurindji people. It wasn't right that that he was a starving beggar at his own table, on his own land. He escalated the strike into a demand for the sacred Gurindji lands to be returned to their rightful owners.

Wirra Woman: You should have heard the outcry! Little Vincent, like David, had slung a sharp pointed rock at a lumbering two headed Goliath: a mega rich lord on one hand and a bunch of racist rednecks, masquerading as the Australian Government, on the other.

Wauwe Woman. Lord Spam (as Vestey was called) was getting really worried. What, his underlings were not kowtowing to him as they should? He offered better wages. Lingiari refused. Fresh meat. Lingiari refused.

Even a tap. Lingiari refused. Sympathetic supporters drove supplies down from Darwin. At least the strikers could eat! In 1967, Lingiari petitioned another of the Queen's lords, the Governor General, Lord Casey. Lingiari meant business!

Lord Vestey was desperate. He offered further inducements. Lingiari refused. Even more money. Lingiari refused.

Wirra Woman: And you know what he said? In his own quiet dignified way? *She swells with pride.*

'We want them Vestey mob – all go away from here. Wave Hill Aboriginal people bin called Gurindji. We bin here long time before them Vestey mob. This is our country, all this bin Gurindji country. Wave Hill bin our country. We want this land; we strike for that. You can keep your gold. We just want our land back. We can wait.'

Wauwe Woman: And boy did he have to wait! While he waited, things were hotting up around the country. Charlie Perkins continued to blaze a storm, and actively campaigned for Aboriginal rights as a member of Federal Council for the Advancement of Aborigines. In Adelaide, the Playford dictatorship was finally over, and Don Dunstan became Minister of Aboriginal Affairs. A long-time champion of Aborigines, he started moving things for our people, before becoming Premier. In the same year, 1967, due to continual bombardment by the Federal Council for the Advancement of Aborigines, a referendum was held which compelled the federal government to take action in the area of Aboriginal Affairs.

Wirra Woman: Then in 1969, Charlie Perkins and his mother Hetti drove into the federal government reserve at Jay Creek, near his home town of Alice Springs. Here, 300 Aboriginal people were corralled into an Australian gulag, living in appalling squalor. The children suffered terrible eye diseases and their stomachs were distended as a result of shit food.

Author: My God! I saw a place like that when I went up to Alice Springs myself in 1967. I saw these Aboriginal children in what looked like pens. I was shocked to the core.

Wirra Woman: Anyway, Charlie and Hetti found the barbed wire gate at Jay Creek locked. A notice said: 'No entry, by ministerial order.'

'What d'you, reckon, mum?' said Charlie.
    'Do it,' said Hetti, The car smashed through the gate.
    'G'day,' said Charlie to the white manager.
    'Where's your bloody permit?'
    'Lost it, mate,' chirped Charlie. 'Now, how come these children look so bloody sick??'
    Yes, Charlie was a hero: a courageous trailblazer who did so much to change the conditions at Jay Creek and in other gulags. You know that when he wanted to demonstrate against something he would ring up the press and say, 'Look, come on down. There's a demo happening.' The press would say, 'How many people will be there?'
    'Well, just me for starters. Hopefully more will turn up!'

Wauwe Woman: Yeah, a real hero. And then there's Lowitja O'Donohue, the one who had to fight to be a nurse in the hallowed white halls of Royal Adelaide Hospital. She went to nurse in Coober Pedy in the late sixties, hoping to find her mother Lily, from whom she had been removed when she was two. Lily was so excited when she heard her girl was back in the neighbourhood that she waited by the side of the road from dawn to dusk for three months. What was another three months after thirty-five years?

Wirra Woman: Our people sure know how to wait.

Wauwe Woman: Vincent Lingiari had to wait for a very long time. The strike lasted over seven years. The sun rose and set over Wave Hill three thousand times. Each time that sun rose, the struggle intensified. The Whitlam government eventually negotiated with Lord Vestey over the pastoral lease. The end result was an enormously important event in our history when, during an emotional ceremony in 1975, Prime Minister Gough Whitlam poured the ancestral Daguragu soil into Vincent Lingiari's hands and handed the Wave Hill station back to the Gurindji people. Vincent Lingiari simply replied, 'We are mates.'

Wirra Woman: Yes, it was very hopeful. Very symbolic. But you know what, we are still not really mates. We are still down the toilet. Even in the 1990s when there was so much hope that things would be different. When Mabo won his land. When Terra Nullius was finally overturned and the Federal Government commissioned so many studies, so many projects, so

323

much research – even a Royal Commission, so many brilliant recommendations. So few implemented.

Author: But what about all the Sorry Day journeys of healing? And the final 'Sorry' from Prime Minister Rudd. I was at Elder Park to see the screening.

Wauwe Woman: Yes, they were wonderful. It showed that there were many white people on our side. They had been moved by our plight and ashamed of Howard's refusal to say sorry for his ancestors' misdeeds.

Wirra Woman: But what has come of it really?

Wauwe Woman: Yes, we want healing. But as Charlie Kumantjayi Perkins said before he died, 'We ask for land rights with tongue in cheek knowing full well that the land belonged to us in the first instance. We wander through Australian society as beggars. We live off the crumbs that fall off the White Australian tables and are told to be grateful.' But like Lowitja O'Donohue, who has become a great spokesperson for our people, we don't want to throw mud or apportion blame.

Wirra Woman: Speak for yourself. I do.

Wauwe Woman: We just want to uncover the big ugly boil of endemic racism and lance it, if necessary. We don't want to put any more dollops of concealer on it. We need to flush out the dead white cells which fester below the surface.

Author: So, my Kaurna grandmothers, how is this to be done?

Wauwe Woman: Well, you whites have to look inside yourself at your racism. Easier said than done. Charlie Perkins is famous for accusing various white Australians of being racists and rednecks. The fact that it got people's backs up shows he hit a nerve. We want to be kinder, and *invite* you whites to look at your racism.

Wirra Woman: We would like to introduce you to our good friend to explain. Nin is our insider name for her. As Lillian Holt, she has been slogging away at this point for a long time.

Nin: Yes. Hello. I was Head of Taoundi College in Port Adelaide for several years in the 1990s. While in the job I met with a bunch of cops in an attempt to ease racial tensions in South Australia. You saw it with your own eyes when you chatted to those Aboriginal boys in Elder Park in 1962. It was very common then for coppers to kick Aboriginal youths about like footballs and lock them up on any flimsy excuse.

Anyway, at this meeting most of the policemen introduced themselves in the usual politically correct way, putting themselves forward as enlightened racial harmonists; a way that whites have spent the last twenty years getting pretty good at. Then there's this cop from Port Augusta who introduces himself and says,

'I godda be straight wi' ya Miss 'olt. I need ya to know I'm a racist.'

The rest of the room froze. Except me. It was like a breath of fresh air in the room. Finally, someone dared say the truth.

I replied, 'I'm so pleased to meet you. I have an excellent feeling that you and I will get along very well indeed.'

And you know, we did. He was a straight talker and so was I.

After the meeting, the police chief wrote me a letter of apology about this man. I replied, no need to apologise. He was great. He was telling the truth and by doing so, showing a willingness to move from there. And he did.

Wirra Woman: Bloody political correctness. Has a lot to answer for.

Wauwe Woman: No need to knock political correctness. It's good that whites are forced to watch their tongues.

Wirra Woman: Oh, you mean their lying tongues!

Author: So, you're saying we have to admit to being racists. Many of us are not.

Nin: I would be surprised by the word 'many'. If you were a white brought up in Australia, it's hard not to be a racist. Even you.

Author: Me?

Nin: Yes, tell me about your racism.

Author: I'm writing a book to try and reconcile black and white.

Nin: All the more reason for you to own up to your own racism. How many black friends do you have?

Author: Well...

Nin: Too long a wait. Tell me about the first time you saw our people.

Author: Well it was when we had our shop in Woodville Gardens and were surrounded by the Housing Trust. It was about 1959 and an Aboriginal family moved in a few streets away. Local people hated them coming into the area and shunned them. I remember some of the

Aborigine kids walking past our shop and the bodgies, you know the greasy rockers of the day, were out the front telling them to piss off.

Nin: Did you stick up for them?

Author: Well no... *Squirming*

Nin: And so how did you feel about them?

Author: I felt sorry for them

Nin: But not enough to stick up for them?

Author: Well, (*taking a deep breath*) you know how I actually felt?

Nin: That is what we want to know.

Author: I was glad there was someone lower down the pecking order than me. It made me feel okay. Yes, I felt glad the bodgies were picking on someone else. I was glad they weren't picking on me. I was glad I was white. There. I've said it.

All the kammammi clap delightedly. I am surprised. I expected disapproval.

Nin: Well done

Wauwe Woman: So you could see that at least you were a white citizen, even if it was a New Australian reffo. We were non-citizens. We women got no maternity benefit, no pension, no nothing. You know Nin wrote a paper entitled 'Psssst ... I Wannabe White.' Kicked up a storm. Had all sorts of people, both black and white, misunderstanding her, accusing her of all sorts of stuff.

Nin: I was just saying the truth. It was my heartfelt cry at having been ravaged by racism all my life. Being called a boongie, a blackgin, all sorts of hurtful names. All the

'I'm proud to be Black' statements didn't stop the hurt. You know, I wanted to be white just for one day so that I could stop feeling the racism that was coming my way. Even from well meaning people. It was well masked, but still there. A bit like what the Milmenrura man, Mongarawata, saw in the eyes of that sailor. But whites won't go looking for their deeply buried racism if they don't need to. They are too comfortable, too superior. Racism just drips off people, unconsciously, in so many subtle hues. And they don't know it.

Anyway, our dear author there must be more.

I think for a bit. A horrible realisation comes over me.

Author: Oh no, I can't tell you that. It is so shameful.

Nin: Come on, my dear. You are among friends.

Author: Well, when I was twenty-one, I got involved in an Aboriginal Rights campaign. I had been appalled by the conditions I'd seen in Alice Springs, so wanted to do something. Don Dunstan was on the way to becoming Premier and was gung-ho about Aboriginal rights. I thought he was great. I stood on street corners spouting about injustices to Aborigines and gathered money for their cause. I was driving home with a chunk of money I'd collected when I saw an Aboriginal bloke hitchhiking along the road. I thought, well I should practise what I preach. I pulled up and offered him a lift. He looked at me rather dubiously: a lone, pretty white woman offering a lift to an Aborigine? Strange.

Anyway, he slid in next to me on the front seat of my two-tone Holden. And I'm ashamed to say this, but what hit me straight away was his smell. It was so horrible I nearly vomited.

I look at the kammammi. Surprisingly they don't look too horrified.

Wauwe Woman: Probably hadn't washed for weeks and was wearing a stinky cast-off nylon shirt from the Salvo Army.

Author: Well yes, he looked pretty filthy and hot. We had an attempt at a conversation but I couldn't wait for him to get out.

Wauwe Woman: Well that's not too bad. Any old white vagrant would smell foul too.

Author: Yes, but it gets worse. I was so put off by this guy that all my lofty ideals sunk into the mire. *I take a deep breath.* I never gave that money to the Aboriginal cause. I kept it.

Wirra Woman: You kept it! What you raised it for the Aborigines? And you kept it. Why?

Author: I was repulsed by the guy. I felt he didn't deserve the money. I was greedy, too. I kept it.

I feel so ashamed and look around. They all look at me with their beautiful black eyes. I feel like a white junkie. I feel all the times I have shot my arm full of white superiority; how I have bowed to greed before sharing.

Wirra Woman: Did it occur to you to give the money to the hitchhiker?

Author: Not at all. There was a strange disassociation between the lofty ideals of preaching about Aboriginal equality and the reality. And you guys want to know the truth, right?

All the Kammammi nod and smile encouragingly.

Wirra Woman: But you whites made him that way…

Wauwe Woman: Shoosh! *She puts a hand on Wirra Woman.* Wait…

Author: I despised him for being black and inferior.
   There is silence.
   I dare not look at all those beautiful eyes. It is like I am staring into the face of God.
   I dare look up at Nin.
   I am surprised to see she has tears in her eyes.

Nin: Thank you. Thank you for coming here with me.

I dare look at them all. They are so beautiful. We are a circle of grandmothers together.

Author: You know, I feel remorseful, but I don't feel like saying sorry.

Wirra Woman: You're as bad as Howard.

Nin: Just wait you feisty Wirra Woman! She can't manufacture a sorry that's not there. Neither can Howard. The difference is he won't even look. Don't worry, my dear. It takes time for the real sorry to emerge. You have taken the first big step. Just to look. Just to be open to the real truth. For that we honour you.

She sees my dejected look. What's happening now?

Author: But I feel a fraud writing this book

Wauwe Woman: What, just because you are not sorry about the hitchhiker?

Author: Partly. But there's more. I didn't give him the money then, and I still wouldn't want to now.

I sit miserably thinking of throwing my whole book out the window.
   The grandmothers wait. And wait.

Nin: How are you doing? *She gives me a little nudge.* Okay, so you don't want to give him the money. How do you actually feel about the hitchhiker?

Author: I feel disgusted. If he was an embodiment of what Aborigines are today I don't want anything to do with it.

Nin: Good. Keep going. Delve deep. *She rocks back and forth, humming.*

Author: Yeah, I don't want to give handouts to Abo slobs

Wirra Woman: Watch it!

Wauwe Woman: Shhhh!

Author: But I don't know what to do. I don't know the answer.

Wauwe Woman: You don't need to figure out the answer. That is white man's disease. Just stay with your truth.

Author: I see dissolute Aborigines who have lost their way and their sense of self. They have disappeared down society's cracks. Handouts can't help that. *I ponder deeply.* Uh oh!

Nin: What?

Author: Now I see what I didn't want to see then. The hitchhiker was a possible version of myself – dispossessed, alienated, lost. Just what happened to my mother and sister. My mother Olga (yes, she is Tatiana) died a vegetable in a mental hospital. My youngest sister was schizophrenic too, and virtually became a vegetable, dying at the age of forty-five. We Russians were pretty well blown up off the face of the earth by Stalin and then Hitler. I know what it was like to be dispossessed, disowned and thrown to a corner of the world that was not my own. Like that black man, I was a second-class citizen too.

I take a deep breath. The grandmothers coo and cluck.

If I look at this hitchhiker in my mind's eye, I think, *There but for the grace of God go I.* I can see a chap who had been deeply traumatised and was unable to know what was saddening him. He had just lost hope. Just like my mother, just like me, deep inside.

I begin to sob. The grandmothers sit quietly knowing that tears, like those of their esteemed ancestor Tjilbruke, are healing.

Wauwe Woman: Yeah, just like Kudnartu. It's the same with young Aboriginal glue-sniffers today. They are just escaping from chronic sadness. Having been hoodwinked out of their past, they have lost connection with their ancestors and live in limbo. Indigenous people have a dark nucleus within them, of death, disease, destruction, loss, and profound grief. The young don't know what ails them. They need encouragement to look into the deep well of their collective psyche and see what is there.

Author: That is what I am trying to do with this book – open up that well and see the good things in there as well as the bad. If all whites and all blacks look down into the well then there may be true healing: a chance to repair the collective self.

Nin: Thank you for journeying with us.

Author: I am starting to feel clearer. I know that in confessing the story of the hitchhiker, I am now able to differentiate my feelings. It's okay to feel angry at the hitchhiker. That is being real. I don't want to give handouts.

Wirra Woman: We don't want them!

Author: Giving handouts is perpetuating the guilt of our ancestors. Murlawirrapurka was so good at teaching differentiation. I am distinguishing between what I want to support and what I don't want to support. I certainly don't support the latest intervention in the Northern territory, which keeps the whole miserable shebang going.

Wauwe Woman: I reiterate. You don't need to know all the answers. You wanting answers and solutions all the time is your white culture's sickness. White Western culture always thinks it knows what's best – or that if enough knowledge, enough research, and enough analyses are gathered then all the questions will be answered. Julia Gillard, the former Prime Minister, wanted to make a second intervention into the Northern Territorry curtailing our peoples' freedom even more. And this is without consulting with the Aboriginal elders and asking what they wanted. Several Aborigines, including Barbara Shaw from Alice Springs, are insisting on being consulted and want to shelve the whole intervention and, in their words, 'Rebuild from the Ground Up'. The true answers will only arise from joint enquiry.

Nin: That is what I want – white people who are willing to journey with me.

Author: Phew! I am so relieved that I don't have to know all the answers.

Wauwe Woman: We don't want any more experts telling us how to restore harmony. They have no idea. Their advice just stirs up more disharmony.

It's enough that you have told your version of a story of Adelaide. It means that at last we can begin.

Author: Begin what?

Wauwe Woman: The long road to REAL reconciliation. And it's for us to find out together. And to honour the book you have written. Honour the vision you had to write it. And you don't have to have the answers.

Author: What a relief!

Nin: Thank you again for journeying with me.

They all clap again. I envisage a film where people are encouraged to look at their racism and, when they do, a black audience claps enthusiastically.

Author: I want to tell you a powerful and vivid dream I've had.

Wauwe Woman: Uh oh, you and your dreams and visions!

Author: I dreamt I was by the Torrens River and that the Adelaide Festival Hall had been replaced by a huge water feature which was full of large fountains. Then out of the top of the central fountain emerged two giant kangaroo foetuses that were doing a beautiful spiralling slow motion dance. I circled around nearer to the river so I could see them more clearly. I was surprised that people picnicking on the grass around the fountain did not appear to notice them. As I was watching, I saw several large stingrays come out of the water and begin to hover quite near to people lying on the grass. Then I saw people diving into the fountain. I was trying to tell them that it was dangerous and full of stingrays but no one was taking any notice. So, my fellow grandmothers, what do you think?

Wauwe Woman: That is an amazing dream. You seem to do well on visions and dreams, don't you? You are our kinda people.

Author: Well thank you. You are now much friendlier than when I started this book.

Wauwe Woman: Well yes. You have done us the honour of looking at your racism. We welcome you because your own liberation is bound with ours.

Author: What about the dream?

Wauwe Woman: Well, the foetal kangaroos are obvious. The giant Tandanya red kangaroo, even though extinct, lives on in spirit and looks like it is due for a rebirth. But the stingray is even more heartening. And when a white-skin like you dreams about stingrays it gives us great hope.

Author: What does it symbolise? Why are you crying?

Wauwe Woman: We think you have been too dredged in our lore for too long. Have you been looking up at the stars lately? How could you possibly know, white girl? Stingrays symbolise our cultural survival.

Author: There's more to the dream. A good looking Aboriginal man, looking smart and sharp in a pale blue Armani suit, was standing by the fountain filling up a bottle. He offered it to me to drink. There was something quite sexual about the offer. I wasn't sure if I should drink it.

Wauwe Woman: Sexy grandmother, aren't you?

Author: I hope so.

Wauwe Woman: The dream shows that we trust you. Water is a powerful symbol in Kaurna lore. Our ancestor, Tjilbruke, brought forth life-giving springs with his tears. We offer you water from our fountain. It shows you have our best interests at heart.

Author: Thank you. I fervently hope so. Baba Yaga was right. I am now in very good hands. I feel healed by my connection with you. I feel welcomed into your circle. I feel we can go forward together.

Wauwe Woman: Now I will tell *you* something. As you wrote in the story, Midlato's *kammammi* had seen a great secret in the sky. A secret that many other civilisations have also read in the stars. But first I must explain something many white people do not understand about us and secrets. We were given different pieces of the puzzle; they were entrusted to us by our elders, and it was our sacred duty to carry the burdens of the truths of our sacred traditions. We are each a repository for this knowledge and can only pass it on when others are ready to hear it. Only then can we reveal it.

However, I can now reveal some of Midlato's *kammammi*'s secret, as many of you are now ready to listen. The messages she saw in both comets with their twin tails is similar to the messages from other cultures, in ancient traditions such as the Mayans, Druids, and American Indians. The Mayan calendar ends in December 2012, 'white time'. Our star system also shows a huge change at that time. It points to a dramatic shift in the consciousness of the peoples of the world. This will allow the human race to work towards a harmonious coexistence which up to now has not been possible.

Wirra Woman: I'm afraid it will be too late. White people won't listen to our wisdom till they have destroyed the planet.

Wauwe Woman: Perhaps. The white people who have invaded our land are just a blip in our 40,000 year history. They arose from a tradition spawned in the northern hemisphere, which is only a few hundred years old. This tradition holds that they know everything through the study of science, therefore thinking they are in control. This has led them to control the world, nature, and cultures like ours. The perpetrators of this tradition have been caught in a spell that has blinded them and led the world to the brink of destruction. Now, at last, they have been pulled up short. Australia is suffering severe difficulties as a result of this 'control game' that has supplanted our ancient law: drought;

pollution; extinction of species, just to name a few. However, this state of affairs is all in the stars.

Wirra Woman: Yeah, it's all written up there, that humanity will take itself to the point of self-destruction.

Wauwe Woman: And that it will take a huge shift to save ourselves. The perpetrators of 'I can control the planet', 'I know all the answers', must learn humility. We indigenous cultures, on the other hand, must claim our inner wisdom, retrieve our knowledge and learn to trust ourselves again. The perpetrators and the people they have trodden down must fuse together and avert global catastrophe. You whites are in the grip of a trance which is destructive and unsustainable. You are beginning to wake up.

Author: I really hope so

Wauwe Woman: As you have shown so clearly in your Adelaide story, it is easy to see the trance the 19th century whites were in. They really believed the Aborigines were inferior. In fact, whites today tut-tut at how racist their ancestors were. But our great grand children will tut-tut at the box you whites are now stuck in.

Wirra Woman: If we are still on the planet.

Wauwe Woman: Hopefully, whites will garner our knowledge. Our dreaming is our particular take on our bit of world – we know what makes our land zing.

Wirra Woman: It took us over 40,000 years. We should have sussed it!

Wauwe Woman: Well, whites haven't. They just think they have.

Wirra Woman: Arrogant dunderheads.

Wauwe Woman: Shutup, will you. I'm trying to think! Anyway, we also know there is a lot more to be discovered. The way we worked it all out before you whites came was unique to that time – the way we work with it now is unique to now – you white people have dropped holus bolus into our pond, and we are all in this together now. You whites and your legacy are now part of our dreamtime. We must find a way of moving forward together: and it isn't that we '*must*', it is inevitable that we will – as predicted in the stars.

If you trust us and we trust you, we have a way forward; and you have to give up thinking you know it all, because you know zilch.

Wirra Woman: You know there are Kaurna plaques now all over Adelaide. River Torrens is also the Karrawirra Parri and Victoria Square, Tartanyanggartu. To me they are just flimsy bandaids on a profound multiple fracture. It will take more than Aboriginal twin naming of places in Adelaide to heal that. Token gestures are much easier than action, aren't they?

Wauwe Woman: But it is a start. And, as we sang at the Sorry Day launch in 2000,

'We must take this journey together as friends.'

And you know, our culture teaches that the unexpected and miraculous can happen any time. Just look at a caterpillar's metamorphosis into a butterfly. Caterpillars are voracious and greedy and strip vegetation at an alarming rate...

Wirra Woman: Over consumptive; a bit like white man

339

Wauwe Woman: Yes, Wirra Woman, you are right. As the 21st century advances, the old system will get more entrenched, more violent, and seemingly more powerful. It is trying to keep itself alive while we know that we need a new system. Just like a caterpillar bloating itself until it just can't function anymore, and then going to sleep with its skin hardening into a chrysalis. What happens is that little imaginal disks (as they're called by biologists), begin to appear in the body of the caterpillar and its immune system attacks them. But they keep coming up stronger and they start to link with each other. As they connect, they mature into fully-fledged cells, and more and more of them aggregate until the immune system of the caterpillar just can't function any more. At that point, the body of the caterpillar melts into a nutritive soup that can feed the butterfly.

I love this metaphor, because it shows us why we who want to change the world are coexisting with the old system for a while. It explains clearly why there is no point in attacking the old system, because you know the caterpillar is unsustainable and will eventually die. What we have to focus on is 'can we build a viable butterfly?' – a butterfly that really can fly.

CHAPTER 15

Threads

Uncle Lewis and I look at the painting of the broken spears and shields of a vanquished race. William Cawthorne sketched the scene in 1844, capturing this defining moment in Kaurna history. *Shields & spears of the natives on the battlefield* is hanging in the Lounge Gallery of the Kaurna Building in the University of South Australia, not far from the Holy Trinity Church.

We stare in silence at the depiction of Murlawirrapurka's aborted last stand to protect his Tandanya plain from the Moorundie.

Uncle Lewis Yerlopurka O'Brien is chief elder of the Kaurna race, direct descendant of Kudnartu, who died so mysteriously at a tender age. A kinder, sweeter man you couldn't hope to meet.

We walk to the Festival Centre where we look at the Kaurna memorial erected on the spot that the Tandanya Rock once proudly stood. Here, as a child, I watched the black swans glide by. Uncle Lewis explains to me the symbols; very simple, very moving. We then take a tour of all the Kaurna historical places. Plaques now commemorate the sites of age old Tandanya haunts.

We walk to Elder Park, where a thousand people watched Prime Minister Kevin Rudd's famous 'Sorry' speech on a large screen and where I innocently chatted to some Aboriginal boys. We walk to the memorial site of Piltawardli where Dresden missionaries assiduously learnt the Kaurna language and argued with Murlawirrapurka, Ityamai-itpina, and Kadlitpina about Jehovah. We walk to the location of the first English school in Kintore Avenue, where Kaurna children were forced to be in the same classrooms as Moorundie children. It is now a migrant museum. I show Uncle Lewis the brick I have laid in memory of my migrant parents. The inscription reads 'Sasha, Olga and Eva Levkowiz, 1950'. To my surprise, Uncle Lewis points to a brick nearby. It is dedicated to Murlawirrapurka.

'Why here?' I ask.

'I just wanted him to be commemorated somewhere,' says Uncle Lewis simply. 'Sadly, they didn't get his date of death right – they've put 1843 instead of 1845.'

I feel deeply honoured that the brick of that great man is so close to my own humble brick. But I feel it is such an inadequate memorial to this great man. It fails dismally to reflect his dynamic personality, his wisdom, his kindness and the multi-dimensional aspect of the relationships that he formed with those 'strange white newcomers'. I feel strongly that a statue should be built for him. The people of Albany built a statue for Mokare in Western Australia. Rymill Park on the eastern edge of Adelaide has recently received the twin name Murlawirrapurka. Perhaps that is where the statue should stand.

We gaze at the side of Old Parliament House. Uncle Lewis asks me if I see a pattern in the old haphazard stonework. I think I see a kangaroo but think I might be imagining it. Then it strikes me. 'Do you think pieces of the Tandanya Rock are in this wall?'

'Highly likely. It was built about the same time the Rock disappeared.'

I look at the Old Parliament House with new reverence. Every time I came out of the Adelaide Railway Station as a child, I would go past this wall. I ponder the vagaries of new civilizations destroying and supplanting far older ones.

Uncle Lewis shows me a string game. He always carries a piece of string and shows anybody who may be interested. He tells me old stories and shares some of his ideas on how to go forward in Adelaide, ecologically. He has a unique contribution to make. I wonder if anyone is listening or values his expertise. He has written a beautiful book, *And the Clock Struck Thirteen*, an evocative story of his life and thoughts, which described great hardship without a trace of bitterness. He has read my first book, *Sasha & Olga*, and has the graciousness to tell me that I had it worse than him.

'No, no,' I say. 'What I learnt in writing *Butterflies & Demons* is that you, the Kaurna people, had it far worse than I did.'

He just smiles benevolently at me, his eyes twinkling.

'You know we the Kaurna were great educators,' Uncle Lewis continues proudly. 'Our people taught us how to learn. For example, the learning that goes into playing these string games can be easily transposed to different situations. This is why Kaurna children learnt so quickly. My great great grandmother Kudnartu is a case in point. She was sent to the English school for three months before she got married, and in that short time learnt how to read and write English very quickly. She was better at it than her husband, John Adams.'

We speak of Kudnartu and her children, Tim and Tom Adams.

'You know we still haven't got the land, Block 386, that rightfully belonged to us. So much for the empty promises the early colonisers made. But at least we have our language.'

Yes, the Kaurna language. What an amazing tale.

—⁓—

When the school at Piltawardli was closed in 1845, preservation of Kaurna written material was not high on any agenda. Some of it had been sent to Dresden. Governor Grey took farewell letters from Kaurna children to his next appointment in South Africa. English was mandatory for Kaurna children from then on. Rations were withheld if they spoke their language. Children, ripped from their land and shipped to missions, were castigated and often beaten if they uttered their beloved words. After the last fluent speaker, Ityamai-itpina's daughter, died in 1929, nothing of the Kaurna language remained on the Tandanya plain; only perhaps in the mumblings of an old Kaurna woman incarcerated in Parkside Mental Hospital.

In World War Two, Dresden was bombed to smithereens by the Allies, and any possible papers or books that lurked in musty rooms were swept up in some of the most dreadful fires that obliterated thousands of civilians. My mother Olga escaped similar lethal firestorms in nearby Magdeburg.

It seemed the Kaurna language was lost. How was it that Midlato's *kammammi* had been so confident that Kaurna would once more be spoken on the Adelaide plain? It was written in the stars, of course.

After 1967, when an Australian referendum finally recognised that Aboriginals were actual human beings with fundamental rights, a few Kaurna people started to trickle back to the Adelaide area. Many did not know where they originally came from, as they had been herded to missions from all over the country. Some, like Lewis Yerlopurka O'Brien, had fortunately retained some contact with family and had the story of his ancestor Kudnartu passed down to him in the oral tradition. The stories referred to Block 386 and the land that rightfully belonged to his great grandmother and her family.

In the 1980s something deep began to stir within Kaurna descendants. Prominent Kaurna *ngankiburka*, Georgina Williams, became involved in a project to revive the Tjilbruke trail. During that time, she heard Tjilbruke speak to her.

'Go wake the people up, my people our people.'

But where was the language? Where were the sounds that rang out over the plain for thousands of years?

In 1989, an unassuming linguist, Rob Amery, who had lived among the indigenous people of Arnhem Land, came to Adelaide University. In conjunction with the emerging Kaurna community, he set about reclaiming the original language of the Adelaide Plains. With a combination of his linguistic skills and utter dedication, he started to gather any recorded snippets of the language that had been forgotten in musty local archives or scattered in faraway places: he was helped by many Kaurna descendants who wanted to revive their oral tradition.

Then a mighty coup: a musty copy of Teichelmann and Schurmann's grammar book was found in a dusty basement. This original work came to be recognised as a huge gift and a godsend. But then came the enormous task of deciphering it and painstakingly piecing the language together. This was an awesome task, which did not lack its fair share of miracles. In 1998, an academic from Germany hand-delivered some vital original Kaurna texts which he found in Leipzig. The Dresden Missionaries had fortuitously moved to Leipzig well before World War Two. Even though Leipzig was also bombed by the Allies, the collections of the missionaries miraculously survived. These precious papers, included letters Kaurna children had written to Governor Gawler, and pages from a copy-book written by Kartanya and other children. Klose had proudly sent these examples to the Society to demonstrate how clever and able his students were. Kartanya's page of biblical truths written in Kaurna, as well as being a crucial part of an elaborate jigsaw puzzle to reclaim the language, has also been an eye-opener to Kaurna descendants. They can see how skilful and clever their ancestors were, a wonderful counter to 19th and 20th century white propaganda that black people were backward.

The upshot of all this work is that Kaurna is now being taught in schools and universities throughout Adelaide. This is an extraordinary feat, as over 90% of all Aboriginal Australian languages have been lost. As Lester Rigney, an influential indigenous Australian educationalist, says of the Kaurna language, 'It is ours. It has been recorded for us and indeed in some of those recordings our people are talking to us. But we need to decode it.'

And Uncle Lewis recognises how the language gives the Kaurna their identity.

'To learn the Kaurna language... is to find out why you speak the way they did – it gives you structure.'

When I hear the Kaurna language spoken it sends shivers down my spine – it is so lyrical, evocative, strong. I can see clearly how it is a slender but strong piece of thread that will connect present Kaurna to past Kaurna, like their string games, like a dripfeed of spiritual nutrition and regeneration. Charlie Perkins hoped whites would learn Aboriginal languages.

'My expectation of a good Australia is when white people would be proud to speak an Aboriginal language, when they realise that Aboriginal culture and all that goes with it, philosophy, art, language, morality, kinship, is all part of their heritage. And that's the most unbelievable thing of all that it's all there waiting for us all. White people can inherit 40,000 or 60,000 years of culture, and all they have to do is reach out and ask for it.

The year 2011 saw the 175th anniversary of the formation of the Dresden missionary society. It had been founded in the same year that Colonel Light landed on the Tandanya plain. Teichelmann and Schurmann were its first two missionaries, followed by Klose. Another missionary had been sent to the Encounter Bay area. To mark the 175th celebration a group of Kaurna and Ngarrindjeri people travelled to Dresden to visit archives and museums that contained documents, artefacts, and natural history specimens sent by the early missionaries.

As well as Kaurna language revival, there has also been revival of ceremony, music, and dance throughout South Australia. A raft of talented indigenous artists sing and play evocative songs.

Rediscovering the Kaurna language has also meant that many places in Adelaide have regained a Kaurna name, in a dual naming project undertaken by the Adelaide City Council. Governor Gawler started this in the 1840s, as he wanted Kaurna names to be retained, but with subsequent administrations this impetus was lost. As well as the River

Torrens being known as Karrawirraparri, the Adelaide City golf links is known as Piltawardli, the former Emigration Square is called Tambawardli, and Rymill Park is named Murlawirrapurka. That's where I think a statue to the great man should be erected.

As Uncle Lewis wisely says, 'I think it's all these things (the revival of the language, dual naming projects) that are helping. It's a very easy step, people need easy steps sometimes.'

However, dreadful problems beset the Aboriginal community: homelessness, high suicide rates, and drug and alcohol addiction to name a few; all consequences of complete loss of power of self-determination, and being victims of a seemingly uncaring, dominant culture.

I went out with Nin, whose name in white culture is Dr Lilian Holt. As we walked into a restaurant in Norwood I experienced a different energy that came towards her and not towards me. Condescension, laced with something deeply buried, perhaps disgust – even fear. I read her paper, *Psst I wanna be white*. What a brave, honest piece. I am humbled by her.

She asked me about my vision. Had I fulfilled it by writing this book? Yes. As well as discovering how amazing the indigenous people of Adelaide are and healing more of my past, I also have greater understanding of the white people of Adelaide. That was how the vision had started. In my vision, the 1950s people, the Guthries, the Taplows, the Portmans, begged me not to forget them. They came from a particular timewarp in Adelaide history; when it was comfortably Anglo-Saxon and provincial, just before their whole world would change. In that staid early 1950s world they were my masters and, despite the legacy they carried, the mock execution, the prejudice, and the mishandling of my mother's illness, they were fundamentally kind.

'What, even Mrs Taplow?' Nin asked

'Even Mrs Taplow,' I answered. 'Like my own mother, she was consumed by her demons. Her craziness just happened to be accommodated by the society she lived in.'

I think the biggest reason why people in Adelaide are so kind is the influence of the Kaurna. It permeates the land. And early colonists did at least attempt to be fair. As South Australian historian, Geoffrey Manning, wrote, 'The history of every State in the Commonwealth is foul with the blood of the unfortunate Aborigines and is marked with deeds of callous brutality on the part of the settlers and natives alike. To this record South Australia is a pleasant exception, an exception, indeed, unique in the annals of white colonisation.'

Not, of course, that blood was not spilt here on both sides, or that many mistakes were not made in dealing with the Aborigines which led to misunderstanding, but as the scene of an honest-to-God attempt to give them a square deal from the outset, South Australia holds pride of place among the countries of the earth which have been invaded and settled by Europeans.

Wirra Woman: Oy, I disagree. Square deal! You must be joking. Whitewash. Whitewash.

Author: Oy, you're not in the story any more. You've had your say.

Wirra Woman: No one will ever shut me up! Ever.

I wonder if Wirra Woman is right. It seems that the 'honest-to God attempt to give them a square deal' still has a long way to go. Rudd's 'Sorry' speech was just a beginning; the continued interference in the Northern Territory is a travesty.

I walk to Victoria Square, dual name Tartanyanggartu. This square has been home to many indigenous ceremonies in the last few years. I sit and remember coming out of the police station with my mother, after the 'shining lights' episode. A terrible day. But the memory has been healed with the thought that Baba Yaga and the Kaurna grandmothers were sitting in the square watching over me.

I take a bus ride to the hills, and am enveloped in the lush greenery of Morialta Falls where my mother used to love to come. I like to think that the Kaurna grandmothers were easing her anguish when she was here. I feel they are with me still.

I go to the Onkaparinga River, and smile that it was once the women's secret river, the Ngankiparringa. It had gone through a few name changes in the early years but, partly due to Governor Gawler's insistence that some Kaurna names be retained, the present name is not dissimilar to the original.

I visit the Aldinga Scrub Conservation Park. It is now recognised officially as Murlawirrapurka's *pangkarra*, and is a significant Kaurna site. Here I sit and soak in that great man's energy. Within its three hundred hectares, many rare plants are protected. Its natural features include mallee scrub, remnant red gum forests and lacy coral lichen. More than 160 different bird species can be seen and heard. I am told if I watch quietly I might spot mistletoe birds, rainbow bee-eaters, and golden whistlers. The park's vegetation provides a variety of host plants for eighteen species of butterflies and 540 species of other insects.

Brushtail possums, short-beaked echidnas, geckoes, and skinks also live in the park. The beautiful red, yellow, and white butterfly, the delias aganippe, once abundant on the Adelaide plain, and Midlato's *pilyabilya*, is rarely seen. But there is hope for this butterfly, as the South Australian Butterfly Conservation Society has taken it on as its mascot, and is working to restore vegetation that would bring it back.

I sit and wait to hear the birds that would have been part of Murlawirrapurka's dawn chorus. I remember what the *kammammi* circle said about his burial – that his energies were suffused throughout this land – I can feel his kindness cradling me. And I feel an overwhelming sadness. Even though care is being taken in this bit of scrub, more than half of plants and wildlife have gone forever. Diversity is what makes this planet so abundant and so alive. I ache for the Kaurna song to rise up from each blade of grass and each beat of the butterflies' wings. Love in its every manifestation. Love that the Kaurna had in abundance and cherished every day of their lives. The myriad verses of the old songs have disappeared forever. I wait for a new song to be sung. It may take a thousand years.

I hope we have that long.

About the Author

Eva Maria Chapman

 A former teacher, psychotherapist, researcher, and successful business-woman, Eva Chapman became an author when nursing her stepfather, Sasha, for the last 2 years of his life. After a 33-year estrangement, they forgave each other and he unburdened the harrowing story of his Jewish family's persecution in Ukraine in WW2, and was able to die a happy man.

This, plus her mentally ill mother's equally harrowing life, led Eva to write S*asha & Olga*, (Lothian Books, 2006). This launched her career as a writer; *Russian Roulette 20:20*, Solaris 2010; *From Russia to Love*, Robson Press 2012; *Sexy at 70, A Spiritual Journey*, Publishing Push 2019.; *Butterflies & Demons* (long-listed for Mslexia novel prize), DoctorZed Publishing, Adelaide 2020

Eva lives on a wildlife sanctuary on the edge of Exmoor England, which she shares with her husband, Jake, of 41 years, on a joint path to greater love. Jake and Eva a currently writing a joint book, *Our Love Story*.

Connect with Eva on:

Website: www.evamariachapman.com
Instagram: @sizzling70s
Facebook: @evamariachapman and Sizzling into my 70s
Twitter: @sizzle70s

Lightning Source UK Ltd.
Milton Keynes UK
UKHW012308070620
364562UK00001B/38